D0319831

Leaves from my Library

An English Anthology

'Knowing I lov'd my books, he furnish'd me,
From my own library, with volumes that
I prize above my dukedom.'

Prospero to his daughter, Miranda, after they came ashore on an uninhabited island.
Shakespeare, *The Tempest*, Act I, sc 2.

Leaves from my Library
An English Anthology

by the Rt Hon

LORD DENNING

London

BUTTERWORTHS

1986

United Kingdom — Butterworth & Co (Publishers) Ltd, 88 Kingsway, LONDON WC2B 6AB and 61A North Castle Street, EDINBURGH EH2 3LJ

Australia — Butterworths Pty Ltd, SYDNEY, MELBOURNE, BRISBANE, ADELAIDE, PERTH, CANBERRA and HOBART

Canada — Butterworths. A division of Reed Inc, TORONTO and VANCOUVER

New Zealand — Butterworths of New Zealand Ltd, WELLINGTON and AUCKLAND

Singapore — Butterworth & Co (Asia) Pte Ltd, SINGAPORE

South Africa — Butterworth Publishers (Pty) Ltd, DURBAN and PRETORIA

USA — Butterworth Legal Publishers, ST PAUL, Minnesota, SEATTLE, Washington, BOSTON, Massachusetts, AUSTIN, Texas and D & S Publishers, CLEARWATER, Florida

British Library Cataloguing in Publication Data

Leaves from my library: an English anthology.
1. English prose literature
I. Denning, Alfred Denning
828'.08 PR1285

ISBN 0 406 17615 9

Typeset by CCC, printed and bound in Great Britain by William Clowes Limited, Beccles and London

Preface

I have managed to write another book – even at the age of eighty-six. I thought of Lord Wavell's charming anthology of poetry which he called *Other Men's Flowers.* At the beginning he quoted Montaigne:

I have gathered a posie of other men's flowers and nothing but the thread that binds them is my own.

As Lord Wavell gathered choice pieces of poetry, why should not I gather choice pieces of prose? And bind them together in a book: in which nothing is my own, except the selection, arrangement and annotations?

That is what I have tried to do. Instead of 'other men's flowers' I have taken 'other men's stories'. Many of them have something to do with the law. But for the most part I have selected them for their literary quality and descriptive force.

I fear that some of the more sophisticated of you may consider them to be outworn tales. You know them all so well. But this book is not intended for such. It is for those who have not hitherto had the time or the opportunity or the inclination to be conversant with the best writers of English prose. Also, I hope it will give pleasure to those of you older ones who knew the stories well when you were young – and like to come upon them again – as meeting old friends. Into which group do you come?

Some anthologies give hundreds of little snippets taken out of many books. Like the *Oxford Book of English Prose.* They are books of quotations – whereas every good piece of descriptive prose should be read in its setting. Just as a good judge does not read one section of a statute by itself, but in the context of the statute as a whole, so ought the reader of a piece of descriptive prose. So you will find that in every case I have told the story for your entertainment, and maybe instruction, as well as for the purple patch.

Perhaps you do not know the origin of the 'purple patch'. It comes from the Roman poet, Horace, who lived in the century just before Christ. He wrote:

> *Inceptis gravibus plerumque et magna professis*
> *Purpureus, late qui splendeat, unus et alter*
> *Adsuitur pannus.* (*De Arte Poetica*, 1.15)

which may be freely translated:

> When you are covering, as with a garment, some weighty or important matter, you should sew on one or two purple passages so as to attract the attention of those who are unfamiliar with it.

My book is not all prose. I have brought in a verse or two of poetry, now and then, usually of a lighter kind.

It has been quite a task – a happy task – very suitable for retirement.

To test your knowledge – as they do on television in 'Master Mind' – I would ask you whether you can answer straightaway, before you read the book, the twenty questions which follow. They are of much the same kind as our master used to ask us at school. Some are easy. Others are difficult. I give the answers separately for you to check them afterwards. If you can answer all twenty correctly, straight off, you deserve to be placed in the top class with special distinction – using the mixed Greek and Latin symbols as at Oxford α++ (alpha plus plus). If you can get half of them right straight off, you are still in the top class of exceptional ability – and should be marked α+ (alpha plus). If you can get one-quarter of them right, you are still in the top class but only of average ability – just α (alpha). If you get less than a quarter right or even none, you deserve to get a good second – just because you have tried. You shall be marked 'L' for 'Learner'.

In any case please do read the book and, if you feel like it, write and tell me how you get on. I will try to reply, but at my age I had better say, for all our sakes, D.V. (*Deo volente*) God willing.

Denning

On my eighty-seventh birthday
23 January 1986

Twenty Questions

1 Who said repeatedly 'Off with his head'?

2 Who said and where 'This was their finest hour'?

3 Who said and where 'I appeal unto Caesar'?

4 Who wrote, and where and when, 'I leave Emma Lady Hamilton therefore a legacy'?

5 Who said and where 'Take away that bauble'?

6 Who said and where 'Take then thy bond'?

7 Who wrote and who first sang the hymn 'Who would true valour see'?

8 Who said and when that he's 'upset my apple-cart'?

9 Which Queen of England often wished herself to be 'a milkmaid all the month of May'?

10 Who shouted out 'For which King?' and at what battle?

11 In *Pride and Prejudice*, who was 'Pride' and who was 'Prejudice'?

12 Who was the girl who became 'Maiden no more'?

13 Who was the gentleman who could not pull off his night-cap?

14 Who said and of whom that he was 'Unwept, unhonour'd and unsung'?

15 Who was the man who falsely claimed to be a baronet?

16 Who was the judge who sat in a fog, and where?

17 Who was the clergyman who secretly enjoyed Rabelais?

18 Where do swallows go in the wintertime, and what naturalist was mistaken about them?

19 Who was the lady who had 'five husbands at church door'?

20 At whose trial did 'the judges walk and the trial stand still'?

[*Answers on p. 255*]

Contents

Bibliography & Acknowledgments

Some of you may like to know the books from which I have taken the 'leaves from my library' – in case you wish to read more of them. The Bible and Shakespeare are everywhere. *Hansard* is in all the great libraries. Others are quite old and a few are now out of date. But some will be found in popular paperback editions and in public libraries.

Chapter 1 Winston Churchill

All extracts of Winston Churchill's speeches in the House of Commons are taken from the official reports of proceedings in that House, *Hansard*, for 13 May, 4 and 18 June and 20 August 1940.

Chapter 2 Lord Nelson

Robert Southey *Life of Nelson* 1813 (International Library of Famous Literature, Vol XIV, London, *The Standard*, 1900).

Chapter 4 John Buchan

John Buchan *Oliver Cromwell* (London, Hodder & Stoughton, 1934). Extracts are reproduced by kind permission of The Rt Hon Lord Tweedsmuir.

Chapter 5 Lord Macaulay

Lord Macaulay's essay *Warren Hastings* from *Essays and Lays* 1843 (London, Longmans Green & Co, 1909).

G M Trevelyan *History of England* 1926 (London, Longmans Green & Co, 3rd edn, 1945).

Chapter 6 Lord Macaulay

Lord Macaulay *The History of England* 1849 (London, Longmans Green & Co, Vol 1, 1880).

Lord Campbell *The Lives of the Lord Chancellors* (London, John Murray (Publishers) Ltd, Vol III, 1845).

Chapter 7 Thomas Hardy

Thomas Hardy *Tess of the d'Urbervilles* 1891 (London, Penguin Books Ltd, 1979).

Gordon Beningfield *Hardy Country* (London, Allen Lane, 1983, © Gordon Beningfield (pictures) Anthea Zeman (text) and Cameron Books Ltd).

Chapter 8 Lewis Carroll

Lewis Carroll *Alice in Wonderland* 1865 (London, Raphael Tuck & Sons, c 1910, pictured by Mabel Lucie Attwell).

Chapter 9 John Bunyan

John Bunyan *The Pilgrim's Progress from this world to that which is to come* 1678 (Pt I) 1684 (Pt II) (Hanserd Knollys Society, 1847).

Chapter 11 Charles Dickens

Charles Dickens *Bleak House* 1852/53 (London, Chapman & Hall, Vol VI of Dickens' work, ?date).

W S Gilbert *Iolanthe* from *The Savoy Operas* (London, Macmillan, 1926).

Chapter 12 Charles Dickens

Charles Dickens *The Pickwick Papers* 1837 (London, Chapman & Hall, 1901).

Chapter 13 Anthony Trollope

Anthony Trollope *The Warden* 1855 (The Shakespeare Head edition, ed Michael Sadler, Oxford, Basil Blackwell, 1929). Extracts are reproduced by kind permission of the publishers.

Chapter 14 Lord Maugham

Lord Maugham *The Tichborne Case* (London, Hodder & Stoughton, 1936). Extracts are reproduced by kind permission of the Executors of the Estate of the late Lord Maugham.

Chapter 15 Basil Williams

Basil Williams *Cecil Rhodes* (series Makers of the 19th Century, London, Constable & Co, 1921). Extracts are reproduced by kind permission of the publishers.

Edward Gibbons *The Memoirs of the Life of Edward Gibbon by himself* 1796 (ed Dr G Birkbeck Hill, London, Methuen & Co, 1900).

Chapter 16 Izaak Walton

Izaak Walton *The Compleat Angler, or the Contemplative Man's Recreation* 1655 (The Winchester Edition, London, Freemantle & Co, 1902).

William Cowper *The Diverting History of John Gilpin* 1785 (International Library of Famous Literature, London, *The Standard*, Vol X, 1900).

Chapter 17 Gilbert White

Gilbert White *The Natural History of Selborne* 1789 (ed Cherry and Richard Kearton, Bristol, J W Arrowsmith Ltd, 1924).

Chapter 18 William Cobbett and others

William Cobbett *Rural Rides* 1830 (ed G D H and Margaret Cole, London, Peter Davies, Vol I, 1930).

H Plunket Greene *Where the Bright Waters Meet* 1924 (London, Philip Allan & Co, 2nd edn, 1929).

Alfred, Lord Tennyson *The Brook* 1865 (The Oxford Edition *Poems of Tennyson*, London, Oxford University Press, 1913).

Chapter 19 Jane Austen

Jane Austen *Pride and Prejudice* 1813 (London, J M Dent & Co, 1892).

Chapter 20 Geoffrey Chaucer

Chaucer *Prologue – The Canterbury Tales* 1387 (*The Canterbury Tales of Geoffrey Chaucer*, London, Jonathan Cape & The Medici Society, 1913).

1 Four months in 1940

Introduction

It is now forty years since the ending of the Second World War. None of you under sixty will have been involved in it to any extent. It must be difficult for you to know what happened in those days. Civilisation itself was threatened. England stood alone in its defence.

I write this on Remembrance Sunday 1985. We have been to Church as usual. We have had read Laurence Binyon's words, 'We will remember them'. But now I ask: How long will the people of England remember those who fell? How long will they remember what they did? Or what we did who survived? And we are getting fewer each year. After we are gone, who will tell them? If you should read *The Family Story* you will see what our family did. But many other families did as much or more: and suffered as much or more. The people of England faced terrific odds. They stood firm and resolute. Four months in 1940 were decisive. It was our finest hour.

1 The first phase

i *Churchill's speeches*

The speeches of Winston Churchill in the dark days of 1940 are outstanding in our English literature. We old folk know them well. We heard and read them at the time. But many of you youngsters will not have known them at all. And you should know them.

In reading them you must remember that there was strict censorship over all news and information. We could not rely on anything in the newspapers. But we could rely on what Winston Churchill said in the House of Commons. He told the truth – both of triumphs and disasters. His speeches will tell you about it better than any history books. Better even than his own history, *The Second World War*.

ii *The 'phoney' war*

For the first eight months of the war – from September 1939 to April 1940 – the war was a 'phoney'war. It made little impact on ordinary life. There was an ill-fated military venture in Norway. We sent a British expeditionary force to France. But there was no fighting there. It was the lull before the storm.

But the next four months – from May to August 1940 – were the most eventful of all time. Hitler with his armies overran much of Europe and threatened us in England. My army brother Reg was in the Southern Command manning our defences against invasion. My naval brother Norman was in the Admiralty seeking the whereabouts of German warships. I was at Leeds – to and fro – detaining those who would betray us – fifth-columnists. My wife Mary and son Robert (aged nearly two) were at home at Cuckfield in Sussex. The German bombers flew right over us on their way to London – and dropped some on us.

Under this threat a National Government of all parties was formed with a new Prime Minister, Winston Churchill. I take my extracts from the contemporary reports in *Hansard* of his speeches.

2 House of Commons: 13 May 1940

i *'Blood, toil, tears, and sweat'*

I beg to move,

That this House welcomes the formation of a Government representing the united and inflexible resolve of the nation to prosecute the war with Germany to a victorious conclusion.

...

To form an administration of this scale and complexity is a serious undertaking in itself, but it must be remembered that we are in the preliminary stage of one of the greatest battles in history, that we are in action at many other points in Norway and in Holland, that we have to be prepared in the Mediterranean, that the air battle is continuous, and that many preparations . . . have to be made here at home. In this crisis I hope I may be pardoned if I do not address the House at any length today . . . I would say to the House, as I said to those who have joined this Government: 'I have nothing to offer but blood, toil, tears, and sweat.'

Those four words struck home. They told us what we were in for.

ii *'Come then, let us go forward'*

We have before us an ordeal of the most grievous kind. We have before us many, many long months of struggle and of suffering. You ask, what is our policy? I will say: It is to wage war, by sea, land, and air, with all our might and with all the strength that God can give us; to wage war against a monstrous tyranny, never surpassed in the dark, lamentable catalogue of human crime. That is our policy. You ask, what is our aim? I can answer in one word: It is victory, victory at all costs, victory in spite of all terror, victory, however long and hard the road may be; for without victory, there is no survival. Let that be realised; no survival for the British Empire, no survival for all that the British Empire has stood for, no survival for the urge and impulse of the ages, that mankind will move forward towards its goal. But I take up my task with buoyancy and hope. I feel sure that our cause will not be suffered to fail among men. At this time I feel entitled to claim the aid of all, and I say: 'Come then, let us go forward together with our united strength.'

3 The next three weeks

i *In grave peril*

That speech was on 13 May 1940. During the next three weeks Hitler struck blow after blow. Holland was overrun. The defences of the French were broken. The Germans swept like a sharp scythe, cutting off all communications between our army and the main French armies. The Belgians surrendered. The British Expeditionary Force was in grave peril. In a desperate effort to save them or part of them, we sent out our finest regiments to Calais. They got there on 23 May 1940.

ii *The 60th Rifles*

The story of Calais has been well told by many. In particular by Airey Neave (who was there) and by Winston Churchill in *Their Finest Hour*.[1] But it is of special interest to us because of our close association with the 60th Rifles. Our gardener, 'Darkie', was a corporal and our neighbour, Brigadier Nicholson, was in command. At one time there was a plan that they should be evacuated. Destroyers were sent to stand off Calais for the purpose but the plan was altered. Instead of being taken off in waiting destroyers, they were ordered to fight to the end. This was the message sent to the Brigadier on 26 May 1940:

Every hour you continue to exist is of the greatest help to the B.E.F. Government has therefore decided you must continue to fight. Have greatest possible admiration for your splendid stand. Evacuation will not (*repeat* not) take place, and craft required for above purposes are to return to Dover.

[1] *The Second World War*, vol II.

So the destroyers went off and our men fought for five days until their ammunition was all spent. Many were killed. Nearly all the rest were taken prisoner. Brigadier Nicholson died in captivity. 'Darkie' was taken prisoner and, after the war, returned home. He worked for us until he had a heart attack and retired. Later on my son Robert, when he was eighteen, did his National Service with the 60th Rifles (the Greenjackets). So we are proud of them. Their headquarters are at Winchester.

4 House of Commons: 4 June 1940

After those three weeks, Winston Churchill told of the disasters and of the miracle of deliverance. First, he told of the stand at Calais:

i *The stand at Calais*

. . . I have said this armoured scythe-stroke almost reached Dunkirk – almost but not quite. Boulogne and Calais were the scenes of desperate fighting. The Guards defended Boulogne for a while and were then withdrawn by orders from this country. The Rifle Brigade, the 60th Rifles, and the Queen Victoria's Rifles, with a battalion of British tanks and 1,000 Frenchmen, in all about 4,000 strong, defended Calais to the last. The British Brigadier was given an hour to surrender. He spurned the offer, and four days of intense street fighting passed before silence reigned over Calais, which marked the end of a memorable resistance. Only 30 unwounded survivors were brought off by the Navy and we do not know the fate of their comrades. Their sacrifice, however, was not in vain. At least two armoured divisions, which otherwise would have been turned against the British Expeditionary Force, had to be sent for to overcome them. They have added another page to the glories of the Light Division, and the time gained enabled the Gravelines waterlines to be flooded and to be held by the French troops.

Then he told of the blow after blow that befell us in the three weeks:

ii *'Hard and heavy tidings'*

Thus it was that the port of Dunkirk was kept open. When it was found impossible for the armies of the north to re-open their communications to Amiens with the main French armies, only one choice remained. It seemed, indeed, forlorn. The Belgian, British, and French armies were almost surrounded. Their sole line of retreat was to a single port and to its neighbouring beaches. They were pressed on every side by heavy attacks and far outnumbered in the air.

When a week ago today I asked the House to fix this afternoon as the occasion for a statement, I feared it would be my hard lot to announce the greatest military disaster in our long history. I thought – and some good judges agreed with me – that perhaps 20,000 or 30,000 men might be re-embarked. But it certainly seemed that the whole of the French First Army and the whole of the British Expeditionary Force north of the Amiens-Abbeville gap, would be broken up in the open field or else would have to capitulate for lack of food and ammunition. These were the hard and heavy tidings for which I called upon the House and the nation to prepare themselves a week ago. The whole root and core and brain of the British Army, on which and around which we were to build, and are to build, the great British armies in the later years of the war, seemed about to perish upon the field or to be led into an ignominious and starving captivity.

iii *The Belgians surrender*

That was the prospect a week ago. But another blow which might well have proved final was yet to fall upon us. The King of the Belgians . . . suddenly, without prior consultation, with the least possible notice, without the advice of his Ministers and upon his own personal act, sent a plenipotentiary to the German Command, surrendered his Army, and exposed our whole flank and means of retreat.

. . . So in doing this and in exposing this flank . . . it seemed impossible that any large number of Allied troops could reach the coast.

iv *'Attacked on all sides'*

The enemy attacked us on all sides:

The enemy attacked on all sides with great strength and fierceness, and their main power, the power of their far more numerous air force, was thrown into the battle or else concentrated upon Dunkirk and the beaches. Pressing in upon the narrow exit, both from the east and from the west, the enemy began to fire with cannon upon the beaches by which alone the shipping could approach or depart. They sowed magnetic mines in the channels and seas; they sent repeated waves of hostile aircraft, sometimes more than 100 strong in one formation, to cast their bombs upon the single pier that remained, and upon the sand dunes upon which the troops had their eyes for shelter. Their U-boats, one of which was sunk, and their motor launches took their toll of the vast traffic which now began. For four or five days an intense struggle reigned. All their armoured divisions – or what was left of them – together with great masses of German infantry and artillery, hurled themselves in vain upon the ever-narrowing, ever-contracting appendix within which the British and French armies fought.

v *The Royal Navy to the rescue*

Meanwhile, the Royal Navy, with the willing help of countless merchant seamen, strained every nerve to embark the British and Allied troops. Two hundred and twenty light warships and 650 other vessels were engaged. They had to operate upon the difficult coast, often in adverse weather, under an almost ceaseless hail of bombs and an increasing concentration of artillery fire. Nor were the seas, as I have said, themselves free from mines and torpedoes. It was in conditions such as these that our men carried on, with little or no rest, for days and nights on end, making trip after trip across the dangerous waters, bringing with them always men whom they had rescued. The numbers they have brought back are the measure of their devotion and their courage. The hospital ships, which brought off many thousands of British and French wounded, being so plainly marked were a special target for Nazi bombs; but the men and women on board them never faltered in their duty.

vi *The Royal Air Force too*

Meanwhile, the Royal Air Force, which had already been intervening in the battle, so far as its range would allow, from home bases, now used part of its main metropolitan fighter strength, and struck at the German bombers, and at the fighters which in large numbers protected them. This struggle was protracted and fierce.

vii *'A miracle of deliverance'*

Suddenly the scene has cleared, the crash and thunder has for the moment – but only for the moment – died away. A miracle of deliverance, achieved by valour, by perseverance, by perfect discipline, by faultless service, by resource, by skill, by unconquerable fidelity, is manifest to us all. The enemy was hurled back by the retreating British and French troops. He was so roughly handled that he did not harry their departure seriously. The Royal Air Force engaged the main strength of the German Air Force, and inflicted upon them losses of at least four to one; and the Navy, using nearly 1,000 ships of all kinds, carried over 335,000 men, French and British, out of the jaws of death and shame, to their native land and to the tasks which lie immediately ahead. We must be very careful not to assign to this deliverance the attributes of a victory. Wars are not won by evacuations. But there was a victory inside this deliverance which should be noted. It was gained by the Air Force. Many of our soldiers coming back have not seen the Air Force at work: they saw only the bombers which escaped its protective attack. They underrate its achievements.

viii *A trial of strength*

... This was a great trial of strength between the British and German air forces. Can you conceive a greater objective for the Germans in the air than to make evacuation from these beaches impossible, and to sink all these ships which were displayed, almost to the extent of thousands? Could there have been an objective of greater military importance and significance for the whole purpose of the war than this? They tried hard, and they were beaten back; they were frustrated in their task. We got the Army away; and they have paid four-fold for any losses which they have inflicted. Very large formations of German aeroplanes – and we know that they are a very brave race – have turned on several occasions from the attack of one-quarter of their number of the Royal Air Force, and have dispersed in different directions. ...

ix *The young airmen*

... I will pay my tribute to these young airmen ... There never had been, I suppose, in all the world, in all the history of war, such an opportunity for youth. The Knights of the Round Table, the Crusaders, all fall back into a prosaic past: not only distant but prosaic; but these young men, going forth every morn to guard their native land and all that we stand for, holding in their hands these instruments of colossal and shattering power, of whom it may be said that

'When every morning brought a noble chance,
And every chance brought out a noble knight,'

deserve our gratitude, as do all of the brave men who, in so many ways and on so many occasions, are ready, and continue ready, to give life and all for their native land.

x *'A colossal military disaster'*

Nevertheless, our thankfulness at the escape of our Army and so many men, whose loved ones have passed through an agonising week, must not blind us to the fact that what has happened in France and Belgium is a colossal military disaster. The French Army has been weakened, the Belgian Army has been lost, a large part of those fortified lines upon which so much faith had been reposed is gone, many valuable mining districts and factories have passed into the enemy's possession, the whole of the Channel ports are in his hands, with all the tragic consequences that follow from that, and we must expect another blow to be struck almost immediately at us or at France. . . .

xi *'We shall never surrender'*

Then Winston Churchill spoke the finest piece of prose in the English language or in any language. It stirred us all greatly.

I have, myself, full confidence that if all do their duty, if nothing is neglected, and if the best arrangements are made, as they are being made, we shall prove ourselves once again able to defend our island home, to ride out the storm of war, and to outlive the menace of tyranny, if necessary for years, if necessary alone. At any rate, that is what we are going to try to do. That is the resolve of His Majesty's Government – every man of them. That is the will of Parliament and the nation. The British Empire and the French Republic, linked together in their cause and in their need, will defend to the death their native soil, aiding each other like good comrades to the utmost of their strength. Even though large tracts of Europe and many old and famous States have fallen or may fall into the grip of the Gestapo and all the odious apparatus of Nazi rule, we shall not flag or fail. We shall go on to the end. We shall fight in France, we shall fight on the seas and oceans, we shall fight with growing confidence and growing strength in the air, we shall defend our island, whatever the cost may be. We shall fight on the beaches, we shall fight on the landing grounds, we shall fight in the fields and in the streets, we shall fight in the hills; we shall never surrender, and even if, which I do not for a moment believe, this island or a large part of it were subjugated and starving, then our Empire beyond the seas, armed and guarded by the British Fleet, would carry on the struggle, until, in God's good time, the new world, with all its power and might, steps forth to the rescue and the liberation of the old.

I remember the impact of that speech on us. That last sentence hit hard. Were we in such peril as that? But so be it. We were told the truth. We knew the dangers ahead. We were determined to fight on.

5 House of Commons: 18 June 1940

That was on 4 June 1940. A fortnight passed. We began to pull round. We had to prepare ourselves against the impending invasion. Many of us were apprehensive about sending too many of our fighter aircraft over to France where they might be lost – and unable to defend us when most needed. We knew also that many of the men returning from Dunkirk had had to abandon much of their artillery and ammunition. Winston Churchill reassured us:

i *Our strength*

... During the last few days we have successfully brought off the great majority of the troops we had on the lines of communication in France – a very large number, scores of thousands – and seven-eighths of the troops we have sent to France since the beginning of the war, that is to say, about 350,000 out of 400,000 men, are safely back in this country ... We have also brought back a great mass of stores, rifles, and munitions of all kinds which had been accumulated in France during the last nine months.

We have, therefore, in this island today a very large and powerful military force. This force includes all our best-trained and finest troops and includes scores of thousands of those who have already measured their quality against the Germans and found themselves at no disadvantage. We have under arms at the present time in this island over a million and a quarter men. Behind these we have the Local Defence Volunteers, numbering half a million, only a portion of whom, however, are yet armed with rifles or other firearms. We have incorporated into our Defence Forces every man for whom we have a weapon.

ii *Air power will be decisive*

... This brings me, naturally, to the great question of invasion from the air and of the impending struggle between the British and German air forces. It seems quite clear that no invasion on a scale beyond the capacity of our land forces to crush speedily is likely to take place from the air until our Air Force has been definitely overpowered. In the meantime, there may be raids by parachute troops and attempted descents of airborne soldiers. We should be able to give those gentry a warm reception both in the air and if they reach the ground in any condition to continue the dispute. But the great question is, Can we break Hitler's air weapon? Now of course it is a very great pity that we have not got an Air Force at least equal to that of the most powerful enemy within striking distance of these shores. But we have a very powerful Air Force which has proved itself far superior in quality, both in men and in many types of machine, to what we have met so far in the numerous fierce air battles which have been fought. In France, where we were at a considerable disadvantage and lost many machines on the ground, we were accustomed to inflict losses of as much as two to two and a half to one. In the fighting over Dunkirk, which was a sort of no man's land, we undoubtedly beat the German Air Force, and this gave us the mastery locally in the air, and we inflicted losses of three or four to one. Anyone who looks at the photographs which were published a week or so ago of the re-embarkation, showing the masses of troops assembled on the beach and forming an ideal target for hours at a time, must realise that this re-embarkation would not have been possible unless the enemy had resigned all hope of recovering air superiority at that point.

iii *A painful decision*

In the defence of this island the advantages to the defenders will be very great ... During the great battle in France, we gave very powerful and continuous aid to the French Army both by fighters and bombers, but in spite of every kind of pressure we never would allow the entire Metropolitan strength of the Air Force, in fighters, to be consumed. This decision was painful, but it was also right, because the fortunes of the battle in France could not have been decisively affected, even if we had thrown in our entire fighter force ...

iv *Our fighter pilots*

But, as it is, I am happy to inform the House that our fighter air strength is stronger at the present time, relatively to the Germans, who have suffered terrible losses, than it has ever been, and consequently we believe ourselves to possess the capacity to continue the war in the air under better conditions than we have ever experienced before. I look forward confidently to the exploits of our fighter pilots, who will have the glory of saving their native land, their island home, and all they love, from the most deadly of all attacks ...

Therefore, in casting up this dread balance-sheet, contemplating our dangers with a disillusioned eye, I see great reason for intense vigilance and exertion, but none whatever for panic or despair ...

v *'Their finest hour'*

Then Winston Churchill finished with this call to us to brace ourselves to our duty:

What General Weygand called the 'Battle of France' is over. I expect that the battle of Britain is about to begin. Upon this battle depends the survival of Christian civilisation. Upon it depends our own British life and the long continuity of our institutions and our Empire. The whole fury and might of the enemy must very soon be turned on us. Hitler knows that he will have to break us in this island or lose the war. If we can stand up to him all Europe may be free, and the life of the world may move forward into broad, sunlit uplands, but if we fail then the whole world, including the United States, and all that we have known and cared for, will sink into the abyss of a new dark age made more sinister, and perhaps more prolonged, by the lights of a perverted science. Let us therefore brace ourselves to our duty and so bear ourselves that if the British Commonwealth and Empire lasts for a thousand years men will say: 'This was their finest hour.'

I remember too the impact of those last words. Everyone realised that the coming battle would be decisive.

6 House of Commons: 20 August 1940

i *We at home*

Two months passed. The battle of Britain began. Enemy aircraft came over day and night. Our fighters went up and shot down all they could. Anti-aircraft batteries brought down many which got closer. Winston Churchill made his next speech to the House of Commons on 20 August 1940. But before I tell you of it, I would give you a few lines from a letter which Mary, my wife, wrote to her close friend in Herefordshire two days before. We had my brother Norman's family evacuated to us at the time. My Robert was nearly two and his cousin John the same age. The letter shows the calmness with which they carried on.

18 August 1940

Dearest Gladys,

We have got little John Denning with us.

We are getting on very well in spite of frequent air-raid warnings. Two days we had two in the day but nothing much happened. However we have an excellent large, under-the-stairs cupboard, and if I hear gun-fire or any ominous sounds, I take the family there. You would have been amused to see the two little boys having their lunches in their own den. We did have a few bombs dropped on Haywards Heath on Thursday night but no damage was done and nobody here really takes much notice of Hitler's increased activity. Tom was in Leeds from Thursday till yesterday – all quiet there, he says – I hope you have not been disturbed.

Now two days later, on 20 August 1940, Winston Churchill told the House of Commons how the battle was going.

ii *'The sole champion'*

. . . Hitler is now sprawled over Europe. Our offensive springs are being slowly compressed, and we must resolutely and methodically prepare ourselves for the campaigns of 1941 and 1942. Two or three years are not a long time, even in our short, precarious lives. They are nothing in the history of the nation, and when we are doing the finest thing in the world, and have the honour to be the sole champion of the liberties of all Europe, we must not grudge these years or weary as we toil and struggle through them. . . .

iii *'A cataract of disaster'*

Rather more than a quarter of a year has passed since the new Government came into power in this country. What a cataract of disaster has poured out upon us since then. The trustful Dutch overwhelmed; their beloved and respected Sovereign driven into exile; the peaceful city of Rotterdam the scene of a massacre as hideous and brutal as anything in the Thirty Years War. Belgium invaded and beaten down; our own fine Expeditionary Force, which King Leopold called to his rescue, cut off and almost captured, escaping as it seemed only by a miracle and with the loss of all its equipment; our Ally, France, out; Italy is against us; all France in the power of the enemy, all its arsenals and vast masses of military material converted or convertible to the enemy's use; a puppet Government set up at Vichy which may at any moment be forced to become our foe; the whole Western seaboard of Europe from the North Cape to the Spanish frontier in German hands; all the ports, all the airfields on this immense front, employed against us as potential springboards of invasion. Moreover, the German air power, numerically so far outstripping ours, has been brought so close to our Island that what we used to dread greatly has come to pass and the hostile bombers not only reach our shores in a few minutes and from many directions, but can be escorted by their fighter aircraft.

iv *Standing erect*

Why, Sir, if we had been confronted at the beginning of May with such a prospect, it would have seemed incredible that at the end of a period of horror and disaster, we should stand erect, sure of ourselves, masters of our fate, and with the conviction of final victory burning unquenchable in our hearts. Few would have believed we could survive; none would have believed that we should today not only feel stronger but should actually be stronger than we have ever been before.

v *'Sure of ourselves'*

Let us see what has happened on the other side of the scales. The British nation and the British Empire finding themselves alone, stood undismayed against disaster. No one flinched or wavered; nay, some who formerly thought of peace, now think only of war. Our people are united and resolved, as they have never been before. Death and ruin have become small things compared with the shame of defeat or failure in duty. We cannot tell what lies ahead. It may be that even greater ordeals lie before us. We shall face whatever is coming to us. We are sure of ourselves and of our cause and here then is the supreme fact which has emerged in these months of trial.

vi *The great air battle*

. . . The great air battle which has been in progress over this Island for the last few weeks has recently attained a high intensity. It is too soon to attempt to assign limits either to its scale or to its duration. We must certainly expect that greater efforts will be made by the enemy than any he has so far put forth. Hostile airfields are still being developed in France and the Low Countries, and the movement of squadrons and materials for attacking us is still proceeding. It is quite plain that Herr Hitler could not admit defeat in his air attack on Great Britain without sustaining most serious injury. . . .

vii *'Never in the field of human conflict . . .'*

Then he told of our gratitude to the young airmen:

The gratitude of every home in our Island, in our Empire, and indeed throughout the world, except in the abodes of the guilty, goes out to the British airmen who, undaunted by odds, unwearied in their constant challenge and mortal danger, are turning the tide of world war by their prowess and by their devotion. Never in the field of human conflict was so much owed by so many to so few. All hearts go out to the fighter pilots, whose brilliant actions we see with our own eyes day after day, but we must never forget that all the time, night after night, month after month, our bomber squadrons travel far into Germany, find their targets in the darkness by the highest navigational skill, aim their attacks, often under the heaviest fire, often with serious loss, with deliberate, careful discrimination, and inflict shattering blows upon the whole of the technical and war-making structure of the Nazi power. On no part of the Royal Air Force does the weight of the war fall more heavily than on the daylight bombers who will play an invaluable part in the case of invasion and whose unflinching zeal it has been necessary in the meanwhile on numerous occasions to restrain.

Amongst those bomber pilots was Leonard Cheshire, then aged 23, the son of our dear friend Professor Geoffrey Cheshire. He was awarded the Victoria Cross, DSO and two bars. After the war, he founded the Cheshire Homes for the Sick, of which I was Chairman for many years.

viii *'Our task'*

. . . But before we can undertake the task of rebuilding we have not only to be convinced ourselves, but we have to convince all other countries that the Nazi tyranny is going to be finally broken. The right to guide the course of world history is the noblest prize of victory. We are still toiling up the hill, we have not yet reached the crest-line of it, we cannot survey the landscape or even imagine what its condition will be when that longed-for morning comes. The task which lies before us immediately is at once more practical, more simple, and more stern. I hope – indeed I pray – that we shall not be found unworthy of our victory if after toil and tribulation it is granted to us. For the rest, we have to gain the victory. That is our task . . .

7 The battle of Britain

i *We won through*

The battle of Britain continued. Day after day, night after night, our fighters and bombers were in action. Day after day fighting in the air and bringing down the enemy. Night after night bombing enemy bases. At home, anti-aircraft batteries rattling. Scores, nay hundreds, of German aircraft shot down. The date of the battle is given as 15 September 1940. But it lasted over several weeks. When it was won, it meant that we had no longer any fear of invasion. But we still had the dreadful bombings of our cities and towns. These our people withstood with undaunted courage – till in the end we gained the victory.

2 England expects

Introduction

Having told you of Winston Churchill's call to arms, I would remind you of Lord Nelson's equally famous call to the fleet at the battle of Trafalgar:

England expects that every man will do his duty.

That one sentence was one of the most effective pieces of prose in our language. It strengthened the morale of the men. It was worth a dozen extra ships.

The nearest parallel in my time is in the words of Lord Haig to us in March 1918 after the enemy had advanced within striking distance of Amiens and Paris. I told you of it in *The Family Story*:

> Every position must be held to the last man: there must be no retirement. With our backs to the wall and believing in the justice of our cause, each one of us must fight on to the end.

1 Before the battle

i *HMS* Euryalus

Nelson's famous message was recorded at the time in the log-book of HMS *Euryalus*. She was a frigate commanded by Nelson's personal friend, Henry Blackwood. She was acting as a 'repeating ship'. That means that she was to repeat signals made by the flagship *Victory* and pass them on to the whole line of battle. Her master (in charge of her navigation and sailing) was Frederick Ruckert. He kept the log recording her movements. It is on a canvas-backed manuscript written up from hour to hour during the battle. It is now in the Nelson collection at Lloyd's in the City of London.

ii *Nelson's prayer*

Nelson himself kept a diary in which he recorded the events day by day. I have quoted from it in *The Family Story*. His entries tell us that at daylight on 21 October 1805 Nelson in his flagship the *Victory* saw the enemy's combined fleet – that is, the combined fleets of France and Spain – in the far distance. He at once gave a signal to the British fleet to prepare for battle. He went down to his cabin and wrote down in his diary this prayer:

> May the great God whom I worship grant to my country and for the benefit of Europe in general a great and glorious victory, and may no misconduct in any one tarnish it, and may humanity after victory be the predominant feature in the British fleet.

He must have had a foreboding that he himself would be killed, for he added this prayer for himself:

> For myself individually I commit my life to Him who made me . . . To Him I resign myself and the just cause which is entrusted to me to defend. Amen, Amen, Amen.

iii *Nelson's will*

On that very morning, on the very next page in his diary, he wrote his will in his own hand, finishing with these bequests:

> I leave Emma Lady Hamilton therefore a legacy to my King and country that they will give her an ample provision to maintain her rank in life. I also leave to the beneficence of my country my adopted daughter Horatia Nelson Thompson and I desire she will use in future the name of Nelson only. These are the only favors I ask of my King and country at this moment when I am going to fight their battle.

It was necessary for his will to be witnessed by two witnesses so at eight o'clock that morning he sent a signal to Henry Blackwood on the *Euryalus* asking him to come over. Blackwood was pulled over in a boat to the *Victory*. Nelson asked the *Victory*'s captain – his dearest friend, Thomas Hardy – to come in. Nelson asked the two of them to witness his signature to his will. They did so in good bold hands.

iv *Prepare for action*

After the signing, Blackwood urged Nelson to shift his flag from the *Victory* to the frigate *Euryalus* so as to be better able to direct the action.

> 'But,' said Blackwood, 'Nelson would not hear of it and gave as his reason the force of example'.

Nelson ordered the *Victory* to set more sail. He then made a tour of his flagship as it was preparing for action. He took Blackwood and Hardy with him.

2 Into battle

i *The message to the fleet*

The enemy were then getting so close that cannon balls were beginning to hit the *Victory*. Then comes the description (in the Nelson collection at Lloyd's) of the way in which the message was sent to the fleet:

Back on the quarter deck, his lordship remarked to Blackwood to the effect that he would make a general signal 'to amuse the fleet'. The French and Spanish battleships less than half a mile away had opened fire at extreme range and were already scoring hits on the *Victory* as Nelson called to his signal lieutenant 'Mr Pasco, I wish to say to the fleet "England confides that every man will do his duty". You must be very quick for I have one more signal to make which is for Close Action'. Lieutenant Pasco suggested that 'expects' might be substituted for 'confides', which was not in the code-book and would have had to be spelt out with seven separate flag hoists. 'That will do' said Nelson, 'make it directly.'

Blackwood . . . said farewell to his chief and was left in no doubt that he would never see Nelson alive again. As he was pulled back to his ship, he must have seen *Euryalus* repeating Lord Nelson's historic signal – eight three-numeral groups – 'England' – 'Expects' – 'That' – 'Every' – 'Man' – 'Will' – 'Do' – 'His' – followed by the alphabetical flags spelling out 'Duty' – a word not thought necessary to be included in the code-book.

As Blackwood's boat drew near the *Euryalus*, Frederick Ruckert '*observed the Royal Sovereign (Admiral Collingwood) leading the Lee line bearing Down on the Enemys Rear line being then nearly within Gun Shot of them Lord Nelson leading the Weather Line bore Down upon the Enemys Center.*'

ii *Nelson is wounded*

After giving the signal, Nelson went on the upper deck of the *Victory*, wearing his Admiral's uniform with epaulets and stars – no doubt to encourage his men so that they could see him in the forefront of the battle. Then the *Victory* closed with the French ship *Redoubtable*. This is Robert Southey's description of Nelson being wounded:

A ball fired from her mizzen top, which, in the then situation of the two vessels, was not more than fifteen yards from that part of the deck where he was standing, struck the epaulet on his left shoulder, about a quarter after one, just in the heat of action. He fell upon his face, on the spot which was covered with his poor secretary's blood. Hardy, who was a few steps from him, turning round, saw three men raising him up. 'They have done for me at last, Hardy', said he. 'I hope not', cried Hardy. 'Yes!' he replied; 'my backbone is shot through.'

iii *Down to the cockpit*

He was carried down to the cockpit. He asked for Hardy to come down to him. But Hardy was in the thick of the battle on deck and could not leave for some time. Later on, he went down twice to see Nelson. On the second time he told him that it was a complete victory. Then the last scene is told by Robert Southey in these words:

'Take care of my dear Lady Hamilton, Hardy: take care of poor Lady Hamilton. Kiss me, Hardy', said he. Hardy knelt down and kissed his cheek; and Nelson said, 'Now I am satisfied. Thank God I have done my duty!' Hardy stood over him in silence for a moment or two, then knelt again and kissed his forehead. 'Who is that?' said Nelson; and being informed, he replied, 'God bless you, Hardy!' And Hardy then left him – for ever.

After Hardy left him:

His articulation now became difficult; but he was distinctly heard to say, 'Thank God, I have done my duty!' These words he repeatedly pronounced; and they were the last words he uttered. He expired at thirty minutes after four, – three hours and a quarter after he had received his wound.

iv *Southey's epitaph*

So Nelson had done his duty as he had exhorted his men to do. Southey's epitaph was:

He has left us, not indeed his mantle of inspiration, but a name and an example which are at this hour inspiring thousands of the youth of England – a name which is our pride, and an example which will continue to be our shield and our strength. Thus it is that the spirits of the great and wise continue to live and to act after them.

Postscript

As I told you before, my eldest brother Jack died in much the same way. He was mortally wounded on 25 September 1916 on the Somme. As he was being carried into the casualty clearing station, he told a comrade, 'I'm done for'. In a letter home found in his valise, he told father and mother, 'You may rest assured that I shall have done my duty'.

A year or two ago the Commander-in-Chief invited us to dine on the *Victory* at Portsmouth. He took us down to the cockpit. It meant going down a rope ladder which went down vertically. It must have been very distressing for the wounded Nelson. I could not have managed it except with the help on one side of the Commander-in-Chief himself and an able-bodied seaman on the other.

3 A pound of flesh

Introduction

In gathering leaves from my library, there is a pile of them from Shakespeare. I know many of the passages by heart. I recite them. I quote them. They illustrate all sides of life. At every turn of a page, I am lost in admiration at his genius. His use of words, his portrayal of action, and his powers of description have had immense influence in forming the English language. So I have pondered, what shall I choose?

Everyone knows the call to courage from *Henry V* before Harfleur:

> Once more unto the breach, dear friends, once more;
> Or close the wall up with our English dead!

Everyone knows the funeral oration of Antony on the death of Julius Caesar:

> Friends, Romans, countrymen, lend me your ears;
> I come to bury Caesar, not to praise him.

Everyone knows the theatrical metaphor of the melancholy Jaques in *As You Like It*:

> All the world's a stage,
> And all the men and women merely players.

I put all those on one side. They are worn thin by usage. At length I decided upon *The Merchant of Venice*: because it contains the most dramatic trial scene in all our literature. The Bar Theatrical Society (of which I am President) have performed it well, especially with our dear friend, Sir Denys Buckley, taking the part of Shylock.

I have drawn parallels between the law of Venice (as painted by Shakespeare) and the law of England (as it was in his time). They are much the same.

1 Venice

i *On the Rialto*

The play, *The Merchant of Venice*, is a combination of two stories: one about the 'pound of flesh'; the other about the elopement of Jessica, Shylock's daughter. I am here only concerned with the first.

The story is set in Venice about the year 1598 AD, contemporary with Shakespeare himself. At that time Venice was a great commercial city, comparable to what London is now. Much of the sea-going trade of the world was in the hands of merchant princes of Venice. They had their great palaces alongside the canals. They patronised the fine arts. They lived in culture and luxury.

When these merchants were doing business, they used to meet on the Rialto (Ponte di Rivo Alto), which means the bridge of the deep stream. It was a beautiful single-span marble bridge across the Grand Canal, newly built towards the end of the sixteenth century. It was the centre of the mercantile quarter of old Venice. Shakespeare knew all about it. He mentions it several times. It is still there.

The City of Venice was at that time a self-governing republic with its own constitution and its own laws. These were administered by the Chief Magistrate who was called the Doge (Duke). He tried all important cases.

ii *Its past glories*

In the following centuries Venice declined. Its trade disappeared. Its palaces decayed. It became a museum-piece. But its past glories were commemorated by Wordsworth in his lovely sonnet, *On the Extinction of the Venetian Republic, 1802*:

> Once did she hold the gorgeous East in fee;
> And was the safeguard of the West: the worth
> Of Venice did not fall below her birth,
> Venice, the eldest Child of Liberty.
> She was a maiden City, bright and free;
> No guile seduced, no force could violate;
> And, when she took unto herself a mate,
> She must espouse the everlasting Sea.
> And what if she had seen those glories fade,
> Those titles vanish, and that strength decay;
> Yet shall some tribute of regret be paid
> When her long life hath reach'd its final day:
> Men are we, and must grieve when even the Shade
> Of that which once was great is pass'd away.

2 Antonio the merchant

i *Is Antonio good for the money?*

Signor Antonio was one of the great merchant princes of Venice. When a question arose as to his credit – whether he was good for 3,000 ducats, that is, 3,000 gold coins – Shylock, the Jewish moneylender, was confident that he was. He discusses it with Bassanio, Antonio's friend:

Shy. Antonio is a good man.

Bass. Have you heard any imputation to the contrary?

Shy. Ho, no, no, no, no: my meaning, in saying he is a good man, is to have you understand me, that he is sufficient. Yet his means are in supposition; he hath an argosy bound to Tripolis, another to the Indies; I understand, moreover, upon the Rialto, he hath a third at Mexico, a fourth for England, and other ventures he hath, squandered abroad. But ships are but boards, sailors but men: there be land-rats and water-rats, water-thieves and land-thieves, I mean pirates; and then there is the peril of waters, winds, and rocks. The man is, notwithstanding, sufficient. Three thousand ducats; I think I may take his bond.

ii *Yes, but it is a risk*

You will notice that Shylock, in his shrewdness, was well aware that even Antonio's means were 'in supposition,' that is, at risk. If a vessel was lost through perils of the sea, the owner had to bear the loss himself. There were no insurers in Venice in those days. Even in London Edward Lloyd did not start his coffee-house in Lombard Street until the eighteenth century. There were no bankers in Venice either, and no commercial credits. If a trader wished to borrow money for his enterprise, he had to go to a moneylender.

3 Bassanio the spendthrift

i *Bassanio wastes money*

Bassanio was a friend of Antonio. He was a very different type. He was 'a scholar and a soldier'. He lived in grand style but much beyond his means. He got through his own money and also much that he had borrowed from his friends. Most of it from Antonio. He confessed himself:

> How much I have disabled mine estate,
> By something showing a more swelling port
> Than my faint means would grant continuance.

ii *Bassanio plans to marry an heiress*

To redeem his fortune, he became suitor to a fair lady named Portia. She was a rich heiress with many suitors seeking her – or her money. Bassanio wished to outdo them all and win her for himself. He voiced it to Antonio:

> O my Antonio, had I but the means
> To hold a rival place with one of them, . . .
> . . . I should questionless be fortunate!

Bassanio told Antonio he had first 'to get clear of all the debts I owe.' He made a plea for help such as is made by every borrower, 'Lend me more, and I will repay all.' He draws an analogy from his experience in archery:

> In my school-days, when I had lost one shaft,
> I shot his fellow of the self-same flight
> The self-same way with more advised watch,
> To find the other forth; and by adventuring both,
> I oft found both: I urge this childhood proof,
> Because what follows is pure innocence.
> I owe you much; and, like a wilful youth,
> That which I owe is lost; but if you please
> To shoot another arrow that self way
> Which you did shoot the first, I do not doubt,
> As I will watch the aim, or to find both,
> Or bring your latter hazard back again,
> And thankfully rest debtor for the first.

4 The bond is given

i *Antonio is willing to guarantee Bassanio*

Antonio was agreeable. He gave this assurance to Bassanio:

> . . . be assured,
> My purse, my person, my extremest means,
> Lie all unlock'd to your occasions.

But he had not enough cash in hand to satisfy Bassanio's request. All his money was invested in his sea-borne trade. He had not got 3,000 ducats (gold coins) available or anything like it. So he authorised Bassanio to pledge his credit without limit so as to further his suit for Portia. I cannot think that in real life any merchant would be so foolish. But this is fiction. This is what Antonio told Bassanio:

> Thou know'st that all my fortunes are at sea;
> Neither have I money, nor commodity
> To raise a present sum: therefore go forth;

Try what my credit can in Venice do:
That shall be rack'd, even to the uttermost,
To furnish thee to Belmont, to fair Portia.
Go, presently inquire, and so will I,
Where money is; and I no question make,
To have it of my trust, or for my sake.

ii *Shylock is cautious*

No doubt Bassanio knew all the money-lenders in Venice. None of them would lend him any money on his own credit. But they might on Antonio's credit. So he went to Shylock:

Shy. Three thousand ducats; well.

Bass. Ay, sir, for three months.

Shy. For three months; well.

Bass. For the which, as I told you, Antonio shall be bound.

Shy. Antonio shall become bound; well.

Bass. May you stead me? will you pleasure me? shall I know your answer?

Shy. Three thousand ducats for three months, and Antonio bound.

Shylock is cautious. He does not commit himself at that point. He wants to speak with Antonio first.

iii *Shylock is aggrieved*

Antonio comes forward. Shylock recalls the abuse and injustice he has already suffered at Antonio's hands:

Signior Antonio, many a time and oft
In the Rialto you have rated me
About my moneys and my usances:
Still have I borne it with a patient shrug;
For sufferance is the badge of all our tribe.
You call me misbeliever, cut-throat dog,
And spit upon my Jewish gaberdine,
And all for use of that which is mine own.
Well then, it now appears you need my help:
Go to, then; you come to me, and you say
'Shylock, we would have moneys:' you say so;
You, that did void your rheum upon my beard,
And foot me as you spurn a stranger cur
Over your threshold: moneys is your suit.
What should I say to you? Should I not say
'Hath a dog money? is it possible
A cur can lend three thousand ducats?' or
Shall I bend low and in a bondman's key,

With bated breath and whispering humbleness,
Say this, –
'Fair sir, you spit on me on Wednesday last;
You spurn'd me such a day; another time
You call'd me dog; and for these courtesies
I'll lend you thus much moneys?'

iv *Antonio presses his request*

Antonio acknowledges the justice of Shylock's rebuke. He asks him to lend the money – not out of friendship – but out of hatred on exacting terms:

But lend it rather to thine enemy;
Who if he break, thou mayest with better face
Exact the penalty.

v *Shylock stipulates for a pound of flesh*

Then Shylock comes out with the penalty, on which the whole story turns. He stipulates for a forfeiture of a pound of Antonio's flesh. Just in fun, he says, but in truth in deadly earnest. He will lend the money to Bassanio on these terms:

Shy. Go with me to a notary, seal me there
Your single bond; and, in a merry sport,
If you repay me not on such a day,
In such a place, such sum or sums as are
Express'd in the condition, let the forfeit
Be nominated for an equal pound
Of your fair flesh, to be cut off and taken
In what part of your body pleaseth me.

Ant. Content, i' faith: I'll seal to such a bond,
And say there is much kindness in the Jew.

Bass. You shall not seal to such a bond for me:
I'll rather dwell in my necessity.

Ant. Why, fear not, man; I will not forfeit it:
Within these two months, that's a month before
This bond expires, I do expect return
Of thrice three times the value of this bond.

vi *Antonio gives the bond*

So Antonio agrees:

Ant. Yes, Shylock, I will seal unto this bond.

Shy. Then meet me forthwith at the notary's;
Give him direction for this merry bond;
And I will go and purse the ducats straight.

Shylock went off to get the ducats. Left alone, Bassanio is fearful:

Bass. I like not fair terms and a villain's mind.

Ant. Come on: in this there can be no dismay;
My ships come home a month before the day.

You will note that Shylock insisted on a deed and Antonio agreed: I will seal unto this bond. At that time, even in English law, the law of contract was not developed. One party to a contract had only an effective remedy if the other party had entered into a covenant under seal. Sometimes called a deed or a bond. So long as the plaintiff had a deed, his position was impregnable. In his book, *History and Sources of the Common Law*, my friend Cecil Fifoot said that 'the action was *stricti juris*. The defendant was bound by the Deed, the whole Deed, and nothing but the Deed.'

You will notice also that Shylock said that the forfeiture claim (of a pound of flesh) was only inserted 'in a merry sport'. That is, for fun, not meaning it to be enforced. But any evidence to that effect was quite inadmissible.

5 Antonio has losses

i *One ship is lost*

Later on comes the news that Antonio's ship has been lost. Two of his friends, Salanio and Salarino, talk of it:

Salan. Now, what news on the Rialto?

Salar. Why, yet it lives there unchecked, that Antonio hath a ship of rich lading wrecked on the narrow seas; the Goodwins, I think they call the place; a very dangerous flat and fatal, where the carcases of many a tall ship lie buried. . . .

. . .

Salar. I would it might prove the end of his losses.

ii *Shylock will have his revenge*

Shylock comes up. He tells in a famous passage how the Jews have been ill-treated:

Salar. ... But tell us, do you hear whether Antonio have had any loss at sea or no?

Shy. There I have another bad match: a bankrupt, a prodigal, who dare scarce show his head on the Rialto; a beggar, that was used to come so smug upon the mart; let him look to his bond: he was wont to call me usurer; let him look to his bond: he was wont to lend money for a Christian courtesy; let him look to his bond.

Salar. Why, I am sure, if he forfeit, thou wilt not take his flesh: what's that good for?

Shy. To bait fish withal: if it will feed nothing else, it will feed my revenge. He hath disgraced me, and hindered me half a million; laughed at my losses, mocked at my gains, scorned my nation, thwarted my bargains, cooled my friends, heated mine enemies; and what's his reason? I am a Jew. Hath not a Jew eyes? hath not a Jew hands, organs, dimensions, senses, affections, passions? fed with the same food, hurt with the same weapons, subject to the same diseases, healed by the same means, warmed and cooled by the same winter and summer, as a Christian is? If you prick us, do we not bleed? if you tickle us, do we not laugh? if you poison us, do we not die? and if you wrong us, shall we not revenge? if we are like you in the rest, we will resemble you in that. If a Jew wrong a Christian, what is his humility? Revenge. If a Christian wrong a Jew, what should his sufference be by Christian example? Why, revenge. The villainy you teach me, I will execute; and it shall go hard but I will better the instruction.

iii *More ships are lost*

At first it was only one ship but more bad news followed. All his other ships perished. A messenger, Salerio, brought the bad news to Bassanio:

Bass. ... But is it true, Salerio?
Have all his ventures fail'd? What, not one hit?
From Tripolis, from Mexico, and England,
From Lisbon, Barbary, and India?
And not one vessel scape the dreadful touch
Of merchant-marring rocks?

Saler. Not one, my lord.
Besides, it should appear, that if he had
The present money to discharge the Jew,
He would not take it. Never did I know
A creature, that did bear the shape of man,
So keen and greedy to confound a man:
He plies the Duke at morning and at night;
And doth impeach the freedom of the state,

If they deny him justice: twenty merchants,
The Duke himself, and the magnificoes
Of greatest port, have all persuaded with him;
But none can drive him from the envious plea
Of forfeiture, of justice, and his bond.

6 The forfeiture is complete

i *Antonio fears the worst*

It is to be inferred from that passage that the three months had expired and that Antonio had not repaid the 3,000 ducats. Any tender after that time would in law have been of no effect. Shylock could refuse it as being too late. The forfeiture was complete as soon as the due date (three months) had gone past without payment. This is still the law in England in shipping cases, see *Mardorf Peach* [1977] AC 850 and *Scandinavian Trading* [1983] 2 AC 694.

When Antonio receives the news that all his ships have sunk, he sends a letter to Bassanio telling him, and that he fears the worst:

> Sweet Bassanio, my ships have all miscarried, my creditors grow cruel, my estate is very low, my bond to the Jew is forfeit; and since in paying it, it is impossible I should live, all debts are cleared between you and I, if I might but see you at my death.

ii *An offer of late payment*

Bassanio reads the letter to Portia. She offers to pay the sum:

Por. What sum owes he the Jew?

Bass. For me three thousand ducats.

Por. What, no more?
Pay him six thousand, and deface the bond;
Double six thousand, and then treble that,
Before a friend of this description
Shall lose a hair through Bassanio's fault.

That offer was no good because it was too late. The forfeiture had accrued. No tender of the sum or any higher sum would do any good. It is the same in English law.

iii *Shylock refuses it*

Shylock now sued to enforce the forfeiture. He used the process then available in the English courts – by arresting the debtor so as to bring him before the court. So we see Antonio in the custody of a gaoler meeting Shylock:

A pound of flesh

Shy. I'll have my bond; speak not against my bond:
I have sworn an oath that I will have my bond.
Thou call'dst me dog before thou hadst a cause;
But, since I am a dog, beware my fangs:
The Duke shall grant me justice . . . .

Ant. I pray thee, hear me speak.

Shy. I'll have my bond; I will not hear thee speak:
I'll have my bond; and therefore speak no more.
I'll not be made a soft and dull-eyed fool,
To shake the head, relent, and sigh, and yield
To Christian intercessors. Follow not;
I'll have no speaking: I will have my bond.

iv *Shylock has the law on his side*

He goes off and then, when Salarino says

> I am sure the Duke
> Will never grant this forfeiture to hold

Antonio answers with reasoning which is valid today in the Commercial Court in London. If a foreigner has a good claim or defence, the court will give effect to it according to law. It will lean in his favour rather than against him. This is important for our international trade.

Ant. The Duke cannot deny the course of law:
For the commodity that strangers have
With us in Venice, if it be denied,
Will much impeach the justice of his state;
Since that the trade and profit of the city
Consisteth of all nations.

7 The trial scene

i *Dramatic licence*

So now we come to the trial scene. It will be well-known to many of you. You will realise that Shakespeare distorts it greatly. It has to fit in with the plot by which Portia is to marry Bassanio. So he dresses Portia up in men's clothes and makes her into a doctor of law. And he makes her combine the roles of both an advocate for Antonio and a judge between Shylock and Antonio. So long as you can swallow these gross distortions, it contains two broad themes. The first is whether the court can grant relief to Antonio so as to relieve him from the forfeiture? The answer is No. The second is whether the penalty is contrary to public policy? The answer is Yes. So far as these two themes are concerned, I think the answers in English law would be the same as Shakespeare gives for the law of Venice.

ii *Issue is joined*

I will start at the point where Portia enters the court in Venice and the presiding judge (The Duke) says to her:

Duke. You are welcome: take your place.
Are you acquainted with the difference
That holds this present question in the court?

Por. I am informed thoroughly of the cause.
Which is the merchant here, and which the Jew?

Duke. Antonio and old Shylock, both stand forth.

Por. Is your name Shylock?

Shy. Shylock is my name.

Por. Of a strange nature is the suit you follow;
Yet in such rule that the Venetian law
Cannot impugn you as you do proceed.
You stand within his danger, do you not?

Ant. Ay, so he says.

Por. Do you confess the bond?

Ant. I do.

iii *Portia pleads for mercy*

She makes her off-quoted speech – the 'Quality of Mercy'.

Por. Then must the Jew be merciful.

Shy. On what compulsion must I? tell me that.

Por. The quality of mercy is not strain'd,
It droppeth as the gentle rain from heaven
Upon the place beneath: it is twice blest;
It blesseth him that gives, and him that takes:
'Tis mightiest in the mightiest: it becomes
The throned monarch better than his crown;
His sceptre shows the force of temporal power,
The attribute to awe and majesty,
Wherein doth sit the dread and fear of kings;
But mercy is above this sceptred sway;
It is enthroned in the hearts of kings,
It is an attribute to God himself;
And earthly power doth then show likest God's
When mercy seasons justice.

iv *She turns to Shylock*

Therefore, Jew,
Though justice be thy plea, consider this,
That, in the course of justice, none of us
Should see salvation: we do pray for mercy;
And that same prayer doth teach us all to render
The deeds of mercy. I have spoke thus much
To mitigate the justice of thy plea;
Which if thou follow, this strict court of Venice
Must needs give sentence 'gainst the merchant there.

Shy. My deeds upon my head! I crave the law,
The penalty and forfeit of my bond.

Por. Is he not able to discharge the money?

v *Bassanio offers to pay*

Bass. Yes, here I tender it for him in the court;
Yea, twice the sum: if that will not suffice,
I will be bound to pay it ten times o'er,
On forfeit of my hands, my head, my heart:
If this will not suffice, it must appear
That malice bears down truth. And I beseech you,
Wrest once the law to your authority:
To do a great right, do a little wrong,
And curb this cruel devil of his will.

vi *But Shylock has the legal right*

Portia states forcibly the doctrine of precedent. Shylock is so pleased that he likens her to Daniel, 'A Daniel come to judgement!' This is a reference to the Book of *Daniel and Susanna* in the *Apocrypha* as I told you in *Landmarks in the Law* p 322.

Por. It must not be; there is no power in Venice
Can alter a decree established:
'Twill be recorded for a precedent,
And many an error, by the same example,
Will rush into the state: it cannot be.

Shy. A Daniel come to judgement! yea, a Daniel!
O wise young judge, how I do honour thee!

Por. I pray you, let me look upon the bond.

Shy. Here 'tis, most reverend doctor, here it is.

Por. Shylock, there's thrice thy money offer'd thee.

Shy. An oath, an oath, I have an oath in heaven:
Shall I lay perjury upon my soul?
No, not for Venice.

vii *Shylock asks for judgment*

Por. Why, this bond is forfeit;
And lawfully by this the Jew may claim
A pound of flesh, to be by him cut off
Nearest the merchant's heart. Be merciful:
Take thrice thy money; bid me tear the bond.

Shy. When it is paid according to the tenour.
It doth appear you are a worthy judge;
You know the law, your exposition
Hath been most sound: I charge you by the law,
Whereof you are a well-deserving pillar,
Proceed to judgement: by my soul I swear
There is no power in the tongue of man
To alter me: I stay here on my bond.

Ant. Most heartily I do beseech the court
To give the judgement.

viii *Portia appears to give judgment for him*

Por. Why then, thus it is:
You must prepare your bosom for his knife.

Shy. O noble judge! O excellent young man!

Por. For the intent and purpose of the law
Hath full relation to the penalty,
Which here appeareth due upon the bond.

Shy. 'Tis very true: O wise and upright judge!
How much more elder art thou than thy looks!

Por. Therefore lay bare your bosom.

Shy. Ay, his breast:
So says the bond: – doth it not, noble judge? –
'Nearest his heart:' those are the very words.

Por. It is so. Are there balance here to weigh
The flesh?

Shy. I have them ready.

ix *But she finds a flaw*

Portia notes the difference between 'flesh' and 'blood'.

Por. Have by some surgeon, Shylock, on your charge,
To stop his wounds, lest he do bleed to death.

Shy. Is it so nominated in the bond?

Por. It is not so express'd: but what of that?
'Twere good you do so much for charity.

Shy. I cannot find it: 'tis not in the bond.

x *She gives judgment*

Then Portia announces the judgment of the court:

Por. A pound of that same merchant's flesh is thine:
The court awards it, and the law doth give it.

Shy. Most rightful judge!

Por. And you must cut this flesh from off his breast:
The law allows it, and the court awards it.

Shy. Most learned judge! A sentence! Come, prepare!

8 Portia turns the tables

i *'Tarry a little'*

Up to that point Portia has insisted on the strict rule of law and strict doctrine of precedent – just as the courts in England do. She has rejected any plea for mercy or relief in equity.

But she goes on to consider the letter of the bond and holds it is contrary to public policy that it should be enforced, because it cannot be achieved without the spilling of blood. She is warmly applauded by Gratiano, another friend of Antonio.

Por. Tarry a little; there is something else.
This bond doth give thee here no jot of blood;
The words expressly are 'a pound of flesh:'
Take then thy bond, take thou thy pound of flesh;
But, in the cutting it, if thou dost shed
One drop of Christian blood, thy lands and goods
Are, by the laws of Venice, confiscate
Unto the state of Venice.

Gra. O upright judge! Mark, Jew: O learned judge!

ii *'Thou shalt have justice'*

Shy. Is that the law?

Por. Thyself shall see the act:
For, as thou urgest justice, be assured
Thou shalt have justice, more than thou desirest.

Gra. O learned judge! Mark, Jew: a learned judge!

Shy. I take this offer, then; pay the bond thrice,
And let the Christian go.

Bass. Here is the money.

Por. Soft!
The Jew shall have all justice; soft! no haste:
He shall have nothing but the penalty.

Gra. O Jew! an upright judge, a learned judge!

iii *Shylock is in peril*

Por. Therefore prepare thee to cut off the flesh.
Shed thou no blood; nor cut thou less nor more
But just a pound of flesh: if thou cut'st more
Or less than a just pound, be it but so much
As makes it light or heavy in the substance,
Or the division of the twentieth part
Of one poor scruple, nay, if the scale do turn
But in the estimation of a hair,
Thou diest and all thy goods are confiscate.

Gra. A second Daniel, a Daniel, Jew!
Now, infidel, I have you on the hip.

Por. Why doth the Jew pause? take thy forfeiture.

Shy. Give me my principal, and let me go.

Bass. I have it ready for thee; here it is.

Por. He hath refused it in the open court:
He shall have merely justice and his bond.

Gra. A Daniel, still say I, a second Daniel!
I thank thee, Jew, for teaching me that word.

Shy. Shall I not have barely my principal?

Por. Thou shalt have nothing but the forfeiture,
To be so taken at thy peril, Jew.

Shy. Why, then the devil give him good of it!
I'll stay no longer question.

iv *Shylock suffers the penalty*

Finally, Portia brings a counter-charge against Shylock on the ground that he has been guilty of a criminal offence and can be punished and his goods forfeited. There used to be a parallel for this in the English criminal law. On conviction for a felony, the felon was liable to be hanged and his goods forfeited to the Crown.

Por. Tarry, Jew:
The law hath yet another hold on you.
It is enacted in the laws of Venice,
If it be proved against an alien

> That by direct or indirect attempts
> He seek the life of any citizen,
> The party 'gainst the which he doth contrive
> Shall seize one half his goods; the other half
> Comes to the privy coffer of the state;
> And the offender's life lies in the mercy
> Of the Duke only, 'gainst all other voice.
> In which predicament, I say, thou stand'st;
> For it appears, by manifest proceeding,
> That indirectly, and directly too,
> Thou hast contrived against the very life
> Of the defendant; and thou hast incurr'd
> The danger formerly by me rehearsed.
> Down, therefore, and beg mercy of the Duke.

Shylock did obtain mercy. He was released on condition that he became a Christian and left all his belongings on his death to his daughter, Jessica, and her husband.

9 In our courts

i *Often cited*

The case has often been mentioned in judgments. For instance, in *Tsakiroglou v Noblee Thorl*,[1] Diplock J said:

> Lawyers have ever been more prone than merchants to cling to the letter of the contract; see, for example, *Shylock v Antonio*, a case which might have been decided on grounds of public policy but, in fact, turned on a pure question of construction.

And in *A-G v Times Newspapers*[2] where *The Sunday Times* publicly criticised the Distillers Company – and in so doing prejudged the issue in pending litigation – Lord Diplock said:

> If Venice had been England and the Doge a judge in an English court of law it would have been contempt of court to hold either Shylock or Antonio to public obloquy on the Rialto because he was seeking to enforce in a court of competent jurisdiction legal rights to which he was entitled under the law as it existed at that time.

ii *In mitigation*

I must confess to some sympathy with Shylock. Antonio had publicly abused him on the Rialto. He had spat on him and treated him as if he were a dog. Bassanio was a good-for-nothing spendthrift who owed money all round and asked for more so as to help his suit with a lady.

[1] [1960] 2 QB 318, 329.
[2] [1974] AC 273, 313.

Yet they came round to Shylock begging his help. He was very generous to them and lent them 3,000 ducats for three months free of interest. Bassanio won the lady. They then defaulted. They did not pay him back a single ducat at the appointed time and had no hope of doing so – unless the lady helped them. No wonder he was aggrieved and sought to hold Antonio to his bond. No doubt he pressed the case too far. But spare a little sympathy for him. The Duke did so. He showed mercy to him. So should we.

4 The death of a king

Introduction

From that trial scene of fiction, I turn to the most memorable trial in our history. The trial of King Charles I in the Great Hall of Westminster. The story is told in our history books and by many writers. You will all know it in broad outline. But you will not know the drama of it all unless you read it in a book written by one of our greatest storytellers. He is a modern, John Buchan. He wrote a book on Oliver Cromwell. I gave it to my first wife, Mary, in 1934 when it was published: and I have it before me now. Oliver Cromwell has always been a hero in our family. My brother, General Denning, admired Cromwell's soldierly qualities. He often quoted his advice to his troops:

Put your trust in God and keep your powder dry.

That sentence has two parts. First, by trusting in God, the morale of the troops was strengthened. The war-cry on their colours and in battle was 'God with us' and 'God our strength'. Second, by keeping their powder dry, they made sure that their weapons were effective. I well remember on this point the broadcast which Winston Churchill made in February 1941 addressed to President Roosevelt. We were fighting for our survival and needed munitions of war from the United States:

Give us the tools and we will finish the job.

I have often repeated this to our good men in the grounds here – Charlie, Bert and Frank – and I have made sure that they have the tools.

1 The King himself

i *A painting in Middle Temple Hall*

Apart from Oliver Cromwell, the most colourful character in the book is the King, Charles the First. He is the subject of a famous painting in the Hall of the Middle Temple – surely the most beautiful hall in all England – going back to the time of the first Elizabeth, and miraculously surviving the bombs of the last war. The painting is large, covering most of the west wall. It is attributed to Van Dyck or one of his school. It has been in the Hall for the last three hundred years. It shows the King on his horse. He is handsome, with a pointed beard, concealing his small height – he was only just over five feet.

ii *Not a saint*

Some people regard Charles I as a saint and a martyr. I would not so describe him myself. Nor would John Buchan have done so. He was a rigid and obstinate authoritarian, claiming a divine right to govern England by his own command. He abused this authority greatly. He was crooked. He was an intriguer. You could not trust him. Worst of all, he claimed a royal prerogative which placed him above the law. He extracted ship money without the authority of Parliament: and when John Hampden challenged the King's authority, most of the judges – to their disgrace – upheld the King's claim. (John Hampden was a Magdalen man. His portrait is in my son's room there now.) The case was argued in 1637 for twelve days before all the twelve judges in Serjeants' Inn Hall. Ten of them were in favour of the King. Two against. The ten were led by Sir John Finch who had been recently appointed to be Chief Justice of the Common Pleas. The general feeling was that Finch was elevated to the Bench for the purpose of carrying through the obnoxious impost. He upheld the King's claim, going so far as to say that 'Acts of Parliament are void if they seek to take away the King's royal prerogative.' He was supported by Mr Justice Berkeley who said:

> I never read or heard that lex was rex, but it is common and most true that rex is lex.

Only two of the judges, Croke and Hutton, dissented. They held that the King was under the law, quoting Bracton:

> The King is under no man save under God and the law.

I am glad to say that in our time it has been held by the House of

Lords that the exercise of the royal prerogative is subject to review by the courts of law, save for some well-known exceptions. It was in *Council for Civil Service Unions v Minister for Civil Service* [1985] AC 374.

iii *'Bloody Tom tyrant'*

The trial and death of Charles I has been described by Dame Veronica Wedgwood as 'one of the great political dramas of European history.' But to understand it, you must know something of the trial and death of his staunch supporter, Thomas Wentworth, the Earl of Strafford. He was nicknamed 'Thorough' by the Royalists because of the thoroughness with which he sought to uphold the supremacy of the King. He was nicknamed 'Bloody Tom Tyrant' by the Parliamentarians because of the oppressive and tyrannical methods that he employed.

Against him were two of my heroes, John Pym and John Hampden. They were leaders of the Commons – and of the people of England. They were the staunch supporters of the rule of law against the autocracy of the Crown. They sat in the Long Parliament when it first assembled in 1640.

iv *Cromwell's plain suit*

Little known then was a new member for Cambridge. His name was Oliver Cromwell. This is the description of him by a contemporary, quoted by Buchan:

> . . . I came into the House one morning, well clad, and perceived a gentleman speaking whom I knew not, very ordinarily apparelled; for it was a plain cloth suit that seemed to have been made by an ill country tailor; his linen was plain, and not very clean, and I remember a speck or two of blood upon his little band which was not much larger than his collar; his hat was without a hatband; his stature was of a good size; his sword stuck close to his side; his countenance swollen and reddish; his voice sharp and untunable, and his eloquence full of fervour. . . .

I may say that our family was in those days for Parliament and against the King. We were Roundheads and not Cavaliers. We were Protestants and not Roman Catholics.

2 Strafford

i *He is impeached*

With Pym at their head, the new Parliament in 1640 made short work of ship money and of all levies made without the authority of

Parliament: and of the Star Chamber and other special courts. They were all abolished. But the urgent task was to get rid of Strafford. The Commons impeached him for high treason. The charge was that

> . . . he had endeavoured to subvert the fundamental laws of England and Ireland, and instead thereof to introduce an arbitrary and tyrannical government against law.

ii *He is tried*

This is the account given by John Buchan:

> The trial began on March 22, 1641, and by dawn each morning the great hall of Westminster was packed. Mr Robert Baillie, the emissary of the Scottish Covenanters, looked on at the spectacle with wondering provincial eyes and has left us a vivid picture; – the tall bowed figure of the accused in deep black wearing the George, the Lords in their robes and the Commons members within and without the rails, the vacant throne, the king in his box breaking the trellis with his own hands that he might hear better, the other boxes to the roof crowded with ladies and foreign notables, the chattering and laughter and guzzling while the grim drama was played out.

You will notice that Buchan refers simply to 'the George.' This was the jewel of the Order of the Garter, with a figure of Saint George armed, on horseback, encountering the dragon.

iii *Not guilty of high treason*

For fifteen days Strafford defended himself with patient reasonableness. Tyranny and misgovernment were conclusively proved against him, but not treason. The Statute of Treason of Edward III was restricted to a levying of war against the King or of compassing the King's death. Strafford had not committed those offences. He had been for the King and not against him.

iv *So he is attainted and executed*

Buchan tells what happened. Seeing that Strafford could not be convicted of treason, the Commons resorted to a Bill of Attainder. This was a process before Parliament by which a man could be sentenced to death without any crime being charged against him. But it had to be passed by Commons and Lords and assented to by the King. Note that fact. The King's assent was essential. In Strafford's case, the King assented to it, although he had personally guaranteed his safety. Buchan tells us:

> It was soon clear that he could not be convicted of treason as the law then stood. After fourteen sittings this became patent to the Commons leaders and they resorted

to other means. There was a general alarm as to what the king might do – march up the army from Yorkshire or seize the Tower to overawe parliament – and on this wave of fear, assisted by organized London mobs, they carried to success a simpler plan. It was Strafford's head or theirs. All pretence of judicial proceedings was relinquished. A bill of attainder was passed by the Commons .... The Lords passed the bill on May 8th; Strafford urged the king to assent to it in the interests of peace, and Charles, renouncing his plighted word, accepted the sacrifice. The doomed man met death with calm eyes; it was all one to him whether he laid his head on the block or was torn to pieces by the mob; his race was accomplished.

v *Oliver Cromwell is watching*

This is how Buchan describes Strafford:

A great man beyond doubt, perhaps the greatest English man of action in two centuries except that member for Cambridge whose harsh face was to be seen among the jostling Commons at the bar.

That member for Cambridge was Oliver Cromwell – one of the greatest of Englishmen.

And this was Buchan's verdict on the execution of Strafford:

Yet beyond question it was an act of revolution, a challenge which, when men began to reflect, was to cause a deep and final division in English minds.

It was the division between Parliament and the King.

3 Crossing the Rubicon

i *Folly upon folly*

After the execution of Strafford, Charles began to plot for armed intervention. He determined to arrest five members of the House of Commons – Pym, Hampden, Holles, Haselrig and Strode. Buchan says:

Then came folly upon folly.... His impatience sent him crashing through all constitutional laws and customs. Next afternoon he went down to the House in a coach, with an armed retinue of three or four hundred men behind him. News of his intention had long before been sent to Pym by Will Murray and by one of the queen's women, Lady Carlisle, and the five members had discreetly withdrawn. Charles strode into the chamber to find the birds flown, and to receive from Speaker Lenthall the classic answer that 'he had neither eyes to see, nor tongue to speak, in this place but as the House is pleased to direct me.' Next day he (the King) sought for the culprits in the city with no better success.

(You will notice Buchan's reference to Lady Carlisle. She was a vain, avaricious, *intrigante*, but though she was a close friend of Strafford there is no evidence that she had been his mistress, and it is highly improbable that she was ever Pym's.)

ii *Charles leaves Whitehall*

That action of Charles was fatal and final. Buchan likens it to the crossing of the Rubicon. You may know that the Rubicon was a small river in Italy which separated the Roman homeland from the outer province of Gaul. In 49 BC Julius Caesar, with his legions, crossed the Rubicon and marched towards Rome. He shouted, '*Alex jacta est*' (the die is cast). The decision was final and irrevocable. There could be no drawing back. By so doing Julius Caesar precipitated the Civil War there. So here Charles's attempt to arrest the five members precipitated our Civil War. This is how Buchan puts it:

> It was for the king the Rubicon which could not be recrossed. By his action he had exasperated the Commons to fury, and alienated the Lords. He had lowered his royal dignity, and convinced the ordinary man that neither his honour nor his judgment was to be trusted. He had attempted violence and failed, and had closed every avenue of reconciliation. On January 10, 1642, he left Whitehall – not to return to it till he returned to die.

He returned seven years later.

iii *The Civil War*

Then came the Civil War. On the one side was Oliver Cromwell who led the Parliament's army. He made it into a well-disciplined, well-equipped, and well-organised force. They were his Ironsides. It was an army of a new model. As Buchan says:

> At forty-three he had found his proper calling, and a force of incalculable velocity had been unloosed on the world.

On the other side was the King, Charles Stuart, who was only forty-one. Buchan rates him very low:

> He had no gift of resolute purpose or single-hearted action; the prominent velvet eyes under the heavy lids were the eyes of an emotional intriguer. They were the eyes, too, of a fanatic . . . .

iv *Personal items*

I do not propose to tell you about the battles, but we in Whitchurch, as I told you in the *Family Story*, are very interested in the second Battle of Newbury; because Charles stayed two nights at the Manor House here, 21 and 22 October 1644, on his way to the battle. (The house was afterwards the vicarage and is now called King's Lodge.) He wrote a letter from here to Prince Rupert at Bristol. (It is now in the British Museum.) After his stay here, he moved with his forces the twelve miles up to Newbury and took up a strong position one mile north of the town. On 25 October 1644 the Parliament's army attacked and nearly succeeded. But Cromwell was let down by some of his officers. The battle was inconclusive. The decisive battle was Naseby in June 1645 when Cromwell with Fairfax routed Charles with Rupert.

The other personal touch is that our direct ancestor Sydenham Poyntz, was a Colonel in the Parliament's army and played a notable part in its victories. Later he became Colonel-General Sir Sydenham Poyntz.

4 House arrest

i *At Carisbrooke Castle*

After the first war, there was a second, ending with the defeat of the Scots. But now I leave the wars and come to the negotiations by Cromwell with the King. These were unduly protracted. In October 1648 the King was virtually the prisoner of Parliament. He was under house arrest in Hampton Court and afterwards in Carisbrooke Castle on the Isle of Wight. Andrew Marvell, a young contemporary, in his *Horatian Ode*, suggests that this was the result of a shrewd scheme by Cromwell. After praising his military genius, Marvell admires Cromwell's diplomatic skill:

> What field of all the civil war
> Where his were not the deepest scar?
> And Hampton shows what part
> He had of wiser art;
>
> Where, twining subtle fears with hope,
> He wove a net of such a scope
> That Charles himself might chase
> To Carisbrooke's narrow case.

ii *At Windsor*

On 19 December 1648 Charles was escorted by a party of horse to Winchester. Thence he was moved to Windsor:

> When he learned that his destination was Windsor, he could not believe that the army intended him any harm, since, as he said, they were moving him from the worst of his castles to the best.... He was also in hourly expectation of a rescue. But the horse, the swiftest in England, which was awaiting him at Bagshot, fell lame, and on the 23rd he arrived at Windsor.

Charles remained at Windsor for some days. He spent a dreary

Christmas there. An envoy was sent to negotiate terms with him but he refused to see him. Buchan tells us:

Weariness and despair had produced a final obstinacy. He would not yield up the ancient rights of the throne or consent to the spoliation of a Church of which he believed himself the divinely appointed head. On the 27th, when the news of this refusal reached London, the council of officers was at last unanimous. There was no way out of the tangle but the king's death.

iii *A proposal for trial*

Oliver Cromwell then saw that the King must be brought to trial. So steps were taken for the purpose. The Commons proposed that the chief judges of England should try him with a jury of commissioners. But the Lords rejected the proposal:

On January 1, 1649, the remnant of the Commons, now the obedient satellites of the army, passed an ordinance to set up a high court of justice for the trial of the king. The court was to consist of Rolle, chief justice of England, St John, chief justice of the Common Pleas, and Wilde, chief baron of the Exchequer, with a jury of 150 commissioners, including six peers. Next day it was sent up to the Lords, accompanied by a resolution which declared that 'by the fundamental laws of this kingdom it is treason for the king of England for the time being to levy war against the Parliament and the kingdom of England.' The Lords, now only twelve in number, summarily rejected both ordinance and resolution. . . . Also the judges nominated refused to take part in the trial.

iv *The Commons assert legislative power*

Then there came a resolution which was quite unlawful:

So on January 4 the Commons passed a new act by a majority of six, which arrogated to a single House the legislative power.

(The journals of the House of Commons record that on the 4th 'a resolution was passed that, since the people were the origin of all just power, the Commons, as representing the people, could pass binding laws without consent of king or Lords.' That resolution would be acceptable to some of our politicians today.)

5 The Court is established

i *A revolutionary act*

Buchan describes the court and shows that it was a revolutionary act:

The court established by it consisted of one hundred and thirty-five commissioners, with no judges among its members, and no peers. The act set forth that Charles Stuart had wickedly designed to subvert the ancient laws and liberties of the people, and had shown himself impenitent in these causes; wherefore he must stand his trial 'for prevention of the like and greater inconveniences, and to the end no chief officer or magistrate whatever may hereafter presume traitorously and maliciously to imagine or contrive the enslaving and destroying of the English nation, and to expect impunity for so doing.' These words, in which we may detect the influence of Oliver, put the thing in its true light as a political act, to meet a present emergency and to provide for the future – a step founded not on legal or constitutional niceties but on a desperate need.

Since there was no High Court judge to preside, John Bradshawe was chosen. He was one of the judges of the Sheriffs' Court of the City of London –equivalent to a circuit judge today. Sir Thomas More had once been a judge of that Court.

ii *The hall is prepared*

Westminster Hall was normally divided by partitions into three courts of law. These were removed for the trial of the King.

Meantime the great hall of Westminster had been set in order for the trial. That hall remains today though all its environs have suffered change, and it is easy to reconstruct the scene. The booths of the tradespeople were cleared from the floor, and the south end, where the courts of Chancery and King's Bench usually sat, was filled with a wooden platform, divided from the rest of the hall by a partition three feet high. . . . The judges were to sit on benches covered with scarlet cloth at the back of the dais under the great south window. In the middle of the front row was a raised desk for the president; the clerks sat at a table beneath him, where lay the mace and the sword of state; at the edge of the dais there were pews for the prosecuting counsel and a crimson-velvet armchair for the king, who would sit with his back to the body of spectators.

iii *The expected first question*

Sir Robert Cotton had a house and garden near to the hall. The King was lodged there for the trial. Everyone knew that the King would dispute the authority of the court to try him. His first question would be and was:

Let me know by what lawful authority I am seated here and I will answer it: otherwise I will not answer it.

iv *'He is come'*

This is what happened according to Buchan:

About two o'clock on the 20th Charles was carried to Whitehall in a sedan-chair and thence by water to Cotton's house. The commissioners in the Painted Chamber saw him arrive before they had decided upon the authority on which they should found their case, for they were well aware of its legal flimsiness. A certain Sir

Purbeck Temple, a royalist who was planning the king's escape, was hidden behind the arras, and at the trial of the regicides deposed as follows:

> When their prayer was over there came news that the King was landing at Sir Robert Cotton's Stairs, at which Cromwell ran to a window, looking on the King as he came up the garden. He turned as white as the wall. Returning to the board . . . he said thus: 'My masters, he is come, he is come, and now we are doing that great work that the whole nation will be full of. Therefore I desire you to let us resolve here what answer we shall give the King when he comes before us, for the first question that he will ask will be by what authority as commissioners we do try him.' To which none answered presently. Then after a little space Henry Marten rose up and said: 'In the name of the Commons in Parliament assembled, and all the good people of England.'

6 The trial

i *The shot-proof hat*

We may discredit certain details, such as Oliver's white face, but there is no reason to disbelieve the substance of the tale. Headed by Bradshawe in his shot-proof hat, the court, having got its formula, marched with its men-at-arms and ushers into Westminster Hall.

ii *Charles refuses to answer*

Charles, in a dark suit and wearing the insignia of the Garter, remained covered and paid no respect to the court. When the roll of judges was called sixty-eight responded. . . . While the charge was read the king's stern face relaxed, and he laughed when he heard himself proclaimed a traitor. He tried to interrupt the clerk by touching him with his cane; its silver head fell off and he had to pick it up himself. Bradshawe called on him to answer, using Henry Marten's new-made formula. . . .

iii *He asks the question*

Then Charles asked the expected question – by what authority he was being tried. England, he said, had never been an elective kingdom; he was monarch not by election but by inheritance, and to acknowledge a usurped authority would be a betrayal of his trust. As he was removed the soldiers by order shouted 'Justice,' but the mass of the spectators cried 'God save the King.'

iv *Again he refuses to plead*

He was next brought before the court on the 22nd, and again refused to plead. . . . So completely did the court fail to overawe the prisoner that Hewson, one of the commanders of the guards, is said to have lost his temper and spat in Charles's face. 'God hath justice in store,' said the king gently, 'both for you and me.' Again on the 23rd he was before the court with the same result.

v *The sentence*

On the 25th it was resolved in a small house that they should proceed to sentence against the king as tyrant, traitor, murderer and public enemy to the commonwealth of England, and that the sentence should be death; and a fuller court next day confirmed the decision. The king was to be brought into Westminster hall on the morrow to hear his doom.

That day, Saturday the 27th, saw the end of the judicial travesty. . . . Bradshawe delivered a vast rambling speech, in which he quoted the Scriptures and the classics, mediaeval lawyers like Bracton, Mariana, Father Parsons and George Buchanan, and made but a poor job of it. Charles asked permission to answer him, but was told that it was too late. The clerk read the sentence, and the prisoner, still struggling to speak, was removed by the guards. The soldiers in the hall and outside it, pursuant to orders, shouted 'Justice' and 'Execution' and blew tobacco-smoke in his face. 'Poor souls,' said the king, 'for sixpence they would do the same for their commanders.' But in the streets the common people were weeping.

7 The last days

i *In contemplation*

On the evening of the 27th, after sentence, Charles was taken to Sir Robert Cotton's house, and thence to Whitehall, where he spent the night. His spirits were equable, almost gay. He gave orders that his dogs should be removed and sent to his wife, that nothing might distract his mind from grave contemplation. On Sunday Juxon, who had been bishop of London, was permitted to attend him, and the day was spent in prayer. . . .

ii *Sunday evening*

On the Sunday evening, through a sudden mercifulness in his gaolers, he was taken to St James's palace that he might not hear the scaffold being hammered together in Whitehall.

iii *The death warrant*

The original death warrant is in the keeping of the House of Lords' Record Office. Historians have inquired closely into it. Names were written in. Then rubbed out and others written in their place. Dates were inserted and afterwards altered. It was addressed to 'Colonell Francis Hacker' and two others. The first signature was that of the President of the court, 'Jo. Bradshawe.' The third was 'O. Cromwell.' There were fifty-nine signatures in all. The date was 29 January 1648 but the then calendar year ended on 25 March. On modern reckoning it was 29 January 1649. The sentence was that 'Charles Steuart Kinge of England . . . be putt to death by the severinge of his head from his body' and 'executed *In the* open Streete before Whitehall uppon the morrowe being the Thirtieth day of this instante moneth of January.'

iv *Monday*

On the Monday the king set about disposing of his few belongings, while the scaffold was rising in Whitehall, and the commissioners were playing strange pranks to secure an adequately signed death warrant. To his family and his friends he gave his books and jewels. His two younger children were admitted to see him, Princess Elizabeth and the Duke of Gloucester. He took them on his knees, dried their tears, and gravely comforted and counselled them. . . .

v *Tuesday, the day of execution*

Tuesday the 30th dawned grey and very cold; so keen was the frost that ice-floes jostled in the Thames. Charles rose shortly after five. He bade Herbert dress him carefully, giving him an extra shirt; 'by reason the season is so sharp as probably may make me shake, which some will imagine proceeds from fear. I would have no such imputation. I fear not death, death is not terrible to me. I bless my God I am prepared.' . . .

In the bitter morning, attended by Juxon and Herbert and a guard of halberdiers, the king walked across the park, briskly, as was his custom. He arrived at Whitehall about ten o'clock. There was no chance of talk on the way, for drums beat continually. At Whitehall he received the sacrament from Juxon and was allowed to rest in a bedchamber for some hours. . . .

8 The execution

i *The scaffold*

The arrangements for the execution were made by Colonel Hacker who commanded the guards:

About half-past one Hacker summoned him to die. He walked to the Banqueting House through the Whitehall galleries which were lined with spectators; most of them were praying, and the guards did not forbid them, 'seeming by their silence and dejected faces afflicted rather than insulting.' From one of the windows he stepped out on to the scaffold. This was railed in, and it and the railings were covered with black cloth. In the centre was the low block. Charles's refusal to plead had led to the fear that he might resist at the last moment, so staples had been fixed in the floor so that if necessary he might be held down by ropes. By the block lay the axe, brought from the Tower, perhaps the very one which had been used at Strafford's death, and beside it stood two masked men, dressed in close-fitting tunics, rough-looking fellows like sailors or butchers, one of them short, and one of them tall with a grey wig. Around the scaffold were lines of horse and foot, and beyond these a packed multitude, while every window and house-top was crowded.

On the scaffold were six figures, the king and Juxon and the two headsmen, Colonel Hacker and Colonel Tomlinson. Since Charles could not speak to the people, he addressed himself to Tomlinson and Juxon. Remembering Strafford, he said that an unjust sentence to which he had been a party was now punished by an unjust sentence upon himself. He submitted himself humbly to God's judgment. He prayed that his enemies might be pardoned, and that the land should be freed from the tyranny of the sword. There could be no peace till men paid their duties to God, people and king. . . .

ii *The axe*

With the assistance of the executioners he put his long hair under a white satin nightcap. For a little he spoke aside with Juxon, handing him the George which he took from his neck, with instructions for its disposal. He removed his cloak and doublet and laid himself down on the scaffold with his head on the block. For a few minutes he lay there praying, his eye, said a watcher, 'as brisk and lively as ever he had seen it.' Then he stretched out his hands, and the grizzled executioner brought down the axe and severed his head. The other held it up in silence to the people. A groan of horror rent the stillness, and the next minute troops of horse were on the move, splitting up the crowd and driving it towards Charing Cross and Westminster.

iii *The Royal actor*

I quote again from Andrew Marvell's *Horatian Ode* which he wrote from his own knowledge. He was twenty-eight in 1649. The King was forty-eight.

That thence the Royal actor borne
The tragic scaffold might adorn:
    While round the armed bands
    Did clap their bloody hands.

He nothing common did or mean
Upon that memorable scene,
    But with his keener eye
    The axe's head did try;

Nor call'd the Gods, with vulgar spite,
To vindicate his helpless right;
    But bow'd his comely head
    Down, as upon a bed.

iv *Buchan's judgment*

It is as well to remember that, if Charles had won the war, he would have seen to it that Cromwell and his colleagues were executed: just as, eleven years later, the regicides were executed.

Buchan says:

As a legal act his death was a travesty of justice; as an incident in a revolutionary war it was as just or as unjust as the other details of that war. Charles lost and had to pay the penalty; if he had won, Oliver, Ireton and many others would have been shorter by their heads.

9 The bauble

i *The 'Rump' is dissolved*

I cannot end this without telling of the end of the Long Parliament. It had started in 1640 and by 1653 there was nothing left except the 'Rump' as it was contemptuously called. It had only a hundred members and the average attendance was only fifty. A Bill was introduced for a new form of government. Sir Henry Vane had introduced it, but he had promised to suspend it and not to proceed with it. On this assurance Cromwell did not intend to go down to the House that day, 20 April 1653. He had put on his old clothes, a plain black suit and grey worsted stockings. But then a message came that Vane had broken his promise and was going to move the Bill that day.

Oliver at once set off for Westminster but first he ordered a party of musketeers from his own regiment to follow him.

ii *'An end to your prating'*

Then we get Buchan's description of the most dramatic moment in the history of Parliament:

Then the Speaker rose to put the third reading of the bill, and Oliver rose with him. 'This is the time,' he muttered to Harrison. 'I must do it.'

... In wild words that tumbled over each other he poured forth his inmost soul. He told the members what was the truth, if not the whole truth. He spoke of their injustice, their corruption, their petty jealousies; he spoke of their private sins, drunkenness, embezzlement, uncleanness, and as he spoke he looked hard at this and that embarrassed member. Then he clapped his hat on his head, to show that his respect for the House had gone, and as he spoke he strode up and down the floor, now and then stamping his foot. 'It is not fit,' he shouted, 'that you should sit as a Parliament any longer. You have sat long enough unless you had done more good.' ... 'I will put an end to your prating,' he cried. 'You are no Parliament. I say you are no Parliament. I will put an end to your sitting.' He turned to Harrison: 'Call them in! Call them in!'

iii *The musketeers come in*

Worsley with his thirty musketeers filed into the chamber. At last Vane found his tongue. 'This is not honest,' he cried. 'It is against morality and common honesty.' Oliver turned on him, and his harsh voice had sadness in it as well as wrath. 'O Sir Henry Vane! Sir Henry Vane! The Lord deliver me from Sir Henry Vane!' He signed to Harrison to deal with the Speaker. Lenthall declined to move, so he was pulled down from his chair. Algernon Sidney, sitting on his right hand, refused to go till he was forced.

iv *'Take it away!'*

Then Oliver's eyes fell on the mace. 'What are we to do with this bauble?' he asked the leader of the musketeers, using the word applied to a jester's staff with its cap and bells. 'Take it away!' As the members hustled out like driven cattle, Oliver gave them his parting words. He told Marten that he was a whore-master, which was undoubtedly true, and Wentworth that he was an adulterer, and a certain alderman that he was a thief, and Challoner that he was a drunkard; even Whitlocke he accused of injustice. Vane he called a juggler without common honesty, and reproached him with being the cause of the whole trouble. 'It's you,' he shouted to the whole body, 'that have forced me to this, for I have sought the Lord night and day that he would rather slay me than put me upon the doing of this work.' From the clerk at the table he snatched the bill, and no man knew what became of it. He saw that the door was locked and went home.

v *He could have been King*

That was the end of the Long Parliament. The army was delighted. All England approved. Cromwell was most popular throughout all the country. He could have made himself King. But he did not. Buchan thinks he should have done:

> England would have had again that mystic and indivisible centre of national unity which in all her history she has demanded. The majesty of the thing restored would have ennobled the restorer.

And the consequence was that:

> Henceforth he is like a hero of tragedy, immeshed in the toils of fate. He was to be a prince, but a prince who must remain standing, since he had no throne.

vi *The Lord Protector*

Oliver Cromwell became Lord Protector. By his military genius he led England to a high standing among the nations of the world. In 1657 there was a new Parliament and there were many who wanted him to become King. But he refused. He was right. As Buchan says:

> To set his house firmly on the throne, he needed some assurance that for a reasonable time he would hold in his own hands the reins of power. His assurance was far otherwise, for he knew now that length of days would be denied him. He was already an old man with a failing body.

He died in the next year – on 3 September 1658 – at the age of fifty-nine.

The two sons of Charles I became successively King of England.

At the Restoration in 1660 the elder son, Charles II, came to the throne. The regicides who signed the death warrant of his father were themselves tried and executed. The monarchy was restored. After him the younger son, James II, became King. But he behaved so badly that he had to fly the realm. We were well rid of those Stuarts from Scotland.

5 The Great Proconsul

Introduction

In the last chapter, I told you of the sombre scenes in Westminster Hall at the trials of Strafford and Charles I. Now I come to a memorable scene in that great Hall – the most memorable in all its long history. It is the trial of Warren Hastings. It is told by Lord Macaulay who was, I believe, the greatest historical writer in the English language. His work excels all others by reason of his immense research and his vivid style.

I have before me a prize which I was awarded at school in 1912 when I was aged 13. It was for English. It is Macaulay's *Essays and Lays*. It is a handsome volume in leather. The print is very small. I have often read his *Essay* on Warren Hastings with its description of India. Lord Macaulay was well fitted to write about India. He had spent many years there and was the architect of the Indian Criminal Code, which has lasted for more than a hundred years and has been adopted by many other countries.

1 An implacable enemy

i *Hastings himself*

Warren Hastings was born in 1732 at Daylesford in Worcestershire. He went to the village school and afterwards to Westminster School. In 1750, at the age of 18, he went to India as a writer in the East India Company. He rose to become Governor-General of Bengal. He did great service to India. He arrived back in England in 1785 at the age of 53. He was entitled to receive, and should have received, recognition by the Government here by the honour of a peerage – just as Robert Clive had been recognised.

ii *His enemy Junius*

But when he got home, he was unjustly attacked by an implacable enemy, Philip Francis, alias Junius. He was that Junius who had written scurrilous letters about the King and Lord Mansfield. I have told you about him in *Landmarks in the Law* (see pages 289 and 290). After writing those iniquitous letters at home, Francis had gone out to India as a member of the Council of the East India Company. He opposed everything that Warren Hastings did.

iii *The duel*

The bitterness between them became so great that Hastings wrote a minute to the Council saying that Francis was void of truth and honour. This was met by a challenge to a duel which Hastings won. This is Macaulay's account of it:

'I do not trust to Mr Francis's promises of candour, convinced that he is incapable of it. I judge of his public conduct by his private, which I have found to be void of truth and honour.' After the Council had risen, Francis put a challenge into the Governor-General's hand. It was instantly accepted. They met, and fired. Francis was shot through the body. He was carried to a neighbouring house, where it appeared that the wound, though severe, was not mortal. Hastings inquired repeatedly after his enemy's health, and proposed to call on him; but Francis coldly declined the visit. He had a proper sense, he said, of the Governor-General's politeness, but could not consent to any private interview. They could meet only at the council-board.

iv *A vendetta against Hastings*

When Francis got home, he conducted a vendetta against Hastings accusing him of gross violence, injustice, robbery and extortion in India. He was so persuasive that Edmund Burke, Charles James Fox and others believed the accusations. They laid charges against Hastings on the table of the House of Commons. The House voted that Hastings should be impeached.

2 Impeachment

i *A true bill*

Impeachment was the ancient process of English law by which persons of importance were indicted of High Misdemeanour. The charges were brought before the House of Commons. If the Commons found 'a true bill', then the trial was held by the House of Lords. As I told you in *Landmarks in the Law*, Francis Bacon was impeached in this way. So now was Warren Hastings. His was the last case of impeachment, save for one case in 1805.

ii *The accusations against Hastings*

In regard to Warren Hastings, the accusers made a formidable case. He had, it was said, sold for a vast sum the services of British troops to crush the free tribes of the Rohillas. He had wrung half a million by oppression from the Rajah of Benares. He had extorted by torture and starvation more than a million from the Princesses of Oude. Nor was this all. At the opening of his career, he had used, it was said, the forms of English law to bring a prosecution against a prominent Hindu, Nuncomar. He had succeeded in getting Nuncomar sentenced to death as a forger. He had used the Chief Justice, Sir Elijah Impey, as a willing tool.

iii *The process of impeachment*

With this introduction I can turn to the magnificent description by Macaulay of the trial. He says of the process of impeachment:

> The High Court of Parliament was to sit, according to forms handed down from the days of the Plantagenets, on an Englishman accused of exercising tyranny over the lord of the holy city of Benares, and over the ladies of the princely house of Oude.

3 The trial

i *Westminster Hall itself*

Westminster Hall is the most famous hall in the whole wide world. By a miracle it was saved from destruction by German bombs in the last war. Often I have walked through it. Always it fills me with a sense of history. A brass slab there commemorates the trial of Warren Hastings.

ii *Pomp and circumstance*

At the trial there was the greatest display that the Hall has ever seen or ever will see. This is Macaulay's description:

> The place was worthy of such a trial. It was the great hall of William Rufus, the hall which had resounded with acclamations at the inauguration of thirty kings, the hall which had witnessed the just sentence of Bacon and the just absolution of Somers, the hall where the eloquence of Strafford had for a moment awed and

melted a victorious party inflamed with just resentment, the hall where Charles had confronted the High Court of Justice with the placid courage which has half redeemed his fame. Neither military nor civil pomp was wanting. The avenues were lined with grenadiers. The streets were kept clear by cavalry. The peers, robed in gold and ermine, were marshalled by the heralds under Garter King-at-arms. The judges in their vestments of state attended to give advice on points of law. Near a hundred and seventy lords, three fourths of the Upper House as the Upper House then was, walked in solemn order from their usual place of assembling to the tribunal. The junior baron present led the way, George Eliott, Lord Heathfield, recently ennobled for his memorable defence of Gibraltar against the fleets and armies of France and Spain. The long procession was closed by the Duke of Norfolk, Earl Marshal of the realm, by the great dignitaries, and by the brothers and sons of the King. Last of all came the Prince of Wales, conspicuous by his fine person and noble bearing. The grey old walls were hung with scarlet. The long galleries were crowded by an audience such as has rarely excited the fears or the emulation of an orator.

iii *The audience*

Then Macaulay tells of the distinguished persons who attended:

There were gathered together, from all parts of a great, free, enlightened, and prosperous empire, grace and female loveliness, wit and learning, the representatives of every science and of every art. There were seated round the Queen the fair-haired young daughters of the house of Brunswick. There the Ambassadors of great Kings and Commonwealths gazed with admiration on a spectacle which no other country in the world could present. There Siddons, in the prime of her majestic beauty, looked with emotion on a scene surpassing all the imitations of the stage. There the historian of the Roman Empire thought of the days when Cicero pleaded the cause of Sicily against Verres, and when, before a senate which still retained some show of freedom, Tacitus thundered against the oppressor of Africa. There were seen, side by side, the greatest painter and the greatest scholar of the age. The spectacle had allured Reynolds from that easel which has preserved to us the thoughtful foreheads of so many writers and statesmen, and the sweet smiles of so many noble matrons. It had induced Parr to suspend his labours in that dark and profound mine from which he had extracted a vast treasure of erudition, a treasure too often buried in the earth, too often paraded with injudicious and inelegant ostentation, but still precious, massive, and splendid. There appeared the voluptuous charms of her to whom the heir of the throne had in secret plighted his faith. There too was she, the beautiful mother of a beautiful race, the Saint Cecilia whose delicate features, lighted up by love and music, art has rescued from the common decay. . . .

Can you place them? Mrs Sarah Siddons, the actress. She was the one great tragedy queen that Britain ever produced. Edward Gibbon, the historian. He wrote *The Decline and Fall of the Roman Empire*. Sir Joshua Reynolds, the great portrait painter. Samuel Parr, a fine Latin scholar but poor writer. Mrs Maria Fitzherbert was the voluptuous woman who had secretly married George, Prince of Wales. Who was the beautiful mother? Samuel Johnson was not there. He had died the year before.

iv *'Mens aequa in arduis'*

Then this moving picture of Hastings the accused – after thirty-five years in India:

> The Sergeants made proclamation. Hastings advanced to the bar, and bent his knee. The culprit was indeed not unworthy of that great presence. He had ruled an extensive and populous country, had made laws and treaties, had sent forth armies, had set up and pulled down princes. And in his high place he had so borne himself, that all had feared him, that most had loved him, and that hatred itself could deny him no title to glory, except virtue. He looked like a great man, and not like a bad man. A person small and emaciated, yet deriving dignity from a carriage which, while it indicated deference to the court, indicated also habitual self-possession and self-respect, a high and intellectual forehead, a brow pensive, but not gloomy, a mouth of inflexible decision, a face pale and worn, but serene, on which was written, as legibly as under the picture in the council-chamber at Calcutta, *Mens aequa in arduis*; such was the aspect with which the great proconsul presented himself to his judges.

How would you translate, '*Mens aequa in arduis*'? Perhaps from Kipling's *If*:

> If you can keep your head when all about you
> Are losing theirs and blaming it on you.

v *The accusers are in green*

The seats and carpets in the chamber of the House of Lords were always red throughout and still are: those in the chamber of the House of Commons green. In Westminster Hall, as the Commons were the accusers, their space was fitted up in green. They wore full dress:

> But neither the culprit nor his advocates attracted so much notice as the accusers. In the midst of the blaze of red drapery, a space had been fitted up with green benches and tables for the Commons. The managers, with Burke at their head, appeared in full dress. The collectors of gossip did not fail to remark that even Fox, generally so regardless of his appearance, had paid to the illustrious tribunal the compliment of wearing a bag and sword. . . . The box in which the managers stood contained an array of speakers such as perhaps had not appeared together since the great age of Athenian eloquence. There were Fox and Sheridan, the English Demosthenes and the English Hyperides. There was Burke, ignorant, indeed, or negligent of the art of adapting his reasonings and his style to the capacity and taste of his hearers, but in amplitude of comprehension and richness of imagination superior to every orator, ancient or modern.

vi *Ladies in the galleries*

Then Burke came to his dramatic peroration with its remarkable effect on the ladies in the galleries – all put on, no doubt:

Having thus attempted to communicate to his hearers an idea of Eastern society, as vivid as that which existed in his own mind, he proceeded to arraign the administration of Hastings as systematically conducted in defiance of morality and public law. The energy and pathos of the great orator extorted expressions of unwonted admiration from the stern and hostile Chancellor, and, for a moment, seemed to pierce even the resolute heart of the defendant. The ladies in the galleries, unaccustomed to such displays of eloquence, excited by the solemnity of the occasion, and perhaps not unwilling to display their taste and sensibility, were in a state of uncontrollable emotion. Handkerchiefs were pulled out; smelling-bottles were handed round; hysterical sobs and screams were heard; and Mrs Sheridan was carried out in a fit. At length the orator concluded. Raising his voice till the old arches of Irish oak resounded, 'Therefore,' said he, 'hath it with all confidence been ordered by the Commons of Great Britain, that I impeach Warren Hastings of high crimes and misdemeanours. I impeach him in the name of the Commons' House of Parliament, whose trust he has betrayed. I impeach him in the name of the English nation, whose ancient honour he has sullied. I impeach him in the name of the people of India, whose rights he has trodden under foot, and whose country he has turned into a desert. Lastly, in the name of human nature itself, in the name of both sexes, in the name of every age, in the name of every rank, I impeach the common enemy and oppressor of all!'

vii *The proceedings become dull*

After that brilliant speech for the prosecution, the trial became deadly dull. The audience departed to other things. There were many points of law which were referred to the judges. They retired to consider them. So often that it was said that the judges walked and the trial stood still:

The interest taken by the public in the trial was great when the Court began to sit, and rose to the height when Sheridan spoke on the charge relating to the Begums. From that time the excitement went down fast. The spectacle had lost the attraction of novelty. The great displays of rhetoric were over. What was behind was not of a nature to entice men of letters from their books in the morning, or to tempt ladies who had left the masquerade at two to be out of bed before eight. There remained examinations and cross-examinations. There remained statements of accounts. There remained the reading of papers, filled with words unintelligible to English ears, with lacs and crores, zemindars and aumils, sunnuds and perwannahs, jaghires and nuzzurs. There remained bickerings, not always carried on with the best taste or with the best temper, between the managers of the impeachment and the counsel for the defence, particularly between Mr Burke and Mr Law. There remained the endless marches and countermarches of the Peers between their House and the Hall: for as often as a point of law was to be discussed, their Lordships retired to discuss it apart; and the consequence was, as a Peer wittily said, that the Judges walked and the trial stood still.

viii *Unprecedented length*

In the session of 1788, when the proceedings had the interest of novelty, and when the Peers had little other business before them, only thirty-five days were given to the impeachment. In 1789, the Regency Bill occupied the Upper House till the session was far advanced. When the King recovered the circuits were beginning. The judges left town; the Lords waited for the return of the oracles of jurisprudence; and the consequence was that during the whole year only seventeen days were given to the case of Hastings. It was clear that the matter would be protracted to a length unprecedented in the annals of criminal law.

ix *Reasons for slow progress*

There were good reasons for the slow progress of the proceedings. The judges had to go off to their judicial duties. The Lords were not going to miss the shooting season for Hastings or anyone else:

The law-lords, whose advice is required to guide the unlearned majority, are employed daily in administering justice elsewhere. It is impossible, therefore, that during a busy session, the Upper House should give more than a few days to an impeachment. To expect that their Lordships would give up partridge-shooting, in order to bring the greatest delinquent to speedy justice, or to relieve accused innocence by speedy acquittal, would be unreasonable indeed. A well-constituted tribunal, sitting regularly six days in the week, and nine hours in the day, would have brought the trial of Hastings to a close in less than three months. The Lords had not finished their work in seven years.

x *The verdict of the Lords*

Eventually the day came when the Lords were to give their verdict. The Hall was crowded once more with sightseers. But not with Peers. Many of those who came on the first day had died in the interval. Only a handful had been present throughout. It may safely be assumed that not one had attended every day. Only twenty-nine felt able to vote.

At length, in the spring of 1795, the decision was pronounced, near eight years after Hastings had been brought by the Sergeant-at-arms of the Commons to the bar of the Lords. On the last day of this great procedure the public curiosity, long suspended, seemed to be revived. Anxiety about the judgment there could be none; for it had been fully ascertained that there was a great majority for the defendant. Nevertheless many wished to see the pageant, and the Hall was as much crowded as on the first day. . . .

xi *Hastings is acquitted*

Only twenty-nine Peers voted. Of these only six found Hastings guilty on the charges relating to Cheyte Sing and to the Begums. On other charges, the majority in his favour was still greater. On some, he was unanimously absolved. He was then called to the bar, was informed from the woolsack that the Lords had acquitted him, and was solemnly discharged. He bowed respectfully and retired.

4 Retirement

i *His resting-place*

Hastings lived on for twenty-three more years. He retired to his birthplace – Daylesford in Worcestershire. He enjoyed good health until he died at the age of 86. Macaulay thought he should have been buried in Westminster Abbey, but ends with this beautiful passage:

Yet the place of interment was not ill chosen. Behind the chancel of the parish church of Daylesford, in earth which already held the bones of many chiefs of the house of Hastings, was laid the coffin of the greatest man who has ever borne that ancient and widely extended name. On that very spot probably, fourscore years before, the little Warren, meanly clad and scantily fed, had played with the children of ploughmen. Even then his young mind had revolved plans which might be called romantic. Yet, however romantic, it is not likely that they had been so strange as the truth. Not only had the poor orphan retrieved the fallen fortunes of his line. Not only had he repurchased the old lands, and rebuilt the old dwelling. He had preserved and extended an empire. He had founded a polity. He had administered government and war with more than the capacity of Richelieu. He had patronised learning with the judicious liberality of Cosmo. He had been attacked by the most formidable combination of enemies that ever sought the destruction of a single victim; and over that combination, after a struggle of ten years, he had triumphed. He had at length gone down to his grave in the fulness of age, in peace, after so many troubles, in honour, after so much obloquy.

ii *The verdict of history*

In his *History of England*,[1] G M Trevelyan sums up:

During the War of American Independence, Warren Hastings was left with very inadequate means to struggle against these external dangers, and at the same time to maintain his internal authority against the faction in his own Council led by his personal enemy, Philip Francis. He saved British rule in India in spite of all, but not without making the kind of mistakes which a strong man is likely to make in difficult emergencies. For these acts, much exaggerated and misconstrued by the malignity of Francis and the imagination of Burke, Fox and Sheridan, he was impeached in Westminster Hall. Those famous proceedings, substantially unjust to Hastings even though they resulted in his acquittal, had the advantage of bringing Indian problems and responsibilities forcibly to the notice of British statesmen and the British public. Burke preached the right ideal of our obligations to the Indians, but misunderstood the relation of Hastings' governorship to the problem.

I am always proud of what the British rule did for the Indian sub-continent. Our soldiers, civil servants and judges gave it a settled government and a just administration under the rule of law for 200 years – which are being carried on into the days of independence.

[1] Bk. V, ch. VI.

iii *Impeachment now obsolete*

Impeachment has never been formally abolished. *Erskine May* says that it 'might still be regarded as an ultimate safeguard of public liberty'.[1] I do not think so. Its use in the case of Warren Hastings was most unjust.

[1] *Parliamentary Practice* (20th edn), p 69.

6 Rebellion in England

Introduction

As I have written in such praise of Lord Macaulay, I must acknowledge my further indebtedness to him. He wrote the *History of England* from the accession of James II in 1685 to the time of William III in 1701. Only 16 years. Yet those years saw the bloody battle of Sedgemoor. They saw the most savage and unjust judge that we have ever had – the notorious Judge Jeffreys. They saw the flight and dethronement of the King, James II. They saw the Glorious Revolution by which Parliament became supreme over the Crown. They saw the Bill of Rights which guaranteed fundamental human rights to our people.

We are fortunate to have Lord Macaulay to chronicle those years: and Lord Campbell in his *Lives of the Lord Chancellors* to fill in some legal details.

1 300 years ago

i *The Western Circuit*

It was 300 years ago. In the summer of the year 1685. Judge Jeffreys went the Western Circuit. 331 prisoners were executed and 849 transported. On the ground that they were traitors. The circuit took only 4½ weeks. Lord Macaulay described it as

> that circuit of which the memory will last as long as our race and language

and said that the sufferers

> were, for the most part, men of blameless life, and of high religious profession. They were regarded by themselves, and by a large proportion of their neighbours, not as wrongdoers, but as martyrs who sealed with blood the truth of the Protestant religion.

ii *Who should be King?*

But how many of you today know anything of it? Even some members of the Circuit do not know. So I venture to tell you. The question was: Who should be King of England? Charles II died on 6 February 1685 after a lingering illness. According to Lord Macaulay:

> He apologised to those who had stood round him all night for the trouble which he had caused. He had been, he said, a most unconscionable time dying; but he hoped that they would excuse it.

Charles II was then aged 55. Who should succeed him as King? He had no children by his lawful wife. He had had three or four mistresses and made them Duchesses: and had three or four sons by them whom he made Dukes. But his first love was Lucy Walter. They lived together in Holland when they were both 18. Their son was born in April 1649 and was christened James Scott. When Charles became King, he made him Duke of Monmouth. There were many rumours that his father, Charles, had married Lucy secretly: and that Monmouth was the legitimate heir. But it was never proved.

When Charles II died in February 1685, his son Monmouth was in Holland. He was in exile there. But he was happy enough. Because Henrietta Wentworth was with him. She was a damsel of high rank and ample fortune. They loved each other dearly. She wanted him to be King of England and herself to be Queen.

iii *James II is on the spot*

But Monmouth's uncle James was at the right place at the right moment. He was in London. He was then aged 52 and the legitimate heir to the throne. He got it and became King as James II. He had, however, a grave defect. He was Roman Catholic. And Papists were unpopular in England. But Monmouth had a considerable asset. He was a Protestant. And there was still in England, especially in the western counties, a strong Protestant fervour. 'No Popery' was its war cry.

iv *Monmouth lands at Lyme*

So Monmouth decided to stake all upon an invasion of England. On 11 June 1685 he arrived with three ships off Lyme in Dorset. (That little town was often called simply Lyme. But its full name has been Lyme Regis ever since the time when Edward I used its harbour during his wars against the French.) Monmouth landed with 83 men and some arms and equipment. Macaulay describes the scene:

> Monmouth commanded silence, kneeled down on the shore, thanked God for having preserved the friends of liberty and pure religion from the perils of the sea, and implored the divine blessing on what was yet to be done by land. He then drew his sword and led his men over the cliffs into the town.
>
> As soon as it was known under what leader and for what purpose the expedition came, the enthusiasm of the populace burst through all restraints. The little town was in an uproar with men running to and fro and shouting 'A Monmouth! a Monmouth! the Protestant religion!' Meanwhile the ensign of the adventurers, a blue flag, was set up in the market place. The military stores were deposited in the town hall; and a declaration setting forth the objects of the expedition was read from the Cross.

v *Monmouth enters Taunton*

Monmouth moved on into Somerset where he had a great welcome. The yeomen, the traders of the towns, the peasants and the artisans were all for him. They abhorred Popery and adored Monmouth. Macaulay describes the entry into Taunton:

> The children of the men who, forty years before, had manned the ramparts of Taunton against the royalists now welcomed Monmouth with transports of joy and affection. Every door and window was adorned with wreaths of flowers. No man appeared in the streets without wearing in his hat a green bough, the badge of the popular cause. Damsels of the best families in the town wove colours for the insurgents. One flag in particular was embroidered gorgeously with emblems of royal dignity, and was offered to Monmouth by a train of young girls. He received the gift with the winning courtesy which distinguished him. The lady who headed the procession presented him also with a small Bible of great price. He took it with a show of reverence. 'I come,' he said, 'to defend the truths contained in this book, and to seal them, if it must be so, with my blood.'

vi *Churchill is for James II*

Meanwhile, however, the news had been flashed to London by the swiftest horsemen. James II called out his troops – both cavalry and foot regiments. With them was a young officer by the name of John Churchill, afterwards the Duke of Marlborough, the greatest soldier of his age. (He was awarded Blenheim Palace for his victories on the Continent.) They were sent to the western counties to put down the rebellion.

Monmouth's men were no match for them. He had a few horsemen but for the most part his troops were peasants and townsmen with no weapons except pikes and scythes and a few muskets. They had no chance at all against the regular royalist troops.

2 The battle of Sedgemoor

i *'For which King?'*

The battle took place at Sedgemoor on the Somerset Marches. Monmouth decided to attack. It was dark, about one o'clock in the early morning of Monday 6 July 1685. As his men went forward, they came upon a deep and muddy trench (called in Somerset a 'rhine') of which Monmouth was not aware. Macaulay describes the encounters of the horse:

'For whom are you?' called out an officer of the Foot Guards. 'For the king,' replied a voice from the ranks of the rebel cavalry. 'For which king?' was then demanded. The answer was a shout of 'King Monmouth,' mingled with the war cry, which forty years before had been inscribed on the colours of the parliamentary regiments, 'God with us.' The royal troops instantly fired such a volley of musketry as sent the rebel horse flying in all directions.

ii *A trench in the way*

So much for the horse. But what about the infantry? Macaulay goes on:

Monmouth was startled by finding that a broad and profound trench lay between him and the camp which he had hoped to surprise. The insurgents halted on the edge of the rhine, and fired. Part of the royal infantry on the opposite bank returned the fire. During three quarters of an hour the roar of the musketry was incessant. The Somersetshire peasants behaved themselves as if they had been veteran soldiers, save only that they levelled their pieces too high.

He then tells us of Monmouth's courage at the outset:

Monmouth had hitherto done his part like a stout and able warrior. He had been seen on foot, pike in hand, encouraging his infantry by voice and by example. But he was too well acquainted with military affairs not to know that all was over. His men had lost the advantage which surprise and darkness had given them.

iii *Monmouth's flight*

Macaulay goes on to tell us of Monmouth's disgraceful flight at the end:

The day was about to break. The event of a conflict on an open plain, by broad sunlight, could not be doubtful. Yet Monmouth should have felt that it was not for him to fly while thousands whom affection for him had hurried to destruction were still fighting manfully in his cause. But vain hopes and the intense love of life prevailed. He saw that if he tarried the royal cavalry would soon be in his rear, and would interrupt his retreat. He mounted and rode from the field.

iv *The Somersetshire peasants*

Yet his foot, though deserted, made a gallant stand. The Life Guards attacked them on the right, the Blues on the left: but the Somersetshire clowns, with their scythes and the butt ends of their muskets, faced the royal horse like old soldiers.

Then came the last charge:

The pikes of the rebel battalions began to shake; the ranks broke. The king's cavalry charged again, and bore down everything before them. The king's infantry came pouring across the ditch. Even in that extremity the Mendip miners stood bravely to their arms, and sold their lives dearly. But the rout was in a few minutes complete. Three hundred of the soldiers had been killed or wounded. Of the rebels more than a thousand lay dead on the moor.

v *The last fight*

Macaulay then tells of the upshot of it all, describing the battle as the last one fought on English ground. It has been far outdone in our day by the Battle of Britain.

So ended the last fight, deserving the name of battle, that has been fought on English ground. The impression left on the simple inhabitants of the neighbourhood was deep and lasting. That impression, indeed, has been frequently renewed. For even in our own time the plough and the spade have not seldom turned up ghastly memorials of the slaughter, skulls, and thighbones, and strange weapons made out of implements of husbandry. Old peasants related very recently that, in their childhood, they were accustomed to play on the moor at the fight between King James's men and King Monmouth's men.

vi *Monmouth is executed*

But what happened to Monmouth? Two days after the battle, he was found hiding, hungry and tired, in ragged clothing, under an oak tree in a ditch full of brambles and bracken. He was taken to London and executed on 15 July. Just five weeks after he had landed at Lyme.

3 The Bloody Assize

i *Dame Alice Lisle*

So much for the bloody battle. Now for the Bloody Assize that followed it. And particularly for one of the most famous trials in English history – the trial of Dame Alice Lisle for High Treason. She was an old lady – a widow – of 70. She was the owner and heiress of a big house and estate in the New Forest called Moyles Court. It is a mile out of a tiny hamlet called Ellingham, and three miles from Ringwood. It is still there. It has been extended and turned into a preparatory school of high repute.

Her husband, John Lisle, had been a strict Puritan in high places in Cromwell's time. He was one of the regicides, but he did not actually sign the death warrant of Charles I. After the Restoration, he had fled to Switzerland, but the royalists had found him and shot him dead. You might think that his widow would have been of his way of thought. But no. At her trial in 1685 she declared she was a royalist and her son was serving with the King's troops. All the gentlemen of Hampshire knew this.

ii *Two on the run*

Now she comes into the story like this: After Sedgemoor, two men fled for their lives. One was a barrister of Gray's Inn called Richard Nelthorpe. (He was one of the men who came from Holland with Monmouth. He landed at Lyme and no doubt fought at Sedgemoor.) The other was John Hickes. He was a Fellow of Trinity College, Dublin, and a distinguished non-conformist Minister of a town near Bath called Keynsham. He believed Monmouth to be the legitimate heir to the throne. No doubt his sympathies were with Monmouth but there is nothing to show he joined his forces or fought at Sedgemoor.

Those two men hoped to make their escape by way of the New Forest on to the coast and get a boat for Holland. They had to hide from the royalist troops. It took them three weeks to get as far as Warminster. Someone there told them that they might get shelter at Moyles Court in the Forest. It was 26 miles on. A baker named James Dunne offered to go on ahead and ask Dame Alice Lisle. She agreed. So Dunne went back to Warminster and rode with them to Moyles Court. But they had been betrayed. They had asked their way of a stranger. He went straight off and told the royalist troops. Macaulay tells us the outcome:

> The same womanly kindness which had led her to befriend the royalists in their time of trouble would not suffer her to refuse a meal and a hiding place to the wretched men who now intreated her to protect them. She took them into her house, set meat and drink before them, and showed them where they might take rest. The next morning her dwelling was surrounded by soldiers. Strict search was made. Hickes was found concealed in the malthouse, and Nelthorpe in the chimney.

Dame Alice was taken off to the gaol at Southampton. Hickes to Taunton Castle. Nelthorpe to London.

iii *Was she guilty?*

To the royalist lawyers of that time it must have seemed clear that Dame Alice was herself Guilty of High Treason. To them the two men, Nelthorpe and Hickes, were obviously Guilty. They were levying war against the King in his realm contrary to the Treason Act 1351. In helping them to escape, Dame Alice was an accessory after the fact and also Guilty of High Treason. There was also a valuable by-product. If she was convicted of High Treason, her great house and estate at Moyles Court would be forfeited to the King for him to give to whomever he chose.

iv *An imposing cavalcade*

So the King and his advisers determined that the case of Dame Alice Lisle should be taken first – as an example to the others. It was not the ordinary summer circuit. A special commission was issued to the Lord Chief Justice Jeffreys and four other judges. Towards the end of August 1685, they left for the west. It was an imposing cavalcade, headed by the Lord Chief Justice in his coach and six. He took the executioner, Jack Ketch, with him. They stayed the weekend with the Bishop of Winchester at Farnham Castle. They went on to Winchester. Next day they went in state to the Cathedral for the Assize Service. They sat in the Great Hall of the Castle to try the cases.

v *She is arraigned*

On 27 August 1685 the case of Dame Alice Lisle was called on. The Clerk of Assize read out the indictment and then the usual formula was gone through:

Clerk of Arraigns. How sayest thou, Alice Lisle, art thou Guilty of the high-treason contained in the indictment or Not Guilty?

Lisle. Not Guilty.

Cl of Ar. Culprit, by whom wilt thou be tried?

Lisle. By God and my country.

Cl. of Ar. God send thee a good deliverance.

The jury were then chosen, and

it being a case of great expectation and moment, the Lord Chief Justice ordered the Sheriff to take care that a very substantial jury should be returned of the best quality in the country.

4 The trial

i *Not proved*

Now I turn, not to Macaulay, but to Lord Campbell who gives a better account of the trial:

The charge against her, which was laid capitally, was that after the battle of Sedgemoor she had harboured in her house one Hickes, who had been in arms with the Duke of Monmouth – *she knowing of his treason.* In truth she had received him into her house, – thinking merely that he was persecuted as a non-conformist minister, and the moment she knew whence he came, she (conveying to him a hint that he should escape) sent her servant to a justice of the peace to give information concerning him. There was the greatest difficulty even to show that Hickes had been in the rebellion, and the Judge was worked up to a pitch of fury by being obliged himself to cross-examine a Presbyterian witness (he was the baker, James Dunne) who had showed a leaning against the prosecution. But the principal traitor had not been convicted, and there was not a particle of evidence to show the *scienter*, *i.e.* that the supposed accomplice, at the time of the harbouring, was acquainted with the treason. Not allowed the benefit of counsel, she herself, prompted by natural good sense, took the legal objection that the principal traitor ought first to have been convicted, 'because, peradventure, he might afterwards be acquitted as innocent after she had been condemned for harbouring him;' and she urged with great force to the jury, 'that at the time of the alleged offence she had been entirely ignorant of any suspicion of Hickes having participated in the rebellion; that she had strongly disapproved of it, and that she had sent her only son into the field to fight under the royal banner to suppress it.'

ii *The jury stand out*

It is said by almost all the contemporary authorities, that thrice did the Jury refuse to find a verdict of *guilty*, and thrice did Lord Chief Justice Jeffreys send them back to reconsider their verdict. In the account of the proceedings in the *State Trials*, which has the appearance of having been taken in short-hand, and of being authentic, the repeated sending back of the Jury is not mentioned; but enough appears to stamp eternal infamy on Jeffreys, if there were nothing more extant against him. After a most furious summing up, the Jury withdrew, and staying out awhile, the Lord Jeffreys expressed a great deal of impatience, and said he wondered that in so plain a case they would go from the bar, and would have sent for them, with an intimation that, if they did not come quickly, he would adjourn, and let them lie by it all night; but, after about half an hour's stay, the Jury returned, and the foreman addressed himself to the Court thus:

Foreman. My Lord, we have one thing to beg of your Lordship some directions in before we can give our verdict: we have some doubt whether there be sufficient evidence that she knew Hickes to have been in the army.

LCJ. There is as full proof as proof can be: but you are judges of the proof; for my part I thought there was no difficulty in it.

Foreman. My Lord, we are in some doubt of it.

LCJ. I cannot help your doubts: was there not proved a discourse of the battle and the army at supper time?

Foreman. But, my Lord, we are not satisfied that she had notice that Hickes was in the army.

iii *They find her Guilty*

LCJ. I cannot tell what would satisfy you. Did she not inquire of Dunne whether Hickes had been in the army? and when he told her he did not know, she did not say she would refuse him if he had been there, but ordered him to come by night, by which it is evident she suspected it. . . . But if there were no such proof, the circumstances and management of the thing is as full a proof as can be. I wonder what it is you doubt of.

Lady Lisle. My Lord, I hope –

LCJ. You must not speak now.

The Jury laid their heads together near a quarter of an hour, and then pronounced a verdict of *Guilty*.

LCJ. Gentlemen, I did not think I should have had any occasion to speak after your verdict; but, finding some hesitancy and doubt among you, I cannot but say I wonder it should come about; for I think in my conscience the evidence was as full and plain as could be, and if I had been among you, and she had been my own mother, I should have found her guilty.

iv *She is sentenced*

He passed sentence upon her with great *sang froid*, and, I really believe, would have done the same had she been the mother that bore him:

'That you be conveyed from hence to the place from whence you came, and from thence you are to be drawn on a hurdle to the place of execution, where your body is to be burnt alive till you be dead. And the Lord have mercy on your soul.'

But Macaulay tells us a little more. The clergy of the Cathedral interceded for her:

On the following morning sentence was pronounced. Jeffreys gave directions that Alice Lisle should be burned alive that very afternoon. This excess of barbarity moved the pity and indignation even of that class which was most devoted to the crown. The clergy of Winchester Cathedral remonstrated with the Chief Justice, who, brutal as he was, was not mad enough to risk a quarrel on such a subject with a body so much respected by the Tory party. He consented to put off the execution five days. During that time the friends of the prisoner besought James to show her mercy. Ladies of high rank interceded for her. . . . But all was vain. The utmost that could be obtained was that her sentence should be commuted from burning to beheading. She was put to death on a scaffold in the market place of Winchester, and underwent her fate with serene courage.

v *The verdict is reversed*

Her estate at Moyles Court was forfeited to the Crown, who gave it to the General who commanded the royalist forces at Sedgemoor. But in 1689 (after James II had fled) her attainder was reversed by the new Parliament on the ground that

the verdict was injuriously extorted by the menaces and violence and other illegal practices of George Lord Jeffreys, Baron of Wem, then Lord Chief Justice of the King's Bench.

So her estate reverted to her descendants.

After her execution, her remains were given to her daughters, who carried them to Ellingham. You will find the church there much as it was in her own day if you turn off the main road to Salisbury soon after leaving Ringwood. Close to the porch on the south side of the church you may see her grave. It is a plain tomb such as she would have desired, inscribed, 'Alicia Lisle, Dyed the Second of Sept. 1685.'

5 The rest of the Circuit

i *Hung with scarlet*

Alice Lisle was the only person executed in Hampshire. For the rest of the Circuit, I must take you back again to Macaulay:

In Hampshire, Alice Lisle was the only victim: but, on the day following her execution, Jeffreys reached Dorchester, the principal town of the county in which Monmouth had landed, and the judicial massacre began.

The court was hung, by order of the Chief Justice, with scarlet; and this innovation seemed to the multitude to indicate a bloody purpose. It was also rumoured that, when the clergyman who preached the assize sermon inforced the duty of mercy, the ferocious mouth of the judge was distorted by an ominous grin. These things made men augur ill of what was to follow.

More than three hundred prisoners were to be tried. The work seemed heavy; but Jeffreys had a contrivance for making it light. He let it be understood that the only chance of obtaining pardon or respite was to plead guilty. Twenty-nine persons, who put themselves on their country and were convicted, were ordered to be tied up without delay. The remaining prisoners pleaded guilty by scores. Two hundred and ninety-two received sentence of death. The whole number hanged in Dorsetshire amounted to seventy-four.

ii *The most fearful vengeance*

From Dorchester Jeffreys proceeded to Exeter. The civil war had barely grazed the frontier of Devonshire. Here, therefore, comparatively few persons were capitally punished. Somersetshire, the chief seat of the rebellion, had been reserved for the last and most fearful vengeance. In this county two hundred and thirty-three prisoners were in a few days hanged, drawn and quartered. At every spot where two roads met, on every market place, on the green of every large village which had furnished Monmouth with soldiers, ironed corpses clattering in the wind, or heads and quarters stuck on poles, poisoned the air, and made the traveller sick with horror. In many parishes the peasantry could not assemble in the house of God without seeing the ghastly face of a neighbour grinning at them over the porch. The Chief Justice was all himself. His spirits rose higher and higher as the work went on. He laughed, shouted, joked, and swore in such a way that many thought him drunk from morning to night.

John Hickes was tried at Taunton and executed for treason on 6 October 1685. Richard Nelthorpe was subjected to many distresses and went mad.

iii *The infamous judge*

Macaulay goes on to tell us more of this infamous judge:

It was not only on the prisoners that his fury broke forth. Gentlemen and noblemen of high consideration and stainless loyalty, who ventured to bring to his notice any extenuating circumstance, were almost sure to receive what he called, in the coarse dialect which he had learned in the pothouses of Whitechapel, a lick with the rough side of his tongue. Lord Stawell, a Tory peer, who could not conceal his horror at the remorseless manner in which his poor neighbours were butchered, was punished by having a corpse suspended in chains at his park gate. In such spectacles originated many tales of terror, which were long told over the cyder by the Christmas fires of the farmers of Somersetshire. Within the last forty years peasants, in some districts, well knew the accursed spots, and passed them unwillingly after sunset.

Jeffreys boasted that he had hanged more traitors than all his predecessors together since the Conquest.

iv *The end of Jeffreys*

On his return to London, the King delivered to Jeffreys the Great Seal as Lord Chancellor of England. But, as some of you may remember, James II in December 1688 fled the country and threw the Great Seal into the river Thames. Jeffreys, disguised as a sailor, went into an ale-house in Wapping. He was recognised, hauled by the mob before the Lord Mayor, and committed to the Tower where he died on 18 April 1689. Macaulay's last words of him are:

He dwindled in a few weeks from a portly and even corpulent man to a skeleton. On the eighteenth of April he died, in the forty-first year of his age. He had been Chief Justice of the King's Bench at thirty-five, and Lord Chancellor at thirty-seven. In the whole history of the English bar there is no other instance of so rapid an elevation, or of so terrible a fall.

7 A pure woman

Introduction

In the last chapter, I told you a true story of how an innocent woman – Alice Lisle – was executed for treason. Now I turn to a fictitious story of how a pure woman was hanged for murder. In each case on the Western Circuit.

The story is of *Tess of the d'Urbervilles* told by Thomas Hardy. He was a man of Wessex. He described its countryside and its people better than any other writer. So much so that it has become known as 'Hardy country'. Our friend Gordon Beningfield, an artist of exceptional merit, has produced a charming book of paintings of it with a delightful introduction in which he says:

> Dorset and its people draw me into the world of Tess the milkmaid in *Tess of the d'Urbervilles* and of Gabriel Oak the shepherd in *Far from the Madding Crowd*. The cows of the Frome Valley today may be the inevitable Friesians, but the watermeadows in the early morning still recall Tess and Angel Clare.

My great-grandfather was born in the Frome Valley in 1798 and no doubt knew the Hardy countryside well. I think that I have inherited his love of it. We have spent several holidays there, looking up the parish registers and tracing our lineage. It is still delightful and only small parts of it spoilt by modern developments.

1 The wrong

i *True to life*

Whenever a prisoner was executed in the prison at Winchester, a black flag was run up on the flagpole. Thomas Hardy uses it as the climax of *Tess of the d'Urbervilles*. He tells of Wessex a hundred years ago. It was then just as I remember it myself in my boyhood. His descriptions of its countryside and the people are true to life. But he also teaches a lesson. In those days lives were ruled – and ruined – by the strict standards of Victorian morality. Such was the case with his heroine, Tess. She was tried for murder at the Castle at Winchester, sentenced to death, and hanged.

In the merciless eyes of the law, she was guilty. She had gone to a lodging-house in Bournemouth with a man who was not her husband. They had registered under the names of Mr and Mrs d'Urberville and occupied a bedroom together. Next morning at breakfast they quarrelled. She picked up a carving-knife and stabbed him through the heart. She put on some clothes and rushed off. She was found some days later amid the monoliths at Stonehenge. She was arrested and charged with murder. She admitted that she had killed the man.

But Hardy's point was this: Although in the eyes of the law she was guilty, yet in the eyes of God she was innocent, or at any rate should be forgiven. His subtitle is *A Pure Woman* with a quotation from Shakespeare:[1]

> . . . Poor wounded name! My bosom as a bed
> Shall lodge thee.

ii *The maiden*

The story opens when Tess was but a child herself. She was only 15. She was the eldest of the several children of a farm labourer in a Dorset village. His name was John Durbeyfield. But a local parson, who was something of an antiquary, had discovered that his name came from the Norman-French. He was a direct descendant of Sir Pagan d'Urberville.

After leaving school Tess went out to work. She went to a country house a few miles away. The name was, strangely enough, d'Urberville, but they were upstarts. They were not truly descended from the Norman family.

iii *Maiden no more*

There was a son of the house, Alec d'Urberville. He was 23 and at once made lustful eyes at her. After a party in a near-by town, he gave her a lift home on his horse. She scrambled into the saddle behind him. But he did not take her home. He took her into a wood far out of the way. Hardy leaves the inference to the reader:

> But, might some say, where was Tess's guardian angel? where was the providence

[1] *Two Gentlemen of Verona* Act I, sc ii, lines 115–116.

of her simple faith? Perhaps, like that other god of whom the ironical Tishbite[1] spoke, he was talking, or he was pursuing, or he was in a journey, or he was sleeping and not to be awaked.

Why it was that upon this beautiful feminine tissue, sensitive as gossamer, and practically blank as snow as yet, there should have been traced such a coarse pattern as it was doomed to receive; why so often the coarse appropriates the finer thus, the wrong man the woman, the wrong woman the man, many thousand years of analytical philosophy have failed to explain to our sense of order.

iv *The consequence*

The encounter left its consequence. Tess was with child. The baby only lived a few days. It fell ill. Little more than a child herself, Tess got a prayer-book, called her young sisters and brothers together and christened the baby with the name, Sorrow:

SORROW, I baptize thee in the name of the Father, and of the Son, and of the Holy Ghost.

And the children said: 'Amen.'

Sorrow passed away. Hardy tells of the burial:

So the baby was carried in a small deal box, under an ancient woman's shawl, to the churchyard that night, and buried by lantern-light, at the cost of a shilling and a pint of beer to the sexton, in that shabby corner of God's allotment where He lets the nettles grow, and where all unbaptized infants, notorious drunkards, suicides, and others of the conjecturally damned are laid.

2 Later – Her wedding-night

i *She falls in love*

Two or three years later Tess left home again and went to work as a dairymaid on a big dairy farm. There she met a young man named Angel Clare, the son of a clergyman. Much higher in the social scale than she. He was learning to be a farmer. They fell in love. Angel Clare wanted to marry Tess. She wondered whether to disclose her past to him. Her mother advised her not to do so. So she did not do so. They were married in church.

[1] You may not know of Hardy's reference to 'the ironical Tishbite'. It is a reference to the occasion when Elijah the Tishbite mocked those who called upon their god (I *Kings* 18:27):

'And it came to pass at noon, that Elijah mocked them, and said, Cry aloud: for he is a god; either he is talking, or he is pursuing, or he is in a journey, or peradventure he sleepeth, and must be awaked.'

ii *His confession*

On their wedding-night, sitting by the fire, each confessed to the other his or her sin. Hardy gives Angel Clare's confession thus:

He then told her of that time of his life . . . when, tossed about by doubts and difficulties in London, like a cork on the waves, he plunged into eight-and-forty hours' dissipation with a stranger.

'Happily I awoke almost immediately to a sense of my folly,' he continued. 'I would have no more to say to her, and I came home. I have never repeated the offence. But I felt I should like to treat you with perfect frankness and honour, and I could not do so without telling this. Do you forgive me?'

She pressed his hand tightly for an answer.

'Then we will dismiss it at once and for ever! – too painful as it is for the occasion – and talk of something lighter.'

iii *Her confession*

'O, Angel – I am almost glad – because now *you* can forgive *me*! I have not made my confession. I have a confession, too – remember, I said so.'

Tess then makes her confession about her baby:

. . . and pressing her forehead against his temple she entered on her story of her acquaintance with Alec d'Urberville and its results, murmuring the words without flinching, and with her eyelids drooping down.

iv *The woman pays*

This is the turning point of the story. If Angel Clare had been a sympathetic character, he would have comforted her. But No:

He turned away, and bent over a chair. Tess followed him to the middle of the room where he was, and stood there staring at him with eyes that did not weep. Presently she slid down upon her knees beside his foot, and from this position she crouched in a heap.

'In the name of our love, forgive me!' she whispered with a dry mouth. 'I have forgiven you for the same!'

And, as he did not answer, she said again –

'Forgive me as you are forgiven! I forgive *you*, Angel.'

'You – yes, you do.'

'But you do not forgive me?'

'O Tess, forgiveness does not apply to the case. You were one person; now you are another. My God – how can forgiveness meet such a grotesque – prestidigitation as that!'

I cannot imagine why Hardy put so absurd a word as 'prestidigitation' into Angel Clare's mouth. He would never have used it.

He left her. He deserted her. The brute. He went off to Brazil.

3 She is tempted

i *In a clerical collar*

The next thing in Hardy's story is that Alec d'Urberville turned up again – in a clerical collar. He went about preaching to others how they should behave. But his sordid character soon disclosed itself. He used every device to try and win her. But she resisted and resisted. Her father had died and the family were turned out of their cottage. Alec d'Urberville sought to bribe her into submission by helping her mother and the other children out of their difficulties. She was sorely tempted in her distress.

ii *'Please come back'*

She wrote a long letter to her husband, Angel Clare, beseeching him to come back to her:

'My own husband, – Let me call you so – I must – even if it makes you angry to think of such an unworthy wife as I. I must cry to you in my trouble – I have no one else! I am so exposed to temptation, Angel. I fear to say who it is, and I do not like to write about it at all. But I cling to you in a way you cannot think! Can you not come to me now, at once, before anything terrible happens? O, I know you cannot, because you are so far away! I think I must die if you do not come soon, or tell me to come to you. The punishment you have measured out to me is deserved – I do know that – well deserved – and you are right and just to be angry with me. But, Angel, please, please, not to be just – only a little kind to me, even if I do not deserve it, and come to me! If you would come, I could die in your arms! I would be well content to do that if so be you had forgiven me! . . .'

iii *He is too late*

His parents sent the letter on to him in Brazil. He determined to return home to Tess. But he arrived back too late. She thought that he would never come back. She wrote one last note to him:

'O why have you treated me so monstrously, Angel! I do not deserve it. I have thought it all over carefully, and I can never, never forgive you! You know that I did not intend to wrong you – why have you so wronged me? You are cruel, cruel indeed! I will try to forget you. It is all injustice I have received at your hands! T.'

4 She gives in

i *In a lodging-house*

Angel Clare did return. Thin and pale. He found her at a lodging-house in Bournemouth with Alec d'Urberville. They had booked in as Mr and Mrs d'Urberville. Then she came downstairs:

'I waited and waited for you,' she went on, her tones suddenly resuming their old fluty pathos. 'But you did not come! And I wrote to you, and you did not come! He kept on saying you would never come any more, and that I was a foolish woman. He was very kind to me, and to mother, and to all of us after father's death. He –'

'I don't understand.'

'He has won me back to him.'

ii *The serpent beguiled her*

Clare looked at her keenly, then, gathering her meaning, flagged like one plague-stricken, and his glance sank; it fell on her hands, which, once rosy, were now white and more delicate.

She continued –

'He is upstairs. I hate him now, because he told me a lie – that you would not come again; and you *have* come! These clothes are what he's put upon me: I didn't care what he did wi' me! But – will you go away, Angel, please, and never come any more?'

It was the same explanation as Eve gave in the beginning of time:

And the Lord God said unto the woman, 'What is this that thou hast done?' And the woman said, 'The serpent beguiled me, and I did eat.'[1]

Angel Clare walked out into the street. Tess went back. The landlady heard her say to Alec d'Urberville:

'. . . O, you have torn my life all to pieces . . . made me be what I prayed you in pity not to make me be again! . . . My own true husband will never, never – O God – I can't bear this! – I cannot!'

5 The murder

i *She kills him*

She seized a knife and pierced him through the heart. She ran out after Angel Clare and caught him up.

'Angel,' she said, as if waiting for this, 'do you know what I have been running after you for? To tell you that I have killed him!' A pitiful white smile lit her face as she spoke.

'What!' said he, thinking from the strangeness of her manner that she was in some delirium.

'I have done it – I don't know how,' she continued. 'Still, I owed it to you, and to myself, Angel. I feared long ago, when I struck him on the mouth with my glove, that I might do it some day for the trap he set for me in my simple youth, and his wrong to you through me. He has come between us and ruined us, and now he can never do it any more. . . .'

[1] *Genesis* 3:13.

ii *Tenderness at last*

. . . Tenderness was absolutely dominant in Clare at last. He kissed her endlessly with his white lips, and held her hand, and said –

'I will not desert you! I will protect you by every means in my power, dearest love, whatever you may have done or not have done!'

They wandered and wandered hand in hand for days and days. They came to Stonehenge. Tess was tired and fell asleep. The police officers found out where she was.

'What is it, Angel?' she said, starting up. 'Have they come for me?'

'Yes, dearest,' he said. 'They have come.'

'It is as it should be,' she murmured. 'Angel, I am almost glad – yes, glad! This happiness could not have lasted. It was too much. I have had enough; and now I shall not live for you to despise me!'

iii *'I am ready'*

She stood up, shook herself, and went forward, neither of the men having moved.

'I am ready' she said quietly.

There Hardy leaves the rest of the story for the reader to fill in. You must imagine that Tess was taken to the prison at Winchester, the trial at the Castle, the sentence of death. Her calmness throughout. The last to visit her was her husband, Angel Clare, and her younger sister, 'Liza-Lu. The execution was to take place at Winchester prison at eight o'clock in the morning.

6 The last chapter

i *Winchester as it was*

It is the last chapter of the book. It describes Winchester much as it is now except for the hospital and some new houses and some other new buildings. But any one of you who knows Winchester will recognise the hill up past the prison, and down in the valley the Cathedral, the College and St Cross. The prison is a gaunt, ugly building with an octagonal tower and flagpole on top. I have been there to see a prisoner in one of the cells. In this passage Hardy tells of two persons. They are Angel Clare and Tess's sister, 'Liza-Lu.

The city of Wintoncester, that fine old city, aforetime capital of Wessex, lay amidst its convex and concave downlands in all the brightness and warmth of a July morning. The gabled brick, tile, and freestone houses had almost dried off for the season their integument of lichen, the streams in the meadows were low, and in the sloping High Street, from the West Gateway to the mediaeval cross, and from the mediaeval cross to the bridge, that leisurely dusting and sweeping was in progress which usually ushers in an old-fashioned market-day.

ii *Two persons walking rapidly*

From the western gate aforesaid the highway, as every Wintoncestrian knows, ascends a long and regular incline of the exact length of a measured mile, leaving the houses gradually behind. Up this road from the precincts of the city two persons were walking rapidly, as if unconscious of the trying ascent – unconscious through preoccupation and not through buoyancy. They had emerged upon this road through a narrow barred wicket in a high wall a little lower down. They seemed anxious to get out of the sight of the houses and of their kind, and this road appeared to offer the quickest means of doing so. Though they were young they walked with bowed heads, which gait of grief the sun's rays smiled on pitilessly.

One of the pair was Angel Clare, the other a tall budding creature –half girl, half woman – a spiritualized image of Tess, slighter than she, but with the same beautiful eyes – Clare's sister-in-law, 'Liza-Lu. Their pale faces seemed to have shrunk to half their natural size. They moved on hand in hand, and never spoke a word, the drooping of their heads being that of Giotto's 'Two Apostles.'[1]

iii *The clocks struck eight*

When they had nearly reached the top of the great West Hill the clocks in the town struck eight. Each gave a start at the notes, and, walking onward yet a few steps, they reached the first milestone, standing whitely on the green margin of the grass, and backed by the down, which here was open to the road. They entered upon the turf, and, impelled by a force that seemed to overrule their will, suddenly stood still, turned, and waited in paralyzed suspense beside the stone.

The prospect from this summit was almost unlimited. In the valley beneath lay the city they had just left, its more prominent buildings showing as in an isometric drawing – among them the broad cathedral tower, with its Norman windows and immense length of aisle and nave, the spires of St Thomas's, the pinnacled tower of the College, and, more to the right, the tower and gables of the ancient hospice, where to this day the pilgrim may receive his dole of bread and ale. Behind the city swept the rotund upland of St Catherine's Hill; further off, landscape beyond landscape, till the horizon was lost in the radiance of the sun hanging above it.

iv *The gaol*

Hardy then describes the prison which looks much the same today:

Against these far stretches of country rose, in front of the other city edifices, a large red-brick building, with level gray roofs, and rows of short barred windows bespeaking captivity, the whole contrasting greatly by its formalism with the quaint irregularities of the Gothic erections. It was somewhat disguised from the road in passing it by yews and evergreen oaks, but it was visible enough up here. The wicket from which the pair had lately emerged was in the wall of this structure. From the middle of the building an ugly flat-topped octagonal tower ascended against the east horizon, and viewed from this spot, on its shady side and against the light, it seemed the one blot on the city's beauty. Yet it was with this blot, and not with the beauty, that the two gazers were concerned.

[1] Part of a fresco in the National Gallery attributed then (not now) to Giotto, the famous Florentine painter (1266–1337 AD).

v *A black flag*

Upon the cornice of the tower a tall staff was fixed. Their eyes were riveted on it. A few minutes after the hour had struck something moved slowly up the staff, and extended itself upon the breeze. It was a black flag.

'Justice' was done, and the President of the Immortals, in Aeschylean phrase, had ended his sport with Tess. And the d'Urberville knights and dames slept on in their tombs unknowing. The two speechless gazers bent themselves down to the earth, as if in prayer, and remained thus a long time, absolutely motionless: the flag continued to wave silently. As soon as they had strength they arose, joined hands again, and went on.

This reference to Aeschylus, a great Athenian poet (525–456 BC), is another example of Hardy's style. Hardy here gives *his* literal translation of the Greek phrase. I do not myself like the introduction of it here because so few people will know to what Hardy is referring.

But, apart from this and other oddities, Hardy's fame rests on his descriptions of our Wessex.

8 The trial of a knave

Introduction

After the tragedy of Tess, I feel you should have something lighter to read. I have chosen Lewis Carroll's *Alice in Wonderland.* Like some other chapters in this book, it depicts a trial scene. It is the trial of the Knave of Hearts. All takes place in a dream. Our dreams are always fantastic. I never remember mine. But many a poet and writer have made use of dreams.

Talking of dreams, I go back to the First World War. We youngsters under training on a route-march singing the contemporary favourite by Stoddard King – to keep our spirits up:

> There's a long, long trail a-winding
> Into the land of my dreams,
> Where the nightingales are singing
> And a bright moon beams.
>
> There's a long, long night of waiting
> Until my dreams all come true,
> Till the day when I'll be going down
> That long long trail with you.

When we got to France, there were no more route-marches in training. No singing. Just the hard foot-slogging, pack on back, up to the line. Yet that sentimental song – now as then – in the night watches – goes through my mind.

The best way to enjoy this chapter is to read the best bits of it aloud to your children or grandchildren. After all, that is what Lewis Carroll intended.

1 The beginning

i *A row on the river*

Everyone has heard of *Alice in Wonderland.* Everyone has heard of the Mad Tea-Party with the March Hare, the Mad Hatter and the

Dormouse. Everyone has heard of the lady who shouted 'Off with his head!' But which of you could tell any more about this classic of English literature? We learnt a little more about it in the summer just recently. Our Whitchurch Amateur Dramatic Society gave a performance of *Alice in Wonderland* in a beautiful setting in our garden. They played it on the island with the audience seated on the opposite bank of the river. Even this did not tell us of the trial of the Knave of Hearts. It is a burlesque caricature of trial by jury. You may be amused to be reminded of it.

But first a little about the beginning of it all. Just over one hundred and twenty years ago there was in Oxford a young teacher of mathematics named Charles Dodgson. He and a friend took two little sisters – one named Alice – for a row on the river. He told them an imaginary story which he made up as they went along. They were so pleased with it that they asked him to write it out for them. He did so, all in his own hand, and gave it as a Christmas gift to Alice. Soon afterwards he turned it into a book, twice as long as the manuscript. He published it under the name of Lewis Carroll, with pictures drawn by John Tenniel. It was called *Alice in Wonderland* and captivated grown-ups as well as children. He recalls its beginning in an opening poem:

All in the golden afternoon
   Full leisurely we glide;
For both our oars, with little skill,
   By little arms are plied,
While little hands make vain pretence
   Our wanderings to guide.
...
Thus grew the tale of Wonderland;
   Thus slowly, one by one,
Its quaint events were hammered out –
   And now the tale is done,
And home we steer, a merry crew,
   Beneath the setting sun.

ii *Alice falls asleep*

Lewis Carroll opens the book by telling how Alice falls asleep and dreams that she is in Wonderland, where she sees a White Rabbit:

Alice was beginning to get very tired of sitting by her sister on the bank, and of having nothing to do: once or twice she had peeped into the book her sister was reading, but it had no pictures or conversations in it, 'and what is the use of a book,' thought Alice, 'without pictures or conversations?'

So she was considering in her own mind (as well as she could, for the hot day made her feel very sleepy and stupid) whether the pleasure of making a daisy-chain would be worth the trouble of getting up and picking the daisies, when suddenly a White Rabbit with pink eyes ran close by her.

There was nothing so *very* remarkable in that; nor did Alice think it so *very* much out of the way to hear the Rabbit say to itself, 'Oh dear! Oh dear! I shall be too late!' (when she thought it over afterwards, it occurred to her that she ought to have wondered at this, but at the time it all seemed quite natural); but when the Rabbit *actually took a watch out of its waistcoat-pocket*, and looked at it, and then hurried on, Alice started to her feet, for it flashed across her mind that she had never before seen a rabbit with either a waistcoat-pocket, or a watch to take out of it, and burning with curiosity, she ran across the field after it, and was just in time to see it pop down a large rabbit-hole under the hedge.

In another moment, down went Alice after it, never once considering how in the world she was to get out again.

2 In Wonderland

i *'Drink me'*

Alice had, of course, fallen asleep: and in her sleep she had fallen into dreamland. It was called Wonderland and was peopled with all sorts of creatures. But Alice was a girl of twelve. And Lewis Carroll had to make her an appropriate size to get into Wonderland. So in her dream she came upon a bottle labelled; 'DRINK ME'. She drank it and found herself shutting up like a telescope. She shrank so that she was only ten inches high (or twenty-five centimetres for children of today). She then took up a cake with 'EAT ME' marked in currants. She ate it and opened up like the largest telescope that ever was. She was so distressed that she shed gallons of tears, making a large pool of water. She then saw a fan dropped by the White Rabbit. She picked it up and fanned herself with it. She got smaller and became the size of all the other creatures in Wonderland. She found herself swimming in the pool of tears with them. They got out and dried off. Alice was one of them – of their size – and took part in all they did.

ii *The creatures*

Lewis Carroll takes many of the creatures from real life. Such as the Rabbit, the Mouse, the Hedgehog, and the Lizard. He takes others from rare or extinct species like the Dodo and the Gryphon: or from invented species like the Cheshire Cat and the Mock Turtle. There are also those attractive personalities, the March Hare and the Mad Hatter. For present purposes the principal characters come from a pack of playing cards. Wonderland had a King and Queen – of Hearts. (It had a Knave too – of Hearts.) It had their ten children – from One (the Ace) to Ten – all ornamented with hearts. It had ten Spades.

They were gardeners, obviously. Also ten Clubs who were soldiers. And ten Diamonds. They were courtiers of course.

iii *The Mouse's 'tail' or 'tale'*

Lewis Carroll loves to play upon words. Although Charles Dodgson was a mathematician (like me), as Lewis Carroll he loved to play upon words (like me too!). He makes play with 'tail' and 'tale'. He draws a mouse with a very long 'tail' made up of words. He gets it to tell a long 'tale' about going to law, ending with a sentence to death. I will print its 'tail' wiggly, as Lewis Carroll did:

Fury said to
a mouse, That
he met in the
house, 'Let
us both go
to law: *I*
will prose-
cute *you*. –
Come, I'll
take no de-
nial: We
must have
the trial;
For really
this morn-
ing I've
nothing
to do.'
Said the
mouse to
the cur,
'Such a
trial, dear
sir, With
no jury
or judge,
would
be wast-
ing our
breath.'
'I'll be
judge,
I'll be
jury,'
said
cun-
ning
old
Fury;
'I'll
try
the
whole
cause
and
con-
demn
you to
death.'

iv *'You are old, Father William'*

Lewis Carroll is good at rhyming. Before he took Alice on the river, he had written an entertaining rhyme about Father William. He brings it into Wonderland for fun. It is, indeed, fun, especially as Father William in his youth 'took to the law'. This is the way in which Lewis Carroll brings it in:

> 'Repeat "*You are old, Father William*,"' said the Caterpillar.
> Alice folded her hands, and began:

'You are old, Father William,' the young man said,
'And your hair has become very white;
And yet you incessantly stand on your head –
Do you think, at your age, it is right?'

'In my youth,' Father William replied to his son,
'I feared it might injure the brain;
But, now that I'm perfectly sure I have none,
Why, I do it again and again.'

(After dinner, I have often used those first two verses [as I told you in *What Next in the Law*] by putting 'Master of the Rolls,' instead of 'Father William'.)

'You are old,' said the youth, 'as I mentioned before,
And have grown most uncommonly fat;
Yet you turned a back-somersault in at the door –
Pray, what is the reason of that?'

'In my youth,' said the sage, as he shook his grey locks,
'I kept all my limbs very supple
By the use of this ointment – one shilling the box –
Allow me to sell you a couple?'

Then Lewis Carroll tells how Father William took to the law:

'You are old,' said the youth, 'and your jaws are too weak
For anything tougher than suet;
Yet you finished the goose, with the bones and the beak –
Pray, how did you manage to do it?'

'In my youth,' said his father, 'I took to the law,
And argued each case with my wife;
And the muscular strength, which it gave to my jaw,
Has lasted the rest of my life.'

'You are old,' said the youth, 'one would hardly suppose
That your eye was as steady as ever;
Yet you balanced an eel on the end of your nose –
What made you so awfully clever?'

'I have answered three questions, and that is enough,'
Said his father; 'don't give yourself airs!
Do you think I can listen all day to such stuff?
Be off, or I'll kick you down stairs!'

3 The Mad Tea-party

i *The Dormouse fast asleep*

Now I come to the most famous tea-party in the whole of English literature or history (apart, of course, from the Boston Tea-Party in 1773 when the settlers threw the tea-chests into the sea). It was a brilliant stroke to bring in the March Hare and the Mad Hatter. Why do we say 'As mad as a March hare'? It is because hares are unusually shy and wild in March. It is their rutting season. And why do we say 'As mad as a hatter'? It is because of the mental illness that was once suffered by hatters owing to the chemical used in treating felt. And of course the White Rabbit and the dear little Dormouse need no explanation – except that they are getting rare nowadays. This is how Lewis Carroll introduces the tea-party:

There was a table set out under a tree in front of the house, and the March Hare and the Hatter were having tea at it; a Dormouse was sitting between them, fast asleep, and the other two were using it as a cushion, resting their elbows on it, and talking over its head. 'Very uncomfortable for the Dormouse,' thought Alice; 'only as it's asleep I suppose it doesn't mind.'

ii *No room for Alice*

The table was a large one, but the three were all crowded together at one corner of it. 'No room! No room!' they cried out, when they saw Alice coming. 'There's *plenty* of room!' said Alice indignantly; and she sat down in a large armchair at one end of the table.

'Have some wine?' the March Hare said, in an encouraging tone.

Alice looked all round the table, but there was nothing on it but tea. 'I don't see any wine,' she remarked.

'There isn't any,' said the March Hare.

'Then it wasn't very civil of you to offer it,' said Alice angrily.

'It wasn't very civil of you to sit down without being invited,' said the March Hare.

'I didn't know it was *your* table,' said Alice; 'it's laid for a great many more than three.'

'Your hair wants cutting,' said the Hatter. He had been looking at Alice for some time with great curiosity, and this was his first speech.

'You should learn not to make personal remarks,' Alice said, with some severity; 'it's very rude.'

iii *The March Hare goes mad*

Then Lewis Carroll remembers that the March Hare only went mad in March and tells of a great concert given by the Queen of Hearts. He puts the Hatter as saying:

'We quarrelled last March – just before *he* went mad, you know –' (pointing with his teaspoon at the March Hare), ' – it was at the great concert given by the Queen of Hearts, and I had to sing

Twinkle, twinkle, little bat!
How I wonder what you're at!'

iv *'It's always six o'clock'*

'Well, I'd hardly finished the first verse,' said the Hatter, 'when the Queen jumped up and bawled out, "He's murdering the time! Off with his head!"'

'How dreadfully savage!' exclaimed Alice.

'And ever since that,' the Hatter went on, in a mournful tone, 'he won't do a thing I ask! It's always six o'clock now.'

A bright idea came into Alice's head. 'Is that the reason so many tea-things are put out here?' she asked.

'Yes, that's it,' said the Hatter, with a sigh: 'it's always tea-time, and we've no time to wash the things between whiles.'

'Then you keep moving round, I suppose?' said Alice.

'Exactly so,' said the Hatter; 'as the things get used up.'

'But what happens when you come to the beginning again?' Alice ventured to ask.

'Suppose we change the subject,' the March Hare interrupted, yawning. 'I'm getting tired of this.'

4 The croquet-ground

'Off with his head'

After the Mad Tea-Party, Lewis Carroll goes on to the Queen's croquet-ground where the balls are live hedgehogs and the mallets are live flamingoes. He brings in again the celebrated sentence of death pronounced by the Queen:

The players all played at once without waiting for turns, quarrelling all the while, and fighting for the hedgehogs; and in a very short time the Queen was in a furious passion, and went stamping about, and shouting 'Off with his head!' or 'Off with her head!' about once a minute.

Alice began to feel very uneasy; to be sure she had not as yet had any dispute with the Queen, but she knew that it might happen any minute, 'and then,' thought she, 'what would become of me? They're dreadfully fond of beheading people here: the great wonder is that there's anyone left alive!'

5 The trial begins

i *Of the Knave of Hearts*

Now I come to the trial scene. It was the trial of the Knave of Hearts. As you may anticipate, he was accused of stealing tarts belonging to the Queen of Hearts on a summer's day. It was tried by the King and a jury with the Queen in attendance. Lewis Carroll assumes that you do know something of trial by jury. Much more than Alice would know. (Children under fourteen are not usually allowed into court.) So Lewis Carroll has to suppose that Alice reads the reports of law cases in the newspaper. Incredible in real life. But this was Wonderland.

ii *The stolen property*

Lewis Carroll describes the scene in court. The stolen property – a dish of tarts – was on a table in the very middle of the court. That is the usual place for stolen property, when it has been produced.

The King and Queen of Hearts were seated on their throne when they arrived, with a great crowd assembled about them – all sorts of little birds and beasts, as well as the whole pack of cards: the Knave was standing before them, in chains, with a soldier on each side to guard him; and near the King was the White Rabbit, with a trumpet in one hand, and a scroll of parchment in the other. In the very middle of the court was a table, with a large dish of tarts upon it: they looked so good, that it made Alice quite hungry to look at them – 'I wish they'd get the trial done,' she thought, 'and hand round the refreshments!' But there seemed to be no chance of this, so she began looking about her, to pass away the time.

iii *The judge*

Every judge in England wears a wig. So the King does here. But he wears it under his crown. (Looking as absurd as we do when we wear three-cornered hats over our wigs to greet the Lord Mayor of London.)

Alice had never been in a court of justice before, but she had read about them in books, and she was quite pleased to find that she knew the name of nearly everything there. 'That's the judge,' she said to herself, 'because of his great wig.'

The judge, by the way, was the King, and as he wore his crown over the wig, he did not look at all comfortable, and it was certainly not becoming.

iv *The jurors*

There were twelve jurors in the jury-box. They had writing materials provided for them. This is not done very often but it is very useful. The writing materials here were slates and pencils (as I had when I first went to school – very convenient, as easy to rub out).

'And that's the jury-box,' thought Alice, 'and those twelve creatures – (she was obliged to say 'creatures', you see, because some of them were animals, and some were birds) – 'I suppose they are the jurors.' She said this last word two or three times over to herself, being rather proud of it; for she thought, and rightly too, that very few little girls of her age knew the meaning of it at all. However, 'jurymen' would have done just as well.

The twelve jurors were all writing very busily on slates. 'What are they all doing?' Alice whispered to the Gryphon. 'They can't have anything to put down yet, before the trial's begun.'

'They're putting down their names,' the Gryphon whispered in reply, 'for fear they should forget them before the end of the trial.'

v *The jurors are stupid*

Lewis Carroll portrays the jurors as stupid. They sometimes are in real life. So also in Wonderland.

'Stupid things!' Alice began, in a loud indignant voice, but she stopped hastily, for the White Rabbit cried out 'Silence in the court!' and the King put on his spectacles and looked anxiously round, to see who was talking.

Alice could see, as well as if she were looking over their shoulders, that all the jurors were writing down 'stupid things!' on their slates, and she could even make out that one of them didn't know how to spell 'stupid', and that he had to ask his neighbour to tell him. 'A nice muddle their slates will be in before the trial's over!' thought Alice.

vi *The pencil that squeaked*

Then there is the delightful incident of the pencil that squeaked:

One of the jurors had a pencil that squeaked. This, of course, Alice could *not* stand, and she went round the court and got behind him, and very soon found an opportunity of taking it away. She did it so quickly that the poor little juror (it was Bill, the Lizard) could not make out at all what had become of it; so, after hunting all about for it, he was obliged to write with one finger for the rest of the day; and this was of very little use, as it left no mark on the slate.

6 The trial itself

i *The prisoner is charged*

Lewis Carroll omits the most important moment in a trial. It is when the prisoner is put up to plead Guilty or Not Guilty. Lewis Carroll only repeats the nursery rhyme. It is not appropriate at this stage of the trial, because it asserts that the prisoner is guilty of theft – before his case is heard:

'Herald, read the accusation!' said the King.

On this the White Rabbit blew three blasts on the trumpet, and then unrolled the parchment scroll, and read as follows:

> The Queen of Hearts, she made some tarts,
> All on a summer day:
> The Knave of Hearts, he stole those tarts,
> And took them quite away!

'Consider your verdict,' the King said to the jury.

'Not yet, not yet!' the Rabbit hastily interrupted. 'There's a great deal to come before that!'

ii *The first witness*

The first witness was the Hatter. He came in with a tea-cup in one hand and a piece of bread-and-butter in the other. 'I beg pardon, your Majesty,' he began, 'for bringing these in; but I hadn't quite finished my tea when I was sent for.'

'You ought to have finished,' said the King, 'When did you begin?'

The Hatter looked at the March Hare, who had followed him into the court, arm-in-arm with the Dormouse. 'Fourteenth of March, I *think* it was,' he said.

'Fifteenth,' said the March Hare.

'Sixteenth,' said the Dormouse.

'Write that down,' the King said to the jury, and the jury eagerly wrote down all three dates on their slates, and then added them up, and reduced the answer to shillings and pence.

iii *The witness is confused*

The judge was rude and overbearing to the witness who got very confused and bit a large piece out of his tea-cup:

'Take off your hat,' the King said to the Hatter.

'It isn't mine,' said the Hatter.

'*Stolen*!' the King exclaimed, turning to the jury, who instantly made a memorandum of the fact.

'I keep them to sell,' the Hatter added as an explanation; 'I've none of my own. I'm a hatter.'

Here the Queen put on her spectacles, and began staring hard at the Hatter, who turned pale and fidgeted.

'Give your evidence,' said the King; 'and don't be nervous, or I'll have you executed on the spot.'

This did not seem to encourage the witness at all; he kept shifting from one foot to the other, looking uneasily at the Queen, and in his confusion he bit a large piece out of his tea-cup instead of the bread-and-butter.

iv *Alice squeezes the Dormouse*

The court was full of sightseers. Alice was sitting next to the Dormouse and squeezed him. So he had to get up and go to the other side of the court:

Just at this moment Alice felt a very curious sensation, which puzzled her a good deal until she made out what it was; she was beginning to grow larger again, and she thought at first she would get up and leave the court. But on second thoughts she decided to remain where she was as long as there was room for her.

'I wish you wouldn't squeeze so,' said the Dormouse, who was sitting next to her. 'I can hardly breathe.'

'I can't help it,' said Alice very meekly: 'I'm growing.'

'You've no right to grow *here*,' said the Dormouse.

'Don't talk nonsense,' said Alice, more boldly; 'you know you're growing too.'

'Yes, but *I* grow at a reasonable pace,' said the Dormouse; 'not in that ridiculous fashion.' And he got up very sulkily and crossed over to the other side of the court.

v *The witness loses his shoes*

The Queen ought not to have been taking part in the proceedings, but she remembered the great concert which was talked about at the Mad Tea-Party. She stared at the Hatter so hard that he lost his shoes:

All this time the Queen had never left off staring at the Hatter, and, just as the Dormouse crossed the court, she said to one of the officers of the court, 'Bring me the list of the singers in the last concert!' On which the wretched Hatter trembled so, that he shook off both his shoes.

'Give your evidence,' the King repeated angrily, 'or I'll have you executed, whether you're nervous or not.'

vi *The guinea-pigs are suppressed*

The Hatter had become so confused that he dropped his tea-cup and went down on one knee. One of the guinea-pigs cheered. He was immediately 'suppressed' by means which would not be tolerated in a court of law, but were permissible in Wonderland.

The miserable Hatter dropped his tea-cup, and bread-and-butter, and went down on one knee. 'I'm a poor man, your Majesty,' he began.

'You're a *very* poor *speaker*,' said the King.

Here one of the guinea-pigs cheered, and was immediately suppressed by the officers of the court. (As that is rather a hard word, I will just explain to you how it was done. They had a large canvas bag, which tied up at the mouth with strings: into this they slipped the guinea-pig, head first, and then sat upon it.)

'I'm glad I've seen that done,' thought Alice. 'I've so often read in the newspapers, at the end of trials, "There was some attempt at applause, which was immediately suppressed by the officers of the court," and I never understood what it meant till now.'

'If that's all you know about it, you may stand down,' continued the King.

'I can't go no lower,' said the Hatter: 'I'm on the floor as it is.'

'Then you may *sit* down,' the King replied.

Here the other guinea-pig cheered, and was suppressed.

'Come, that finishes the guinea-pigs!' thought Alice. 'Now we shall get on better.'

vii *The Hatter leaves the court without his shoes*

'You may go,' said the King; and the Hatter hurriedly left the court, without even waiting to put his shoes on.

'And just take his head off outside,' the Queen added, to one of the officers; but the Hatter was out of sight before the officer could get to the door.

viii *The next witness*

'Call the next witness!' said the King.

The next witness was the Duchess's cook. She carried the pepper-box in her hand, and Alice guessed who it was, even before she got into court, by the way people near the door began sneezing all at once.

'Give your evidence,' said the King.

'Sha'n't,' said the cook.

The King looked anxiously at the White Rabbit, who said in a low voice, 'Your Majesty must cross-examine *this* witness.'

'Well, if I must, I must,' the King said with a melancholy air, and, after folding his arms and frowning at the cook till his eyes were nearly out of sight, he said in a deep voice: 'What are tarts made of?'

'Pepper, mostly,' said the cook.

'Treacle,' said a sleepy voice behind her.

'Collar that Dormouse,' the Queen shrieked out. 'Behead that Dormouse! Turn that Dormouse out of court! Suppress him! Pinch him! Off with his whiskers.'

For some minutes the whole court was in confusion getting the Dormouse turned out, and, by the time they had settled down again, the cook had disappeared.

ix *Alice is called*

Lewis Carroll tells a delightful story of how Alice knocked over the jury-box when she was called as the next witness:

Alice watched the White Rabbit as he fumbled over the list, feeling very curious to see what the next witness would be like – 'for they haven't got much evidence *yet*,' she said to herself. Imagine her surprise, when the White Rabbit read out, at the top of his shrill little voice, the name 'Alice!'

'Here!' cried Alice, quite forgetting, in the flurry of the moment, how large she had grown in the last few minutes, and she jumped up in such a hurry that she tipped over the jury-box with the edge of her skirt, upsetting all the jurymen on to the heads of the crowd below, and there they lay sprawling about, reminding her very much of a globe of gold-fish she had accidentally upset the week before.

'Oh, I *beg* your pardon!' she exclaimed, in a tone of great dismay, and began picking them up again as quickly as she could, for the accident of the gold-fish kept running in her head, and she had a vague sort of idea that they must be collected at once and put back into the jury-box, or they would die.

'The trial cannot proceed,' said the King in a very grave voice, 'until all the jurymen are back in their proper places – *all*,' he repeated with great emphasis, looking hard at Alice as he said so.

Alice looked at the jury-box, and saw that, in her haste, she had put the Lizard in head downwards, and the poor little thing was waving its tail about in a melancholy way, being quite unable to move. She soon got it out again, and put it right; 'not that it signifies much,' she said to herself; 'I should think it would be *quite* as much use in the trial one way up as the other.'

As soon as the jury had a little recovered from the shock of being upset, and their slates and pencils had been found and handed back to them, they set to work very diligently to write out a history of the accident, all except the Lizard, who seemed too much overcome to do anything but sit with its mouth open, gazing up into the roof of the court.

x *Alice knows nothing*

Whenever a witness is called, counsel should have a brief instructing him as to what the witness can say. But Alice knew nothing about the stolen tarts. Some said her evidence was important. Others that it was unimportant.

'What do you know about this business?' the King said to Alice.

'Nothing,' said Alice.

'Nothing *whatever*?' persisted the King.

'Nothing whatever,' said Alice.

'That's very important,' the King said, turning to the jury. They were just beginning to write this down on their slates, when the White Rabbit interrupted: '*Un*important, your Majesty means, of course,' he said in a very respectful tone, but frowning and making faces at him as he spoke.

'*Un*important, of course, I meant,' the King hastily said, and went on to himself in an undertone, 'important – unimportant – unimportant – important –' as if he were trying which word sounded best.

Some of the jury wrote it down 'important,' and some 'unimportant'. Alice could see this, as she was near enough to look over their slates; 'but it doesn't matter a bit,' she thought to herself.

xi *Alice is too tall*

Alice had grown so tall that the judge looked up the rules and said she must leave the court. She refused to do so.

At this moment the King, who had been for some time busily writing in his note-book, called out 'Silence!' and read out from his book, 'Rule Forty-two. *All persons more than a mile high to leave the court.*'

Everybody looked at Alice.

'*I'm* not a mile high,' said Alice.

'You are,' said the King.

'Nearly two miles high,' added the Queen.

'Well, I sha'n't go, at any rate,' said Alice; 'besides, that's not a regular rule: you invented it just now.'

'It's the oldest rule in the book,' said the King.

'Then it ought to be Number One,' said Alice.

The King turned pale, and shut his note-book hastily. 'Consider your verdict,' he said to the jury, in a low, trembling voice.

xii *A letter is produced*

Then a letter was produced. It was a set of verses. It was said that the prisoner wrote it. He denied it. It ought not to have been admitted in evidence. But this was Wonderland where any evidence was admissible.

'There's more evidence to come yet, please your Majesty,' said the White Rabbit, jumping up in a great hurry; 'this paper has just been picked up.'

'What's in it?' said the Queen.

'I haven't opened it yet,' said the White Rabbit, 'but it seems to be a letter, written by the prisoner to – to somebody.'

'It must have been that,' said the King, 'unless it was written to nobody, which isn't usual, you know.'

. . .

'Please your Majesty,' said the Knave, 'I didn't write it, and they can't prove that I did: there's no name signed at the end.'

'If you didn't sign it,' said the King, 'that only makes the matter worse. You *must* have meant some mischief, or else you'd have signed your name like an honest man.'

There was a general clapping of hands at this: it was the first really clever thing the King had said that day.

'That *proves* his guilt, of course,' said the Queen; 'so, off with –'

'It doesn't prove anything of the sort!' said Alice.

xiii *Has the letter any meaning?*

After the White Rabbit had read out the verses, there was a controversy about whether they had any meaning. They had none and should have been ignored.

'That's the most important piece of evidence we've heard yet,' said the King, rubbing his hands; 'so now let the jury –'

'If any one of them can explain it,' said Alice (she had grown so large in the last few minutes that she wasn't a bit afraid of interrupting him), 'I'll give him sixpence. *I* don't believe there's an atom of meaning in it.'

The jury all wrote down on their slates, '*She* doesn't believe there's an atom of meaning in it;' but none of them attempted to explain the paper.

'If there's no meaning in it,' said the King, 'that saves a world of trouble, you know, as we needn't try to find any. And yet I don't know,' he went on, spreading out the verses on his knee, and looking at them with one eye; 'I seem to see some meaning in them, after all.'

xiv *There is no verdict*

The jury were asked to consider their verdict but the Queen intervened and prevented it.

'Let the jury consider their verdict,' the King said, for about the twentieth time that day.

'No, no!' said the Queen. 'Sentence first – verdict afterwards.'

'Stuff and nonsense!' said Alice loudly. 'The idea of having the sentence first!'

'Hold your tongue!' said the Queen, turning purple.

'I won't,' said Alice.

'Off with her head!' the Queen shouted at the top of her voice. Nobody moved.

'Who cares for *you*?' said Alice (she had grown to her full size by this time). 'You're nothing but a pack of cards!'

7 The end

The whole pack comes down

Then the whole pack came flying down upon Alice and woke her up.

At this the whole pack rose up into the air, and came flying down upon her; she gave a little scream, half of fright and half of anger, and tried to beat them off, and found herself lying on the bank, with her head in the lap of her sister, who was gently brushing away some dead leaves that had fluttered down from the trees on to her face.

'Wake up, Alice dear!' said her sister. 'Why, what a long sleep you've had!'

'Oh, I've had such a curious dream!' said Alice, and she told her sister, as well as she could remember them, all these strange Adventures of hers that you have just been reading about; and when she had finished, her sister kissed her, and said: 'It *was* a curious dream, dear, certainly; but now run in to your tea; it's getting late.' So Alice got up and ran off, thinking while she ran, as well she might, what a wonderful dream it had been.

9 Seeking Salvation

Introduction

Now we come to another dream but very different from the last. Here we have no fun or games. No playing-cards. Everything very serious and very earnest. For we go back to the Puritan Revolution and to John Bunyan who expressed the spirit of it in his *Pilgrim's Progress*. He sees in a dream a poor man seeking salvation with tears and with no guide save his Bible in his hand. G M Trevelyan tells of its impact in his *English Social History*:

> That man multiplied, congregated, regimented was a force of tremendous potency, to make and to destroy. It was the force by which Oliver Cromwell and George Fox and John Wesley wrought their wonders, being men of a like experience themselves.

There is a trial here too. It is the trial of *Faithful* who was sentenced to death and burnt at the stake. John Bunyan brings out his allegory. He has in mind *Revelation* 2.10:

> Behold the devil shall cast some of you into prison, that ye may be tried; and ye shall have tribulation ten days: be thou *faithful* unto death, and I will give thee a crown of life.

1 John Bunyan

John Bunyan's greatest book, *The Pilgrim's Progress*, ranks next to the *Bible* in its influence world-wide. It has been translated into 108 different languages and dialects. It is remarkable for the beauty and simplicity of its language. Also for the powerful use of names which Bunyan invented to suit his book. Such as the fair which was called Vanity-Fair. In my young days, many still read *The Pilgrim's Progress* or had it read to them. But nobody does now. So I will introduce it to you.

i *A voice from heaven*

John Bunyan was born at Elstow, within a little mile of Bedford, in 1628. We are told that he was 'so addicted to vice, even from his childhood, that he had few equals in wickedness.' But one day, at play with his companions, a voice suddenly darted from heaven into his soul, saying, 'Wilt thou leave thy sins, and go to heaven; or have thy sins, and go to hell?' He elected to go to heaven. Rather like St Paul on the road to Damascus.

In the Civil War, he was a soldier in the Parliament's army. At the siege of Leicester in 1645, he was drawn out to stand sentinel, but another soldier voluntarily desired to go in his place. That soldier went and, as he stood sentinel there, was shot in the head with a musket-bullet, and died. John Bunyan often mentioned it, but never without thanksgiving to God.

ii *In prison for twelve years*

After the Civil War, he was baptised and admitted a member of the Baptist church at Bedford. He was a tinker, and went about preaching. In 1660 at the Bedford quarter sessions he was indicted for unlawful assembly and not conforming to the Church of England. That was the usual formula used in prosecuting dissenters. He was imprisoned for twelve years. He had only two books with him, the *Bible* and Foxe's *Book of Martyrs*. While in prison, he wrote several religious books, including the first part of *The Pilgrim's Progress from this world to that which is to come.*[1]

iii *An allegory*

It is an allegory. That is to say, it is a theological experience dressed up as an earthly story. It speaks of a man with a heavy pack on his back who flees from his own home and, after many difficulties and dangers, gets rid of his pack and reaches his goal. But the pack is full of sins for which he seeks forgiveness and redemption, and his goal is spiritual calm.

2 He tells of a dream

i *Christian with his book*

Bunyan writes the story as if he is telling of a dream; and he names his places and characters by reference to their attributes: places such

[1] All extracts are from the 1847 edition accurately printed for the Hanserd Knollys Society from the first edition with notices of all the subsequent additions and alterations by the author himself.

as the City of Destruction or the Slough of Dispond (Despond) and persons such as Christian or Faithful. In the dream he sees a man – Christian – with a great burden on his back, a burden full of sins, reading in a book from which he learns that the city in which he and his family dwell will be burned with fire. On the advice of Evangelist, Christian flees from the City of Destruction, leaving his wife and children behind. The book is the *Bible* and Bunyan repeatedly quotes from it.

ii *'What shall I do?'*

Christian is in sore plight because of his sins:

As I walk'd through the wilderness of this world, I lighted on a certain place, where was a Denn; And I laid me down in that place to sleep: And as I slept I dreamed a Dream. I dreamed, and behold *I saw a Man cloathed with Raggs, standing in a certain place, with his face from his own House, a Book in his hand, and a great burden upon his back.* I looked, and saw him open the Book, and Read therein; and as he Read, he wept and trembled: and not being able longer to contain, he brake out with a lamentable cry; saying, *what shall I do*?

In this plight therefore he went home, and refrained himself as long as he could, that his Wife and Children should not perceive his distress; but he could not be silent long, because that his trouble increased: wherefore at length he brake his mind to his Wife and Children; and thus he began to talk to them, *O my dear Wife,* said he, *and you the Children of my bowels, I your dear friend, am in my self undone, by reason of a burden that lieth hard upon me: moreover, I am for certain informed, that this our City will be burned with fire from Heaven, in which fearful overthrow, both myself, with thee, my Wife, and you my sweet babes, shall miserably come to ruine; except (the which, yet I see not) some way of escape can be found, whereby we may be delivered.*

iii *Evangelist shows him the way*

Christian's relations thought he was mad and were unkind to him. He was so distressed that he walked alone in the fields, reading and praying. He often burst out crying, 'What shall I do to be saved?' Then a man called Evangelist came to him and asked, 'Wherefore dost thou cry?' Christian answered, 'Because I fear this burden which is upon my back.' Evangelist pointed him to a wicket-gate. (That meant, in Bunyan's time, and still means, a small door or gate for foot-passengers. The 'wicket' in cricket only came into use in 1738.)

Then said *Evangelist*, If this be thy condition, why standest thou still? He answered, Because I know not whither to go. Then he gave him a *Parchment Roll*, and there was written within, *Fly from the wrath to come.*

The Man therefore Read it, and looking upon *Evangelist* very carefully; said, Whither must I fly? Then said *Evangelist*, pointing with his finger over a very wide Field, Do you see yonder *Wicket-gate*? The Man said, No. Then said the other, Do you see yonder shining light? He said, I think I do. Then said *Evangelist*, Keep that light in your eye, and go up directly thereto, so shalt thou see the Gate; at which when thou knockest, it shall be told thee what thou shalt do.

So I saw in my Dream, that the Man began to run; now he had not run far from his own door, but his Wife and Children perceiving it, began to cry after him to return: but the Man put his fingers in his Ears, and ran on crying, Life, Life, Eternal Life: so he looked not behind him, but fled towards the middle of the Plain.

3 The Slough of Despond

i *They fall in*

His neighbours ran after him and tried to get him to come back. One was called Obstinate. The other Pliable. Soon afterwards, Obstinate turned back, but Pliable went on with Christian, talking together. Then they came to the Slough of Despond. Both fell in but Pliable got out and went back. Christian went on. There were some steps by which people could get out of the mire, but Christian did not see them.

Pli. *Well, my good Companion, glad am I to hear of these things: Come on, let us mend our pace.*

Chr. I cannot go so fast as I would, by reason of this burden that is upon my back.

Now I saw in my Dream, that just as they had ended this talk, they drew near to a very *Miry Slough*, that was in the midst of the Plain, and they being heedless, did both fall suddenly into the bogg. The name of the Slow was *Dispond.*[1] Here therefore they wallowed for a time, being grieviously bedaubed with the dirt; and *Christian*, because of the burden that was on his back, began to sink in the Mire.

Pli. *Then said* Pliable, *Ah, Neighbour* Christian, *where are you now?*

Chr. Truly, said *Christian*, I do not know.

Pli. At that *Pliable* began to be offended; and angerly said to his Fellow, *Is this the happiness you have told me all this while of? if we have such ill speed at our first setting out, what may we expect, 'twixt this, and our Journeys end? May I get out again with my life, you shall possess the brave Country alone for me.* And with that he gave a desperate struggle or two, and got out of the Mire, on that side of the Slough which was next to his own House: So away he went, and *Christian* saw him no more.

ii *Help comes*

A man called Help came and helped Christian out of the mire:

Wherefore *Christian* was left to tumble in the Slough of *Dispondency* alone, but still he endeavoured to struggle to that side of the Slough, that was still further from his own House, and next to the Wicket-gate; the which he did, but could not get out,

[1] Bunyan spells it *Dispond.*

because of the burden that was upon his back. But I beheld in my Dream, that a Man came to him, whose name was *Help*, and asked him, *What he did there*?

Chr. Sir, said *Christian*, I was directed this way, by a man called *Evangelist*; who directed me also to yonder Gate, that I might escape the wrath to come: And as I was going thither, I fell in here.

Help. But why did you not look for the steps?

Chr. Fear followed me so hard, that I fled the next way, and fell in.

Help. Then, said he, *Give me thy hand*! So he gave him his hand, and he drew him out, and set him upon sound ground, and bid him go on his way.

iii *Why it is called Despond*

It is called the Slough of Despond because it is the place where people fall into sin. There are steps to get out of it but they are often not seen.

Then I stepped to him that pluckt him out; and said; Sir, Wherefore (since over this place, is the way from the City of *Destruction*, to yonder *Gate*) is it, that *this* Plat is not mended, that poor Travellers might go thither with more security? And he said unto me, this *Miry slough* is such a place as cannot be mended: It is the descent whither the scum and filth that attends conviction for sin, doth continually run, and therefore it is called the *Slough of Dispond*: for still as the sinner is awakened about his lost condition, there ariseth in his soul many fears, and doubts, and discouraging apprehensions, which all of them get together, and settle in this place: And this is the reason of the badness of this ground. . . .

True, there are by the direction of the Law-giver, certain good and substantial Steps, placed even through the very midst of this *Slough*; but at such time as this place doth much spue out its filth, as it doth against change of weather, these steps are hardly seen; or if they be, Men through the diziness of their heads, step besides; and then they are bemired to purpose, notwithstanding the steps be there; but the ground is good when they are once got in at the Gate.

4 The redemption of Christian

i *Christian is taught the Gospel*

Eventually Christian got to the gate. Over it was written, 'Knock and it shall be opened unto you.' Christian knocked. Good Will opened it.

Chr. Here is a poor burdened sinner. I come from the City of *Destruction*, but am going to Mount *Zion*, that I may be delivered from the wrath to come; I would therefore, Sir, since I am informed that by this Gate is the way thither, know if you are *willing* to let me in.

Good Will. I am *willing* with all my heart, said he; and with that he opened the Gate.

Good Will sent him over to the House of the Interpreter who explained the Gospel to Christian. At the end of their talk:

Then said the *Interpreter* to *Christian, Hast thou considered all these things*?

Chr. Yes, and they put me in *hope* and *fear*.

Inter. Well, keep all things so in thy mind, that they may be as a *Goad* in thy sides, to prick thee forward in the way thou must go.

Then *Christian* began to gird up his loins, and to address himself to his Journey. Then said the *Interpreter*, The Comforter be always with thee good *Christian*, to guide thee in the way that leads to the City.

ii *Christian gets rid of his burden*

Believing in the Gospel, Christian is on the way to salvation:

Now I saw in my Dream, that the high way up which *Christian* was to go, was fenced on either side with a Wall, and that Wall is called *Salvation*. Up this way therefore did burdened *Christian* run, but not without great difficulty, because of the load on his back.

He ran thus till he came at a place somewhat ascending; and upon that place stood a *Cross*, and a little below in the bottom, a Sepulcher. So I saw in my Dream, that just as *Christian* came up with the *Cross*, his burden loosed from off his Shoulders, and fell from off his back; and began to tumble, and so continued to do, till it came to the mouth of the Sepulcher, where it fell in, and I saw it no more.

Then was *Christian* glad and lightsom, and said with a merry heart, *He hath given me rest, by his sorrow; and life, by his death.*

5 The Devil

i *The armour of God*

Next, Christian came up against evil in the shape of Apollyon, a foul fiend: but Christian was prepared. He wore the armour described in *Ephesians* 6:11: 'Put on the whole armour of God that ye may be able to stand against the wiles of the devil.'

In my own 1814 edition of *The Pilgrim's Progress* there is a fine engraving of the fight. We used to pore over it when we were children. Christian has all the armour described in *Ephesians* – 'the breastplate of righteousness', 'the shield of faith', 'the helmet of salvation' and 'the sword of the Spirit'. And Apollyon is a hideous monster with all 'the fiery darts of the wicked'.

ii *Christian stands his ground*

But now in this Valley of *Humiliation* poor *Christian* was hard put to it, for he had gone but a little way before he espied a foul *Fiend* coming over the field to meet him; his name is *Apollyon*. Then did *Christian* begin to be afraid, and to cast in his mind whither to go back, or to stand his ground. But he considered again, that he had no Armour for his back, and therefore thought that to turn the back to him, might give him greater advantage with ease to pierce him with his Darts; therefore he resolved to venture, and stand his ground. For thought he, had I no more in mine eye, then the saving of my life, 'twould be the best way to stand.

iii *The Monster Apollyon*

So he went on, and *Apollyon* met him; now the Monster was hidious to behold, he was cloathed with scales like a Fish (and they are his pride) he had Wings like a Dragon, feet like a Bear, and out of his Belly came Fire and Smoak, and his mouth was as the mouth of a Lion. When he was come up to *Christian*, he beheld him with a disdainful countenance, and thus began to question with him.

Apol. *Whence come you, and whither are you bound?*

Chr. I am come from the City of *Destruction*, which is the place of all evil, and am going to the City of *Zion*.

Apollyon claimed to be the Prince of that country. But Christian said that the Prince whom he served was merciful and ready to forgive.

Apol. *Then Apollyon* broke out into a grievous rage, saying, *I am an Enemy to this Prince: I hate his Person, his Laws, and People: I am come out on purpose to withstand thee.*

Chr. *Apollyon* beware what you do, for I am in the Kings High-way, the way of Holiness, therefore take heed to your self.

iv *Apollyon blocks the way*

Apol. Then *Apollyon* strodled quite over the whole breadth of the way, and said, I am void of fear in this matter, prepare thy self to dye, for I swear by my Infernal Den, that thou shalt go no further, here will I spill thy soul; and with that, he threw a flaming Dart at his brest, but *Christian* had a Shield in his hand, with which he caught it, and so prevented the danger of that. Then did *Christian* draw, for he saw 'twas time to bestir him; and *Apollyon* as fast made at him, throwing Darts as thick as Hail; by the which, notwithstanding all that Christian could do to avoid it, *Apollyon* wounded him in his head, his hand and foot; this made *Christian* give a little back: *Apollyon* therefore followed his work amain, and *Christian* again took courage, and resisted as manfully as he could. This sore Combat lasted for above half a day, even till *Christian* was almost quite spent. For you must know that *Christian* by reason of his wounds, must needs grow weaker and weaker.

v *Christian wins through*

Then *Apollyon* espying his opportunity, began to gather up close to *Christian*, and wrestling with him, gave him a dreadful fall; and with that, *Christians* Sword flew out of his hand. Then said *Apollyon, I am sure of thee now*: and with that, he had almost prest him to death, so that *Christian* began to despair of life. But as God would have it, while *Apollyon* was fetching of his last blow, thereby to make a full end of this good Man, *Christian* nimbly reached out his hand for his Sword, and caught it, saying, *Rejoyce not against me, O mine Enemy! when I fall, I shall arise*; and with that, gave him a deadly thrust, which made him give back, as one that had received his mortal would: *Christian* perceiving that, made at him again, saying, *Nay, in all these things we are more than Conquerors, through him that loved us.* And with that *Apollyon* spread forth his Dragons wings, and sped him away, that *Christian* for a season saw him no more.

vi *Christian gives thanks*

In this Combat no man can imagine, unless he had seen and heard as I did, what yelling, and hideous roaring *Apollyon* made all the time of the fight, he spake like a Dragon: and on the other side, what sighs and groans brast from *Christians* heart. I never saw him all the while, give so much as one pleasant look, till he perceived he had wounded *Apollyon* with his two edged Sword, then indeed he did smile, and look upward: but 'twas the dreadfullest sight that ever I saw.

So when the Battel was over, *Christian* said, I will here give thanks to him that hath delivered me out of the mouth of the Lion; to him that did help me against *Apollyon.*

6 Vanity-Fair

i *They get to Vanity-Fair*

After getting through the Valley of Humiliation, Christian passed through the Valley of the Shadow of Death. On getting out of it, he caught up with Faithful. They went on together, talking of their experiences up to that time. They met Talkative, who lived up to his name. Then they came to Vanity-Fair. It had been set up by three evil ones: Beelzebub, Apollyon and Legion.

Then I saw in my Dream, that when they were got out of the Wilderness, they presently saw a Town before them, and the name of that Town is *Vanity*; and at the Town there is a *Fair* kept, called Vanity-Fair: It is kept all the Year long, it beareth the name of *Vanity-Fair*, because the Town where tis kept, *is lighter then* Vanity; and also, because all that is there sold, or that cometh thither, is *Vanity.* As is the saying of the wise, *All that cometh is Vanity.*

This Fair is no new erected business, but a thing of Ancient standing; I will shew you the original of it.

ii *'All sorts of vanity'*

Almost five thousand years agone, there were Pilgrims walking to the Celestial City, as these two honest persons are; and *Beelzebub, Apollyon*, and *Legion*, with their Companions, perceiving by the path that the Pilgrims made, that their way to the City lay through *this Town of Vanity*, they contrived here to set up a Fair; a Fair wherein should be sold of *all sorts of Vanity*, and that it should last all the year long. Therefore at *this Fair* are all such Merchandize sold, As Houses, Lands, Trades, Places, Honours, Preferments, Titles, Countreys, Kingdoms, Lusts, Pleasures and Delights of all sorts, as Whores, Bauds, Wives, Husbands, Children, Masters, Servants, Lives, Blood, Bodies, Souls, Silver, Gold, Pearls, precious Stones, and what not.

And moreover, at this Fair there is at all times to be seen Juglings, Cheats, Games, Plays, Fools, Apes, Knaves, and Rogues, and that of all sorts.

Here are to be seen too, and that for nothing, Thefts, Murders, Adultries, False-swearers, and that of a blood-red colour.

iii *Disorder in the Fair*

When Christian and Faithful went through the fair, they did not buy any of the merchandise there, but only the truth. This gave rise to much disorder, so much so that they were taken in for questioning. Many in the fair were against the two pilgrims, but some were on their side. The two behaved themselves so well that it converted several to their point of view.

. . . Thus, after divers words had passed on both sides, (the men themselves behaving themselves all the while very wisely and soberly before them,) they fell to some Blows, among themselves, and did harm one to another. Then were these two poor men brought before their Examiners again, and there charged as being guilty of the late Hubbub that had been in the *fair*. So they beat them pitifully, and hanged Irons upon them, and led them in Chaines up and down the *fair*, for an example and a terror to others, lest any should further speak in their behalf, or joyn themselves unto them. But *Christian* and *Faithful* behaved themselves yet more wisely, and received the ignominy and shame that was cast upon them, with so much meekness and patience, that it won to their side (though but few in comparison of the rest) several of the men in the *fair*. This put the other party yet into a greater rage, insomuch that they concluded the death of these two men. Wherefore they threatned that the Cage nor Irons should serve their turn, but that they should die, for the abuse they had done, and for deluding the men of the *fair*.

Then they were remanded to the Cage again until further order should be taken with them. So they put them in, and made their feet fast in the Stocks.

7 The trial

i *The pilgrims are brought to trial*

Then Christian and Faithful are brought to trial. You will see how closely Bunyan follows the course of proceedings in those days (about 1670) before a judge and jury.

Then a convenient time being appointed, they brought them forth to their Tryal in order to their Condemnation. When the time was come, they were brought before their Enemies and arraigned; the Judge's name was Lord *Hategood.* Their indictment was one and the same in substance, though somewhat varying in form; the Contents whereof was this.

That they were enemies to, and disturbers of their Trade; that they had made Commotions and Divisions in the Town, and had won a party to their own most dangerous opinions, in contempt of the Law of their Prince.

ii *Faithful makes his defence*

Then *Faithful* began to answer, That he had only set himself against that which had set it self against him that is higher then the highest. And said he, As for Disturbance, I make none, being my self a man of Peace; the Party that were won to us, were won by beholding our Truth and Innocence, and they are only turned from the worse to the better. And as to the King you talk of, since he is *Beelzebub*, the Enemy of our Lord, I defie him and all his Angels.

iii *Witnesses for the prosecution*

Evidence was called for the prosecution. Envy was first called.

Then Proclamation was made, that they that had ought to say for their Lord the King against the Prisoner at the Bar, should forthwith appear and give in their evidence. So there came in three Witnesses, to wit, *Envy, Superstition*, and *Pickthank*. They was then asked, If they knew the Prisoner at the Bar? and what they had to say for their Lord the King against him?

Then stood forth *Envy*, and said to this effect; My Lord, I have known this man a long time, and will attest upon my Oath before this honourable Bench, That he is –

Judge. Hold, give him his Oath;

So they sware him. Then he said, My Lord, This man, notwithstanding his plausible name, is one of the vilest men in our Countrey; he neither regardeth Prince nor People, Law nor Custom: but doth all that he can to possess all men with certain of his disloyal notions, which he in the general calls Principles of Faith and Holiness. And in particular, I heard him once my self affirm, *That Christianity and the Customs of our Town of* Vanity, *were Diametrically opposite, and could not be reconciled.* By which saying, my Lord, he doth at once, not only condemn all our laudable doings, but us in the doing of them.

Judge. Then did the Judge say to him, Hast thou any more to say?

Envy. My Lord, I could say much more, only I would not be tedious to the Court.

Then Superstition and Pickthank were called to the same effect.

iv *The Judge abuses Faithful*

It is interesting first to see that the Judge abused the accused in much the same way as the Recorder abused William Penn (as I told you in *Landmarks in the Law*).

When this *Pickthank* had told his tale, the Judge directed his speech to the Prisoner at the Bar, saying, Thou Runagate, Heretick, and Traitor, hast thou heard what these honest Gentlemen have witnessed against thee?

Faith. *May I speak a few words in my own defence?*

Judge. Sirrah, Sirrah, thou deserveth to live no longer, but to be slain immediately upon the place; yet that all men may see our gentleness towards thee, let us see what thou vile Runagate hast to say.

Faith. I say then in answer to what Mr *Envy* hath spoken, I never said ought but this, *That what Rule, or Laws, or Custom, or People, were flat against the Word of God, are diametrically opposite to Christianity.*

v *The Judge addresses the jury*

Then the Judge called to the Jury (who all this while stood by, to hear and observe) Gentlemen of the Jury, you see this man about whom so great an uproar hath been made in this Town: you have also heard what these worthy Gentlemen have witnessed against him; also you have heard his reply and confession: It lieth now in your brests to hang him, or save his life. . . .

vi *Verdict and sentence*

The jury went out to consider their verdict. Bunyan gives the descriptive name of each of them:

Then went the Jury out, whose names were, Mr *Blind-man*, Mr *No-good*, Mr *Malice*, Mr *Love-lust*, Mr *Live-loose*, Mr *Heady*, Mr *High-mind*, Mr *Enmity*, Mr *Lyar*, Mr *Cruelty*, Mr *Hate-light*, and Mr *Implacable*, who every one gave in his private Verdict against him among themselves, and afterwards unanimously concluded to bring him in guilty before the Judge. And first among themselves, Mr *Blindman* the foreman, said, *I see clearly that this man is an Heretick.* Then said Mr *No-good, Away with such a fellow from the Earth. Ay*, said Mr *Malice, for I hate the very looks of him.* Then said Mr *Love-lust, I could never endure him. Nor I*, said Mr *Live-loose, for he would alwayes be condemning my way. Hang him, hang him*, said Mr *Heady. A sorry Scrub*, said Mr *High-mind. My heart riseth against him*, said Mr *Enmity. He is a Rogue*, said Mr *Lyar. Hanging is too good for him*, said Mr *Cruelty. Lets dispatch him out of the way*, said Mr *Hate-light.* Then said Mr *Implacable, Might I have all the World given me, I could not be reconciled to him, therefore let us forthwith bring him in guilty of death*; And so they did, therefore he was presently Condemned. To be had from the place where he was, to the place from whence he came, and there to be put to the most cruel death that could be invented.

8 The end of Faithful

i *Burnt at the stake*

They therefore brought him out, to do with him according to their Law; and first they Scourged him, then they Buffetted him, then they Lanced his flesh with

Knives; after that, they Stoned him with Stones, then prickt him with their Swords, and last of all they burned him to Ashes at the Stake. Thus came *Faithful* to his end. Now, I saw that there stood behind the multitude, a Chariot and a couple of Horses, waiting for *Faithful*, who (so soon as his adversaries had dispatched him) was taken up into it, and straightway was carried up through the Clouds, with sound of Trumpet, the nearest way to the Celestial Gate.

ii *Christian escapes*

But as for Christian, he had some respit, and was remanded back to prison, so he there remained for a space: But he that over-rules all things, having the power of their rage in his own hand, so wrought it about, that *Christian* for that time escaped them, and went his way.

9 The Celestial City

i *They get there*

I have not space here to go through all the difficulties that Christian surmounted. He was accompanied by Hopeful. They got to Doubting Castle of which the owner was Giant Despair. They overcame him and eventually got to the Celestial City:

Now I saw in my Dream, that these two men went in at the Gate; and loe, as they entered, they were transfigured, and they had Raiment put on that shone like Gold. There was also that met them with Harps and Crowns, and gave them to them; the Harp to praise withall, and the Crowns in token of honour; Then I heard in my Dream that all the Bells in the City Rang again for joy; and that it was said unto them, *Enter ye into the joy of your Lord.* I also heard the men themselves, say, that they sang with a loud voice, saying, *Blessing, Honour, Glory and Power, be to him that sitteth upon the Throne, and to the Lamb, for ever and ever.*

ii *Christian's wife and family follow*

That ends Part I. But Bunyan, when he was out of prison, wrote Part II. Christian's wife, Christiana, and their four sons, followed Christian. They went through all the trials that beset Christian. They were much helped by Mr Great-heart.

iii *The shepherd's boy*

They came upon a shepherd's boy who sang a lovely song:

Now as they were going along, and talking, they espied a Boy feeding his Fathers Sheep. The Boy was in very mean Cloathes, but of a very fresh and welfavoured Countenance, and as he sate by himself he Sung. Hark, said Mr *Great-heart*, to what the Shepherds Boy saith. So they hearkened, and he said,

He that is down, needs fear no fall,
He that is low, no Pride:
He that is humble, ever shall
Have God to be his Guide.
I am content with what I have,
Little be it, or much:
And, Lord, contentment still I crave,
Because thou savest such.
Fulness to such a burden is
That go on Pilgrimage:
Here little, and hereafter Bliss,
Is best from Age to Age,

Then said their *Guide*, do you hear him? I will dare to say, that this Boy lives a merrier Life, and wears more of that Herb called *Hearts-ease* in his Bosom, then he that is clad in Silk, and Velvet.

iv *Mr Valiant-for-Truth*

They also met Mr Valiant-for-Truth who was a pilgrim and was going to the Celestial City. He told them of his difficulties and how he had overcome them. His hymn of courage, which has been set to an English traditional melody, has put heart into many from that time to this:

Who would true Valour see,
Let him come hither;
One here will constant be,
Come Wind, come Weather.
There's no Discouragement,
Shall make him once Relent,
His first avow'd Intent,
To be a Pilgrim.

Who so beset him round,
With dismal Storys,
Do but themselves confound;
His Strength the more is
No Lyon *can him fright,*
He'l with a Gyant *Fight,*
But he will have a right,
To be a Pilgrim.

Hobgoblin, *nor foul* Fiend,
Can daunt *his Spirit:*
He knows, he at the end,
Shall Life Inherit.
Then Fancies fly away,
He'l fear not what men say,
He'l labor Night and Day,
To be a Pilgrim.

v *His death*

Then comes a passage which ranks with the highest in all literature. It is the death of Mr Valiant-for-Truth.

Then said he, I am going to my Fathers, and tho with great Difficulty I am got hither, yet now I do not repent me of all the Trouble I have been at to arrive where I am. *My Sword*, I give to him that shall succeed me in my Pilgrimage, and my *Courage* and *Skill*, to him that can get it. My *Marks* and *Scarrs* I carry with me, to be a Witness for me, that I have fought his Battels, who now will be my Rewarder.

When the Day that he must go hence, was come, many accompanied him to the River side, into which, as he went, he said, *Death, where is thy Sting*? And as he went down deeper, he said, *Grave, where is thy Victory*? So he passed over, and all the Trumpets sounded for him on the other side.

Bunyan goes on to Part III of his book and deals with other pilgrims. Then at the end the gates of the Celestial City are opened to them:

So they entered in, and just at the entrance one met them and said unto them, *Come, ye blessed of my Father, inherit the kingdom prepared for you from the foundation of the world; enter you into the joy of your Lord.* Then a multitude of the heavenly host, with harps in their hands, met them, and sang a song which no man understood but themselves, and such as are thought worthy to be admitted into that blessed place.

So I awoke, and, behold, it was a dream.

10 Preaching Christianity

Introduction

As I have told you of the Pilgrim with a Bible in his hand, I leap across three centuries and ask myself: How many households in England have a Bible now? In my boyhood, there was a Bible in nearly every home. Our mother used to read a passage from it every day. In my library here we have five copies of the Authorised Version. There is the Old Family Bible with the names and dates of birth of those long passed, but we have not kept it up in our generation. There is a big old Bible – bound in beautifully tooled leather – dated 1821, which was used in the Rolls Chapel in Chancery Lane until it was turned into a museum. There are three other Bibles of the Authorised Version, tattered and torn with use. They were given as presents at Confirmations and the like. We have also the New Testament with large print for me to read in Church. We have the Revised Version. We have the Children's Bible. We have two copies of the New English Bible, but we do not think much of that Bible. Its English is nothing like as good as that of the Authorised Version.

I have asked our grandchildren whether they have Bibles in their homes. Most of them have not. And they do not read them anyway. This makes me wonder. How many of you have a Bible nowadays at home? And how many of you ever read it?

The Authorised Version of the Bible has done more than anything else to form our English language and to spread its use through all the world. So you should have some acquaintance with it.

1 A Roman citizen

i *Hogarth's painting*

In the Old Hall of Lincoln's Inn there is a famous painting by Hogarth of *Paul before Felix*. It is rich in colour and has been recently restored.

It has dominated our Hall for over two centuries, going back to the days when the Lord Chancellor sat there. No doubt most people in those days knew all about Paul before Felix. They knew their Bible. But how many of you know of it today? When I take visitors into the Hall, they shake their heads. They know nothing about one of the great trials of history. I tell you of it now. First, because it is one of the early episodes which brought Christianity to the fore. Next, because it is a good illustration of the rich literature of the Authorised Version of the Bible. It was William Tyndale whose translation from the Greek in 1525 formed the basis of it. (In telling you the story I have looked again at the copy of H V Morton's *In the Steps of St Paul* which I gave to my first wife, Mary, when it was published in 1936.)

ii *The Roman Empire*

You must first know that, in the first century after Christ, the Roman Empire bestrode all the known world. Its centre was Rome. It stretched from Britain in the west to Palestine in the Middle East. It had its outlying provinces, each of which had a Governor at the head of the administration, and a Chief Captain at the head of the armed forces. They allowed the natives to keep their own laws and exercise jurisdiction over their own people – so far as possible. In Judaea (Palestine) the High Priest and Council had jurisdiction over the life and death of the Jewish subjects – subject to the sanction of the Roman Governor. But not over Roman citizens.

iii 'Civis Romanus Sum'

The Roman Empire boasted proudly that it protected its citizens wherever they might be. So did we. It was Palmerston who said in 1850 in his greatest speech:

> As the Roman, in days of old, held himself free from indignity, when he could say *Civis Romanus Sum*; so also a British subject, in whatever land he may be, shall feel confident that the watchful eye and the strong arm of England will protect him against injustice and wrong.

I am afraid that we can no longer make that proud boast. Only too often we hear of Englishmen working abroad being arrested and there imprisoned for long periods without charge and without trial. We can do nothing about it – except make diplomatic representations which are ignored.

iv *The citizen's right*

In the Roman Empire the plea *Civis Romanus Sum* carried with it important rights. A Roman citizen was entitled to the protection of the Roman Governor. He could not be condemned unheard. He could not be bound, or scourged, or beaten with rods, or put to death, *except after a trial before the Roman Governor.* But he could 'leap-frog'. A Roman citizen, when accused, had the right to *elect* – either to be tried by the Roman Governor – or he could appeal to the Emperor (often called Caesar) at Rome. If he elected to go to Rome, the Roman Governor had no further jurisdiction. He had to let him go to Rome before the Emperor – Caesar.

2 Saint Paul

i *Born a Jew*

These principles are well shown by the case of St Paul. He lived in the same period of time as Jesus Christ but was a good deal younger. He was a Jew by birth and education but became a Christian by conversion about 30–35 AD in a vision on the road to Damascus. He was a preacher of Christianity. He travelled all over Asia Minor enlisting followers. But for present purposes the important thing is that he was born at Tarsus (now far below the surface of the ground) and his family had the privilege of Roman citizenship. So Paul was a Roman citizen. This was a rare and great honour, conferred for distinguished services to the Roman Empire.

When Paul was born a Jew in Tarsus, his name was Saul. But after his conversion, he was called Paul. Like many people in those days, he spoke Greek and wrote in Greek. He also spoke Hebrew. His life story is told in the *Acts of the Apostles* which were probably written by St Luke.

ii *A great preacher*

Paul was by far the most outstanding preacher of his time. His advocacy of Christianity made him hated by the great majority of Jews in Asia Minor. They were so alarmed by his success that they determined to get rid of him. One particular incident was at Ephesus.

3 At Ephesus

i *The silversmiths*

Not only did Paul antagonise the Jews, he also antagonised the members of other established religions. There is this graphic description of his visit to the city of Ephesus. The people there worshipped a goddess called Diana. The silversmiths made silver images which they sold for profit. Paul sought to convert them from the worship of Diana to the worship of the God whom he believed to be the one true God.

ii *Their wrath*

The silversmiths were furious. This is how the story is told in the *Acts of the Apostles*:[1]

And the same time there arose no small stir about that way. For a certain man named Demetrius, a silversmith, which made silver shrines for Diana, brought no small gain unto the craftsmen; Whom he called together with the workmen of like occupation, and said, 'Sirs, ye know that by this craft we have our wealth. Moreover ye see and hear, that not alone at Ephesus, but almost throughout all Asia, this Paul hath persuaded and turned away much people, saying that they be no gods, which are made with hands; So that not only this our craft is in danger to be set at nought; but also that the temple of the great goddess Diana should be despised, and her magnificence should be destroyed, whom all Asia and the world worshippeth.' And when they heard these sayings, they were full of wrath, and cried out, saying, 'Great is Diana of the Ephesians.'

iii *A protest meeting*

The excitement in the city of Ephesus became so great that the silversmiths speedily arranged a protest meeting in the amphitheatre. Paul wanted to go himself to address the meeting: but his followers persuaded him not to do so. Instead, they put forward a man called Alexander to speak to the people. They listened quietly for a little while, but soon they discovered that Alexander was a Jew like Paul. This made them more furious than ever. They went on for two hours:[2]

And the whole city was filled with confusion: and having caught Gaius and Aristarchus, men of Macedonia, Paul's companions in travel, they rushed with one accord into the theatre. . . . Some therefore cried one thing, and some another: for the assembly was confused; and the more part knew not wherefore they were come together. And they drew Alexander out of the multitude, the Jews putting him forward. And Alexander beckoned with the hand, and would have made his defence unto the people. But when they knew that he was a Jew, all with one voice about the space of two hours cried out, 'Great is Diana of the Ephesians.'

iv *The civic authorities restore order*

Then the town clerk came up. He was the chief magistrate of the city. He read to the crowd the 'Riot Act.' He told them that, if they had a

[1] 19:23–28.
[2] 19:29, 32–34.

grievance against Paul and his followers, they should take it to the courts of law. He called upon them to disperse and they did so. We may assume that Paul got few converts at Ephesus:[1]

And when the townclerk had appeased the people, he said, 'Ye men of Ephesus, what man is there that knoweth not how that the city of the Ephesians is a worshipper of the great goddess Diana, and of the image which fell down from Jupiter? Seeing then that these things cannot be spoken against, ye ought to be quiet, and to do nothing rashly. For ye have brought hither these men, which are neither robbers of churches, nor yet blasphemers of your goddess. Wherefore if Demetrius, and the craftsmen which are with him, have a matter against any man, the law is open, and there are deputies: let them implead one another. But if ye enquire any thing concerning other matters, it shall be determined in a lawful assembly. For we are in danger to be called in question for this day's uproar, there being no cause whereby we may give an account of this concourse.' And when he had thus spoken, he dismissed the assembly.

4 In Jerusalem

i *In the Temple*

Over some years Paul went to many places in Asia Minor. Eventually he came to Caesarea on the Mediterranean coast some sixty miles from Jerusalem. It was the seat of the Roman Governor of Judaea (now Palestine). Paul went up from Caesarea to Jerusalem. Everyone there had heard of his preaching of Christianity. He went into the Temple. Then we are told that[2]

the Jews which were of Asia, when they saw him in the temple, stirred up all the people, and laid hands on him, Crying out, 'Men of Israel, help: This is the man, that teacheth all men every where against the people, and the law, and this place: and further brought Greeks also into the temple, and hath polluted this holy place.' . . . And all the city was moved, and the people ran together: and they took Paul, and drew him out of the temple: and forthwith the doors were shut.

ii *The riot*

The crowd wanted to kill Paul. There was an uproar. The chief captain immediately took soldiers and centurions, and ran down unto them. He took Paul, and commanded him to be carried into the castle.

[1] 19:35–41.
[2] 21:27–28, 30.

iii *'A citizen of no mean city'*

And as Paul was to be led into the castle, he said unto the chief captain, . . . 'I am a man which am a Jew of Tarsus, a city in Cilicia, a citizen of no mean city: and, I beseech thee, suffer me to speak unto the people.' And when he had given him licence, Paul stood on the stairs, and beckoned with the hand unto the people. And when there was made a great silence, he spake unto them in the Hebrew tongue.[1]

iv *Paul speaks to the people*

Paul then made his defence to the people. He told them of his Jewish origin, how he had persecuted non-believers, how he himself had been converted to Christianity in a vision on the road to Damascus, and how afterwards in Jerusalem the Lord said unto him:

'Depart: for I will send thee far hence unto the Gentiles.' And they gave him audience unto this word, and then lifted up their voices, and said, 'Away with such a fellow from the earth: for it is not fit that he should live.'[2]

v *Paul claims that he is a Roman citizen—'born free'*

The chief captain decided to inquire why the multitude were so incensed against Paul. He ordered that he be examined by scourging. Then Paul made his great assertion, 'I am a Roman citizen. I cannot be scourged until I am tried and found guilty.' So the chief captain did not scourge him.

This passage in the *Acts* throws much light on the Roman law at the time. It also shows that Roman citizenship could be acquired by birth (as Paul did) but also by purchase (as the chief captain did):[3]

And as they cried out, and cast off their clothes, and threw dust in to the air, the chief captain commanded him to be brought into the castle, and bade that he should be examined by scourging; that he might know wherefore they cried so against him. And as they bound him with thongs, Paul said unto the centurion that stood by, 'Is it lawful for you to scourge a man that is a Roman, and uncondemned?' When the centurion heard that, he went and told the chief captain, saying, 'Take heed what thou doest: for this man is a Roman.' Then the chief captain came, and said unto him, 'Tell me, art thou a Roman?' He said, 'Yea.' And the chief captain answered, 'With a great sum obtained I this freedom.' And Paul said, 'But I was free born.' Then straightway they departed from him which should have examined him: and the chief captain also was afraid, after he knew that he was a Roman, and because he had bound him.

[1] 21:37, 39–40.
[2] 22:21–22.
[3] 22:23–29.

5 The High Priest

i *Of what offence?*

The chief captain thought it necessary to find out what was the offence, if any, which Paul had committed. In particular, to see if it was an offence punishable by death or scourging: because, if it was, as Paul was a Roman citizen, it had to be tried by the Roman Governor. In order to ascertain this, the chief captain ordered Paul to be brought before the supreme Jewish tribunal – the High Priest and Council:[1]

On the morrow, because he would have known the certainty wherefore he was accused of the Jews, he loosed him from his bands, and commanded the chief priests and all their council to appear, and brought Paul down, and set him before them.

ii *'Thou whited wall'*

The proceedings before the Council were inconclusive, because there was dissension between two groups. So much so that the chief captain had to intervene and save Paul from the mob:[2]

And Paul, earnestly beholding the council said, 'Men and brethren, I have lived in all good conscience before God until this day.' And the high priest Ananias commanded them that stood by him to smite him on the mouth. Then said Paul unto him, 'God shall smite thee, thou whited wall: for sittest thou to judge me after the law, and commandest me to be smitten contrary to the law?' And they that stood by said, 'Revilest thou God's high priest?' Then said Paul, 'I wist not, brethren, that he was the high priest: for it is written, Thou shalt not speak evil of the ruler of thy people.' . . . And when there arose a great dissension, the chief captain, fearing lest Paul should have been pulled in pieces of them, commanded the soldiers to go down, and to take him by force from among them, and to bring him into the castle. And the night following the Lord stood by him, and said, 'Be of good cheer, Paul: for as thou has testified of me in Jerusalem, so must thou bear witness also at Rome.'

6 The Jews conspire to kill Paul

i *Forty conspirators*

The Jews were angry. They had been thwarted of their prey. So they plotted against Paul at a secret conclave. Forty and more of them got together and conspired to kill him. They told the High Priest and Council about it. They approved of the plot. It was this:

The Council were to tell the chief captain that the Council would like to see Paul again so as to ask him some more questions. Then,

[1] 22:30.
[2] 23:1–5, 10–11.

whilst Paul was being brought down, the forty conspirators would kill him:[1]

And when it was day, certain of the Jews banded together, and bound themselves under a curse, saying that they would neither eat nor drink till they had killed Paul. And they were more than forty which had made this conspiracy. And they came to the chief priests and elders, and said, 'We have bound ourselves under a great curse, that we will eat nothing until we have slain Paul. Now therefore ye with the council signify to the chief captain that he bring him down unto you to morrow, as though he would enquire something more perfectly concerning him: and we, or even he come near, are ready to kill him.'

ii *The chief captain takes action*

Paul's nephew got to know of this plot. He told Paul, who told a centurion, who told the chief captain. He regarded it as most serious. It amounted to a rebellion against the authority of the Romans. They were going to take Paul – a Roman citizen. They were going to condemn him without a hearing – contrary to the law. They were to kill him – without the authority of the Roman Governor – contrary to the law. They were going to do it by force of arms – contrary to the law. So the chief captain decided to make an impressive show of force. He got together an army of cavalry, infantry and spearmen to take Paul down to Caesarea – where he would be tried by the Roman Governor. At that time (56 AD), it was Felix.

iii *He writes to Felix*

So the chief captain wrote to the Roman Governor, Felix, with a report in which he set out the position:[2]

And he called unto him two centurions, saying, 'Make ready two hundred soldiers to go to Caesarea, and horsemen threescore and ten, and spearmen two hundred, at the third hour of the night; and provide them beasts, that they may set Paul on, and bring him safe unto Felix the governor.' And he wrote a letter after this manner:

> 'Claudius Lysias unto the most excellent governor Felix sendeth greeting,
>
> This man was taken of the Jews, and should have been killed of them: then came I with an army, and rescued him, having understood that he was a Roman. And when I would have known the cause wherefore they accused him, I brought him forth into their council: Whom I perceived to be accused of questions of their law, but to have nothing laid to his charge worthy of death or of bonds. And when it was told me how that the Jews laid wait for the man, I sent straightway to thee, and gave commandment to his accusers also to say before thee what they had against him.
>
> Farewell.'

[1] 23:12–15.
[2] 23:23–33.

Then the soldiers, as it was commanded them, took Paul and brought him by night to Antipatris. On the morrow they left the horsemen to go with him, and returned to the castle: Who, when they came to Caesarea, and delivered the epistle to the governor, presented Paul also before him.

7 The trial before Felix

i *Paul is remanded in custody*

On arriving at Caesarea, Paul was brought before Felix the governor. He remanded him in custody. He was kept in Herod's judgment hall which was the most splendid in Caesarea:[1]

And when the governor had read the letter, he asked of what province he was. And when he understood that he was of Cilicia; 'I will hear thee,' said he, 'when thine accusers are also come.' And he commanded him to be kept in Herod's judgment hall.

Then we come to the trial before Felix. He had been in office for some four years. He was a Roman and had, as a third wife, a Jewess, the Princess Drusilla.

ii *Case for the prosecution*

The case was opened by a Jewish advocate, Tertullus. He laid an information on behalf of the Jews against Paul, accusing him of sedition and heresy; in particular, of profaning the Temple:[2]

And after five days Ananias the high priest descended with the elders, and with a certain orator named Tertullus, who informed the governor against Paul. And when he was called forth, Tertullus began to accuse him, saying, 'Seeing that by thee we enjoy great quietness, and that very worthy deeds are done unto this nation by this providence, we accept it always, and in all places, most noble Felix, with all thankfulness. Notwithstanding, that I be not further tedious unto thee, I pray thee that thou wouldest hear us of thy clemency a few words. For we have found this man a pestilent fellow, and a mover of sedition among all the Jews throughout the world, and a ringleader of the sect of the Nazarenes: Who also hath gone about to profane the temple: whom we took, and would have judged according to our law. But the chief captain Lysias came upon us, and with great violence took him away out of our hands, Commanding his accusers to come unto thee: by examining of whom thyself mayest take knowledge of all these things, whereof we accuse him.' And the Jews also assented, saying that these things were so.

[1] 23:34–35.
[2] 24:1–9.

iii *Case for the defence*

Paul conducted his own defence. He confessed to preaching Christianity. He said he worshipped the same God as did his accusers: and that the Council of the Jews had found him guilty of nothing except that he believed in the resurrection of the dead:[1]

Then Paul, after that the governor had beckoned unto him to speak, answered, 'Forasmuch as I know that thou hast been of many years a judge unto this nation, I do the more cheerfully answer for myself: Because that thou mayest understand, that there are yet but twelve days since I went up to Jerusalem for to worship. And they neither found me in the temple disputing with any man, neither raising up the people, neither in the synagogues, nor in the city; Neither can they prove the things whereof they now accuse me. But this I confess unto thee, that after the way which they call heresy, so worship I the God of my fathers, believing all things which are written in the law and in the prophets: and have hope toward God, which they themselves also allow, that there shall be a resurrection of the dead, both of the just and unjust. And herein do I exercise myself, to have always a conscience void of offence toward God, and toward men. Now after many years I came to bring alms to my nation, and offerings. Whereupon certain Jews from Asia found me purified in the temple, neither with multitude, nor with tumult. Who ought to have been here before thee, and object, if they had ought against me. Or else let these same here say, if they have found any evil doing in me, while I stood before the council, except it be for this one voice, that I cried standing among them, "Touching the resurrection of the dead I am called in question by you this day."'

iv *Adjourned for further consideration*

Felix found the case so difficult that he adjourned it for further consideration. During the adjournment he heard the evidence of the chief captain and also heard Paul further about Christianity. Even then he could not make up his mind. So he adjourned the case *sine die*:[2]

And when Felix heard these things, having more perfect knowledge of that way, he deferred them, and said, 'When Lysias the chief captain shall come down, I will know the uttermost of your matter.' And he commanded a centurion to keep Paul, and to let him have liberty, and that he should forbid none of his acquaintance to minister or come unto him.

8 Hearing about Christ

i *Drusilla was there*

And after certain days, when Felix came with his wife Drusilla, which was a Jewess, he sent for Paul, and heard him concerning the faith in Christ. And as he reasoned

[1] 24:10–21.
[2] 24:22–23.

of righteousness, temperance, and judgment to come, Felix trembled, and answered, 'Go thy way for this time; when I have a convenient season, I will call for thee.'[1]

ii *Drusilla is taken out*

That scene is the subject of the Hogarth painting of which I have already told you. But there is a true story about it. When Hogarth first painted it, he included Drusilla sitting beside Felix; and Paul, with outstretched hands, addressing them. But his left hand appeared to be suggestively close to Drusilla's bosom. Some 'thought St Paul's hand was improperly placed'. So the figure of Drusilla was taken out. It is not there now. You can see the two versions in the library of Lincoln's Inn.

iii *More talks*

Felix hoped that Paul would give him money to be set free. But Paul did not give it. So Felix let him stay a prisoner. After two years, Felix retired. He was succeeded as governor by Festus:[2]

Felix hoped also that money should have been given him of Paul, that he might loose him: wherefore he sent for him the oftener, and communed with him. But after two years Porcius Festus came into Felix' room: and Felix, willing to shew the Jews a pleasure, left Paul bound.

9 Trial before Festus

i *The plot is revived*

When Festus arrived, the High Priest and Jews in Jerusalem revived their plot against Paul. They asked Festus to bring Paul up from Caesarea to Jerusalem, meaning to kill him on the way. But Festus had heard, no doubt, of the previous plot (to kill Paul on the way). So he did not accede to their request. He said that he would try Paul at Caesarea:[3]

And when he had tarried among them more than ten days, he went down unto Caesarea; and the next day sitting on the judgment seat commanded Paul to be brought.

ii *'I appeal unto Caesar'*

Yet Festus still wanted to do something to please the Jews. So he offered to go to Jerusalem (as they wished) and to try Paul himself at Jerusalem. But Paul could see that a trial before Festus – if held at Jerusalem – might go against him. At Jerusalem, Festus would be

[1] 24:24–25.
[2] 24:26–27.
[3] 25:6.

under much pressure from the Jews. So Paul exercised the right of election given to him, as a Roman citizen, by the Roman law. Instead of being tried by the Roman governor in the province, he elected to go before the Emperor – Caesar – himself at Rome. Once he made his election, it was final. So he made his famous declaration, 'I appeal unto Caesar.'[1]

And when he was come, the Jews which came down from Jerusalem stood round about, and laid many and grievous complaints against Paul, which they could not prove. While he answered for himself, 'Neither against the law of the Jews, neither against the temple, nor yet against Caesar, have I offended any thing at all.' But Festus, willing to do the Jews a pleasure, answered Paul, and said, 'Wilt thou go up to Jerusalem, and there be judged of these things before me?' Then said Paul, 'I stand at Caesar's judgment seat, where I ought to be judged: to the Jews have I done no wrong, as thou very well knowest. For if I be an offender, or have committed any thing worthy of death, I refuse not to die: but if there be none of these things whereof these accuse me, no man may deliver me unto them. I appeal unto Caesar.' Then Festus, when he had conferred with the council, answered, 'Hast thou appealed unto Caesar? unto Caesar shalt thou go.'

10 Hearing before Agrippa

i *A visit by Agrippa*

After Paul had made his election, he was kept in custody pending his departure for Rome. Whilst he was waiting to go; there came an important visitor to Caesarea. It was King Agrippa – who was the King of the Jews. He had come with his Queen, Bernice. He had no actual jurisdiction in the case, but he expressed such an interest in Paul and his cause, that arrangements were made for him to hear Paul. Festus agreed to this and arranged it for the morrow:[2]

And after certain days king Agrippa and Bernice came unto Caesarea to salute Festus. And when they had been there many days, Festus declared Paul's cause unto the king, saying, 'There is a certain man left in bonds by Felix: About whom, when I was at Jerusalem, the chief priests and the elders of the Jews informed me, desiring to have judgment against him. To whom I answered, "It is not the manner of the Romans to deliver any man to die, before that he which is accused have the accusers face to face, and have licence to answer for himself concerning the crime laid against him." Therefore, when they were come hither, without any delay on the morrow I sat on the judgment seat, and commanded the man to be brought forth. Against whom when the accusers stood up, they brought none accusation of such things as I supposed: But had certain questions against him of their own superstition, and of one Jesus, which was dead, whom Paul affirmed to be alive. And because I doubted of such manner of questions, I asked him whether he would go to Jerusalem, and there be judged of these matters. But when Paul had appealed to be

[1] 25:7–12.
[2] 25:13–22.

reserved unto the hearing of Augustus, I commanded him to be kept till I might send him to Caesar.' Then Agrippa said unto Festus, 'I would also hear the man myself.' 'To morrow,' said he, 'thou shalt hear him.'

ii *Festus addresses Agrippa*

There was a hearing before King Agrippa. It could have no legal effect because Paul had already elected to appeal to Caesar, the Emperor, at Rome. But Festus acceded to Agrippa's request so that he could have material to write to Rome:[1]

And on the morrow, when Agrippa was come, and Bernice, with great pomp, and was entered into the place of hearing, with the chief captains, and principal men of the city, at Festus' commandment Paul was brought forth. And Festus said, 'King Agrippa, and all men which are here present with us, ye see this man, about whom all the multitude of the Jews have dealt with me, both at Jerusalem, and also here, crying that he ought not to live any longer. But when I found that he had committed nothing worthy of death, and that he himself hath appealed to Augustus, I have determined to send him. Of whom I have no certain thing to write unto my lord. Wherefore I have brought him forth before you, and specially before thee, O king Agrippa, that, after examination had, I might have somewhat to write. For it seemeth to me unreasonable to send a prisoner, and not withal to signify the crimes laid against him.'

iii *Paul is eloquent*

Paul made an eloquent speech before Agrippa. He recounted once again his own persecution of the Jews, then his conversion on the Damascus road:[2]

Then Agrippa said unto Paul, 'Thou art permitted to speak for thyself.' Then Paul stretched forth the hand, and answered for himself: 'I think myself happy, king Agrippa, because I shall answer for myself this day before thee touching all the things whereof I am accused of the Jews: Especially because I know thee to be expert in all customs and questions which are among the Jews: wherefore I beseech thee to hear me patiently. My manner of life from my youth, which was at the first among mine own nation at Jerusalem, know all the Jews; Which knew me from the beginning, if they would testify, that after the most straitest sect of our religion I lived a Pharisee. And now I stand and am judged for the hope of the promise made of God unto our fathers: Unto which promise our twelve tribes, instantly serving God day and night, hope to come. For which hope's sake, king Agrippa, I am accused of the Jews. Why should it be thought a thing incredible with you, that God should raise the dead? . . .'

iv *'The heavenly vision'*

Then, after telling of his experiences and of his vision on the road to Damascus, Paul went on:[3]

[1] 25:23–27.
[2] 26:1–8.
[3] 26:19–23.

'Whereupon, O king Agrippa, I was not disobedient unto the heavenly vision: But shewed first unto them of Damascus, and at Jerusalem, and throughout all the coasts of Judaea, and then to the Gentiles, that they should repent and turn to God, and do works meet for repentance. For these causes the Jews caught me in the temple, and went about to kill me. Having therefore obtained help of God, I continue unto this day, witnessing both to small and great, saying none other things than those which the prophets and Moses did say should come: That Christ should suffer, and that he should be the first that should rise from the dead, and should shew light unto the people, and to the Gentiles.'

v *Festus is scornful*

Festus intervened with a scornful comment, often quoted:[1]

And as he thus spake for himself, Festus said with a loud voice, 'Paul, thou art beside thyself; much learning doth make thee mad.' But he said, 'I am not mad, most noble Festus; but speak forth the words of truth and soberness.'

vi *King Agrippa is almost converted*

Paul turned to King Agrippa and addressed him:[2]

'King Agrippa, believest thou the prophets? I know that thou believest.' Then Agrippa said unto Paul, 'Almost thou persuadest me to be a Christian.'

vii *'Except these bonds'*

Then there is the dramatic picture in these eloquent words:[3]

And Paul said, 'I would to God, that not only thou, but also all that hear me this day, were both almost, and altogether such as I am, except these bonds.'

viii *A judicial conference*

This is followed by the account of a brief judicial conference. They agreed that, as Paul had elected to go to Rome, his election was binding. But otherwise, they would have set him free:[4]

And when he had thus spoken, the king rose up, and the governor, and Bernice, and they that sat with them: And when they were gone aside, they talked between themselves, saying, 'This man doeth nothing worthy of death or of bonds.' Then said Agrippa unto Festus, 'This man might have been set at liberty, if he had not appealed unto Caesar.'

[1] 26:24–25.
[2] 26:27–28.
[3] 26:29.
[4] 26:30–32.

11 The shipwreck

i *A gale of great force*

So Paul had to make his way to Rome. By ship. He must have had a good deal of money behind him. Perhaps it was provided by his followers. There was no legal aid in the Roman Empire. On his way he was shipwrecked. The story is told vividly. It is very accurate in describing the geography of the Mediterranean and the handling of the sailing ships of those days. In reading it you must remember that the 'boat' was the small rowing boat pulled behind or carried on board the 'ship':[1]

And when the ship was caught, and could not bear up into the wind, we let her drive. And running under a certain island which is called Clauda, we had much work to come by the boat: Which when they had taken up, they used helps, undergirding the ship; and, fearing lest they should fall into the quicksands, strake sail, and so were driven. And we being exceedingly tossed with a tempest, the next day they lightened the ship; And the third day we cast out with our own hands the tackling of the ship. And when neither sun nor stars in many days appeared, and no small tempest lay on us, all hope that we should be saved was then taken away.

ii *Paul is courageous*

Although it was a desperate situation, Paul exhorted them to be courageous: and to put their trust in God:[2]

But after long abstinence Paul stood forth in the midst of them, and said, 'Sirs, ye should have hearkened unto me, and not have loosed from Crete, and to have gained this harm and loss. And now I exhort you to be of good cheer: for there shall be no loss of any man's life among you, but of the ship. For there stood by me this night the angel of God, whose I am, and whom I serve, Saying, "Fear not, Paul; thou must be brought before Caesar: and, lo, God hath given thee all them that sail with thee." Wherefore, sirs, be of good cheer: for I believe God, that it shall be even as it was told me. Howbeit we must be cast upon a certain island.'

iii *On the rocks of Malta*

There is a dramatic story of their nearing the rocks of Malta. The sailors (called 'shipmen') were proposing to save themselves by the 'boat' and to let the rest on board go down. But Paul stopped this plan by cutting the ropes;[3]

But when the fourteenth night was come, as we were driven up and down in Adria, about midnight the shipmen deemed that they drew near to some country;

[1] 27:15–20.
[2] 27:21–26.
[3] 27:27–32.

and sounded, and found it twenty fathoms: and when they had gone a little further, they sounded again, and found it fifteen fathoms. Then fearing lest we should have fallen upon rocks, they cast four anchors out of the stern, and wished for the day. And as the shipmen were about to flee out of the ship, when they had let down the boat into the sea, under colour as though they would have cast anchors out of the foreship, Paul said to the centurion and to the soldiers, 'Except these abide in the ship, ye cannot be saved.' Then the soldiers cut off the ropes of the boat, and let her fall off.

iv *They all are saved*

Then there is the exciting story of how the ship ran aground and all on board – 276 all told – got ashore:[1]

And while the day was coming on, Paul besought them all to take meat, saying, 'This day is the fourteenth day that ye have tarried and continued fasting, having taken nothing. Wherefore I pray you to take some meat: for this is for your health: for there shall not an hair fall from the head of any of you.' And when he had thus spoken, he took bread, and gave thanks to God in presence of them all: and when he had broken it, he began to eat. Then were they all of good cheer, and they also took some meat. And we were in all in the ship two hundred threescore and sixteen souls. And when they had eaten enough, they lightened the ship, and cast out the wheat into the sea. And when it was day, they knew not the land: but they discovered a certain creek with a shore, into the which they were minded, if it were possible, to thrust in the ship. And when they had taken up the anchors, they committed themselves unto the sea, and loosed the rudder bands, and hoised up the mainsail to the wind, and made toward shore. And falling into a place where two seas met, they ran the ship aground; and the forepart stuck fast, and remained unmovable, but the hinder part was broken with the violence of the waves. And the soldiers' counsel was to kill the prisoners, lest any of them should swim out, and escape. But the centurion, willing to save Paul, kept them from their purpose; and commanded that they which could swim should cast themselves first into the sea, and get to land: And the rest, some on boards, and some on broken pieces of the ship. And so it came to pass, that they escaped all safe to land.

12 At Rome

i *Paul gets to Rome*

Paul eventually got to Rome. He called the Jews together there and told them that he appealed unto Caesar and so was brought to Rome 'bound with this chain':[2]

And when we came to Rome, the centurion delivered the prisoners to the captain of the guard: but Paul was suffered to dwell by himself with a soldier that kept him. And it came to pass, that after three days Paul called the chief of the Jews together: and when they were come together, he said unto them, 'Men and

[1] 27:33–44.
[2] 28:16–23.

brethren, though I have committed nothing against the people, or customs of our fathers, yet was I delivered prisoner from Jerusalem into the hands of the Romans. Who, when they had examined me, would have let me go, because there was no cause of death in me. But when the Jews spake against it, I was constrained to appeal unto Caesar; not that I had ought to accuse my nation of. For this cause therefore have I called for you, to see you, and to speak with you: because that for the hope of Israel I am bound with this chain.' And they said unto him, 'We neither received letters out of Judaea concerning thee, neither any of the brethren that came shewed or spake any harm of thee. But we desire to hear of thee what thou thinkest: for as concerning this sect, we know that every where it is spoken against.' And when they had appointed him a day, there came many to him into his lodging; to whom he expounded and testified the kingdom of God, persuading them concerning Jesus, both out of the law of Moses, and out of the prophets, from morning till evening.

ii *He stays in Rome*

We are not told what happened to Paul's appeal. It is probable that the proceedings against him were dropped: either because the Jews in Jerusalem did not press them; or because the Emperor, having read the report of Festus, directed that they be stayed. At any rate, it is clear that he was set free.

iii *He writes letters*

Throughout his travels and later in Rome, Paul wrote letters to his followers in many places. These letters have had much effect in spreading the Christian religion. Extracts from them are set out in the *Book of Common Prayer* and are appointed to be read for every Sunday in the year. In the *Second Letter to the Corinthians* he tells of his experiences in a famous passage:[1]

Howbeit whereinsoever any is bold, (I speak foolishly,) I am bold also. Are they Hebrews? so am I. Are they Israelites? so am I. Are they the seed of Abraham? so am I. Are they ministers of Christ? (I speak as a fool) I am more; in labours more abundant, in stripes above measure, in prisons more frequent, in deaths oft. Of the Jews five times received I forty stripes save one. Thrice was I beaten with rods, once was I stoned, thrice I suffered shipwreck, a night and a day I have been in the deep; In journeyings often, in perils of waters, in perils of robbers, in perils by mine own countrymen, in perils by the heathen, in perils in the city, in perils in the wilderness, in perils in the sea, in perils among false brethren; In weariness and painfulness, in watchings often, in hunger and thirst, in fastings often, in cold and nakedness. Beside those things that are without, that which cometh upon me daily, the care of all the churches.

[1] *2 Corinthians* 11:21–28.

iv *The end*

It is probable that Paul stayed in Rome until he died. He was there in 64 AD when Nero fiddled while Rome was burning. These are the final words about Paul in the *Acts of the Apostles*:[1]

And Paul dwelt two whole years in his own hired house, and received all that came in unto him, Preaching the kingdom of God, and teaching those things which concern the Lord Jesus Christ, with all confidence, no man forbidding him.

[1] *Acts of the Apostles* 28:30–31.

11 Thick fog

Introduction

Every lawyer has heard of the case of *Jarndyce v Jarndyce*. It is often mentioned in court with a smile: but it is never quoted. For the simple reason that it was never reported anywhere. It was the invention of Charles Dickens himself. He brought it into his novel, *Bleak House*. He got the idea of it from the intestacy of one William Jennings who died in 1798, leaving property at Birmingham worth many millions. Dickens used the case to make a vigorous satire on the abuses of the Court of Chancery. The delays and costs of that court brought misery and ruin on the suitors.

In his 'Author's Preface' in 1853, Dickens claimed that it was substantially true. He gave two examples, which are very striking when you remember how the value of money has changed in the last hundred and thirty years.

> Everything set forth in these pages concerning the Court of Chancery is substantially true, and within the truth. . . . At the present moment there is a suit before the Court which was commenced nearly twenty years ago; in which from thirty to forty counsel have been known to appear at one time; in which costs have been incurred to the amount of seventy thousand pounds; which is a *friendly suit*; and which is (I am assured) no nearer to its termination now than when it was begun. There is another well-known suit in Chancery, not yet decided, which was commenced before the close of the last century, and in which more than double the amount of seventy thousand pounds has been swallowed up in costs.

1 *Jarndyce v Jarndyce*

i *The Old Hall*

Dickens sets the scene in the first chapter of *Bleak House*. It is in the Old Hall of Lincoln's Inn. It was here that the Lord Chancellor sat in vacation. (In term-time he sat in Westminster Hall.) Dickens gives a marvellous description of it. I have tried to find out who was the

Lord Chancellor whom he describes. I fancy it was that erudite lawyer, Lord St Leonards, who knew all about wills. He was Lord Chancellor in November 1852 when Dickens was writing *Bleak House*. By a strange irony Lord St Leonards himself made an elaborate will which was lost or destroyed and gave rise to most expensive litigation, see *Sugden v Lord St Leonards* (1876) P 154. It runs to nearly a hundred pages in the *Law Reports*.

ii *'Fog everywhere'*

This is how Dickens starts:

LONDON. Michaelmas Term lately over, and the Lord Chancellor sitting in Lincoln's Inn Hall. Implacable November weather. As much mud in the streets, as if the waters had but newly retired from the face of the earth. . . .

Fog everywhere. Fog up the river. . . . Fog down the river. . . . Fog in the eyes and throats. . . .

Gas looming through the fog in divers places in the streets. . . .

The raw afternoon is rawest, and the dense fog is densest, and the muddy streets are muddiest, near the leaden-headed old obstruction, appropriate ornament for the threshold of a leaden-headed old corporation: Temple Bar. And hard by Temple Bar, in Lincoln's Inn Hall, at the very heart of the fog, sits the Lord High Chancellor in his High Court of Chancery.

Never can there come fog too thick, never can there come mud and mire too deep, to assort with the groping and floundering condition which this High Court of Chancery, most pestilent of hoary sinners, holds, this day, in the sight of heaven and earth.

The old Temple Bar was removed in 1878 and taken to Theobalds Park, Cheshunt. There is now a prospect of it being brought back near St Paul's.

iii *'An endless cause'*

Then Dickens goes on to tell of the Lord Chancellor and the members of the Bar:

On such an afternoon, if ever, the Lord High Chancellor ought to be sitting here – as here he is – with a foggy glory round his head, softly fenced in with crimson cloth and curtains, addressed by a large advocate with great whiskers, a little voice, and an interminable brief, and outwardly directing his contemplation to the lantern in the roof, where he can see nothing but fog. On such an afternoon, some score of members of the High Court of Chancery bar ought to be – as here they are – mistily engaged in one of the ten thousand stages of an endless cause, tripping one another up on slippery precedents, groping knee-deep in technicalities, running their goat-hair and horse-hair warded heads against walls of words, and making a pretence of equity with serious faces, as players might.

iv *'Costly nonsense'*

He tells of the solicitors with their 'mountains of costly nonsense' which I mentioned in *What Next in the Law*:

Thick fog

On such an afternoon, the various solicitors in the cause, some two or three of whom have inherited it from their fathers, who made a fortune by it, ought to be – as are they not? – ranged in a line, in a long matted well (but you might look in vain for Truth at the bottom of it), between the registrar's red table and the silk gowns, with bills, cross-bills, answers, rejoinders, injunctions, affidavits, issues, references to masters, masters' reports, mountains of costly nonsense, piled before them.

v *'Its owlish aspect'*

Well may the court be dim, with wasting candles here and there; well may the fog hang heavy in it, as if it would never get out; well may the stained glass windows lose their colour, and admit no light of day into the place; well may the uninitiated from the streets, who peep in through the glass panes in the door, be deterred from entrance by its owlish aspect, and by the drawl languidly echoing to the roof from the padded dais where the Lord High Chancellor looks into the lantern that has no light in it, and where the attendant wigs are all stuck in a fog-bank!

vi *The appalling state of Chancery*

This is the Court of Chancery; which has its decaying houses and its blighted lands in every shire; which has its worn-out lunatic in every madhouse, and its dead in every churchyard; which has its ruined suitor, with his slipshod heels and threadbare dress, borrowing and begging through the round of every man's acquaintance; which gives to monied might the means abundantly of wearying out the right; which so exhausts finances, patience, courage, hope; so overthrows the brain and breaks the heart; that there is not an honourable man among its practitioners who would not give – who does not often give – the warning, 'Suffer any wrong that can be done you, rather than come here!'

vii *The case is called on*

Everyone goes off when the case of *Jarndyce v Jarndyce* is called on:

Who happen to be in the Lord Chancellor's court this murky afternoon besides the Lord Chancellor, the counsel in the cause, two or three counsel who are never in any cause, and the well of solicitors before mentioned? There is the registrar below the Judge, in wig and gown; and there are two or three maces, or petty-bags, or privy-purses, or whatever they may be, in legal court suits. These are all yawning; for no crumb of amusement ever falls from JARNDYCE AND JARNDYCE (the cause in hand), which was squeezed dry years upon years ago. The short-hand writers, the reporters of the court, and the reporters of the newspapers, invariably decamp with the rest of the regulars when Jarndyce and Jarndyce comes on. Their places are a blank.

viii *What is the case about?*

What is this case of *Jarndyce v Jarndyce*? All we are told is that

A certain Jarndyce, in an evil hour, made a great fortune, and made a great Will.

We are left to infer that he had a great family and left a great number of descendants – to the third and fourth generations. First cousins and second cousins without number. All these were beneficiaries under his will – or one or other of his wills – for he made several. The estate was so complicated and the beneficiaries so numerous that it had to be administered in Chancery. Every beneficiary – and every child born or unborn – had to be separately represented by counsel and solicitors. It had been going on for fifty years already. As always in Chancery, the costs of the lawyers had to come out of the estate. Their slice came first.

ix *The length of the case*

Dickens, in a passage of superb irony, shows that no one now knows what the case means. It has been going on so long.

> Jarndyce and Jarndyce drones on. This scarecrow of a suit has, in course of time, become so complicated, that no man alive knows what it means. The parties to it understand it least; but it has been observed that no two Chancery lawyers can talk about it for five minutes, without coming to a total disagreement as to all the premises. Innumerable children have been born into the cause; innumerable young people have married into it; innumerable old people have died out of it. Scores of persons have deliriously found themselves made parties in Jarndyce and Jarndyce, without knowing how or why; whole families have inherited legendary hatreds with the suit. The little plaintiff or defendant, who was promised a new rocking-horse when Jarndyce and Jarndyce should be settled, has grown up, possessed himself of a real horse, and trotted away into the other world. Fair wards of court have faded into mothers and grandmothers; a long procession of Chancellors has come in and gone out; the legion of bills in the suit have been transformed into mere bills of mortality; there are not three Jarndyces left upon the earth perhaps, since old Tom Jarndyce in despair blew his brains out at a coffee-house in Chancery Lane; but Jarndyce and Jarndyce still drags its dreary length before the Court, perennially hopeless.

2 Bleak House

i *What is Bleak House?*

One of the Jarndyces had a house which became as bleak as the suit itself. He called it Bleak House. Dickens describes it:

> He gave it its present name, and lived here shut up: day and night poring over the wicked heaps of papers in the suit, and hoping against hope to disentangle it from its mystification and bring it to a close. In the meantime, the place became dilapidated, the wind whistled through the cracked walls, the rain fell through the broken roof, the weeds choked the passage to the rotting door.

ii *Who is John Jarndyce?*

John Jarndyce is a kind, well-to-do, elderly man of the Jarndyce family. He is unmarried and has acquired Bleak House. He has a large number of cousins of the Jarndyce tribe. Two of these cousins – several times removed – are two young orphans, Richard Carstone aged nineteen and Ada Clare aged seventeen. They are made wards of court in *Jarndyce v Jarndyce*. John Jarndyce offers to have them reside with him at Bleak House.

iii *An application to the court*

We are told nothing of the actual discussion in court until the Chancellor is about to rise for the day. Then counsel for Richard and Ada, the two wards of court, gets up and makes an application. He asks permission for them to reside with their 'uncle', John Jarndyce. Now John Jarndyce was not their uncle. His counsel gets up. Dickens tells us what happened:

Suddenly a very little counsel, with a terrific bass voice, arises, fully inflated, in the back settlements of the fog, and says, 'Will your lordship allow me? I appear for him. He is a cousin, several times removed. I am not at the moment prepared to inform the Court in what exact remove he is a cousin; but he *is* a cousin.'

Leaving this address (delivered like a sepulchral message) ringing in the rafters of the roof, the very little counsel drops, and the fog knows him no more. Everybody looks for him. Nobody can see him.

'I will speak with both the young people,' says the Chancellor anew, 'and satisfy myself on the subject of their residing with their cousin. I will mention the matter tomorrow morning when I take my seat.'

iv *The Chancellor rises*

Then the Lord Chancellor bows to the bar and goes out of the court.

... Everybody else quickly vanishes too. A battery of blue bags is loaded with heavy charges of papers and carried off by clerks; ... the empty court is locked up. If all the injustice it has committed, and all the misery it has caused, could only be locked up with it, and the whole burnt away in a great funeral pyre, – why, so much the better for other parties than the parties in Jarndyce and Jarndyce!

3 Wards of court

i *The jurisdiction of the court*

Dickens knew something about the jurisdiction of the court over wards of court. It was exercised when there was property belonging to an 'infant' to be taken care of. The two young people in *Jarndyce v*

Jarndyce had been made wards of court because they were both under twenty-one and were entitled to an interest in the Jarndyce millions. The court exercised its supervision over them so as to ensure their good education and proper protection. No important step could be taken in the child's life without the court's consent. The court had to approve their tutors, their schooling and their place of residence. In particular it was settled law that a girl ward could not marry without the court's consent. If a man married her without the court's consent, he was guilty of a contempt of court and could be sent to prison. This was because, at that time, when a young lady married, all her property automatically belonged to her husband. He took the lot. This was well known to many an unprincipled adventurer. He would marry a girl, get hold of her money, and then forsake her. There was no divorce available at that time.

ii *Exercised by the Lord Chancellor*

This jurisdiction over wards was exercised by the Lord Chancellor. He sat in his private room. No outsiders were allowed in. This state of the law was ridiculed by W S Gilbert in his musical comedy, *Iolanthe*, produced in 1882. He brings the Lord Chancellor on to the stage to sing his famous song. (Today, Lord Elwyn-Jones, who was himself Lord Chancellor, gives a delightful rendering of it in his attractive Welsh intonation.)

> The Law is the true embodiment
> Of everything that's excellent.
> It has no kind of fault or flaw,
> And I, my Lords, embody the Law.
> The constitutional guardian I
> Of pretty young Wards in Chancery.
> All very agreeable girls – and none
> Are over the age of twenty-one.
>   A pleasant occupation for
>   A rather susceptible Chancellor!
>
> But though the compliment implied
> Inflates me with legitimate pride,
> It nevertheless can't be denied
> That it has its inconvenient side.
> For I'm not so old, and not so plain,
> And I'm quite prepared to marry again,
> But there'd be the deuce to pay in the Lords
> If I fell in love with one of my Wards!
>   Which rather tries my temper, for
>   I'm *such* a susceptible Chancellor!

And every one who'd marry a Ward
Must come to me for my accord,
And in my court I sit all day,
Giving agreeable girls away,
With one for him – and one for he –
And one for you – and one for ye –
And one for thou – and one for thee –
But never, oh, never one for me!
  Which is exasperating for
  A highly susceptible Chancellor!

iii *A woolsack stuffed with thorns*

Then W S Gilbert allows the Lord Chancellor to tell their Lordships of his feelings:

The feelings of a Lord Chancellor who is in love with a Ward of Court are not to be envied. What is his position? Can he give his own consent to his own marriage with his own Ward? Can he marry his own Ward without his own consent? And if he marries his own Ward without his own consent, can he commit himself for contempt of his own Court? And if he commit himself for contempt of his own Court, can he appear by counsel before himself, to move for arrest of his own judgment? Ah, my Lords, it is indeed painful to have to sit upon a woolsack which is stuffed with such thorns as these!

4 In private

i *In the Lord Chancellor's private room*

In *Jarndyce v Jarndyce* John Jarndyce wanted to take the two wards under his care: and in particular to have Ada Clare, aged seventeen, to live at Bleak House. It was necessary for her to have a female companion: and the approval for this to be obtained from the Lord Chancellor. John Jarndyce proposed that the female companion should be Esther Summerson. (He was her guardian and she herself was the illegitimate daughter of a Jarndyce daughter. She becomes the heroine of the story.) She is conducted by her guardian's solicitor, Mr Kenge, into the Lord Chancellor's private room with the two wards. Dickens puts the story into the mouth of Esther Summerson:

There, plainly dressed in black, and sitting in an arm-chair at a table near the fire, was his lordship, whose robe, trimmed with beautiful gold lace, was thrown upon another chair. He gave us a searching look as we entered, but his manner was both courtly and kind.

The gentleman in the bag wig laid bundles of papers on his lordship's table, and his lordship silently selected one, and turned over the leaves.

'Miss Clare,' said the Lord Chancellor. 'Miss Ada Clare!'

Mr Kenge presented her, and his lordship begged her to sit down near him. That he admired her, and was interested by her, even *I* could see in a moment. It touched me, that the home of such a beautiful young creature should be represented by that dry official place. The Lord High Chancellor, at his best, appeared so poor a substitute for the love and pride of parents.

'The Jarndyce in question,' said the Lord Chancellor, still turning over leaves, 'is Jarndyce of Bleak House.'

'Jarndyce of Bleak House, my lord,' said Mr Kenge.

'A dreary name,' said the Lord Chancellor.

'But not a dreary place at present, my lord,' said Mr Kenge.

'And Bleak House,' said his lordship, 'is in –

'Hertfordshire, my lord.'

'Mr Jarndyce of Bleak House is not married?' said his lordship.

'He is not, my lord,' said Mr Kenge.

A pause.

'Young Mr Richard Carstone is present?' said the Lord Chancellor, glancing towards him.

Richard bowed and stepped forward.

'Hum!' said the Lord Chancellor, turning over more leaves.

'Mr Jarndyce of Bleak House, my lord,' Mr Kenge observed, in a low voice, 'if I may venture to remind your lordship, provides a suitable companion for –'

'For Mr Richard Carstone?' I thought (but I am not quite sure) I heard his lordship say, in an equally low voice, and with a smile.

'For Miss Ada Clare. This is the young lady. Miss Summerson.'

His lordship gave me an indulgent look, and acknowledged my curtsey very graciously.

'Miss Summerson is not related to any party in the cause, I think?'

'No, my lord.'

ii *A private whisper*

Mr Kenge leant over before it was quite said, and whispered. His lordship, with his eye upon his papers, listened, nodded twice or thrice, turned over more leaves, and did not look towards me again, until we were going away.

We are not told why Mr Kenge whispered to the Lord Chancellor. I expect he told the Lord Chancellor he was the family solicitor. He knew the truth about Esther. She was the illegitimate daughter of one of the family. She was in fact a cousin of the two wards.

iii *The Lord Chancellor approves*

After that private whisper, the Lord Chancellor announced his decision.

'Very well!' said his lordship aloud. 'I shall make the order. Mr Jarndyce of Bleak House has chosen, so far as I may judge,' and this was when he looked at me, 'a very good companion for the young lady and the arrangement altogether seems the best of which the circumstances admit.'

5 A detective story

Here I leave *Jarndyce v Jarndyce* because *Bleak House* deteriorates into a detective story which is as dense as the fog in the Old Hall. It takes up eight hundred pages of close print. Mysterious characters come in and out. You have to guess who they are and what they are up to. You have to grope your way – as we had to do in a London fog in my young days – staggering from lamp-post to lamp-post, going up the wrong street and knocking at the wrong door. Occasionally the fog lifts a bit. But nothing is clear in the story until near the very end. Then you come upon a suicide, and a murder and find out who did it. It was one whom you would never have expected. That is usual with thrillers. But this is nowhere near as good a thriller as any one of Agatha Christie's. So I am missing out all that dreary stuff. I go straight to the last scene in *Jarndyce v Jarndyce*.

6 In the list again

i *Hopes are high*

When you get towards the end of the book, the two wards of court, Richard and Ada, have married one another. Richard has been working in the office of Mr Kenge, the solicitor for John Jarndyce. He studies the papers in *Jarndyce v Jarndyce* and deludes himself into believing that, when it is brought to judgment, he and Ada will get a substantial share of the millions.

Esther Summerson has discovered that she is the illegitimate daughter of a Jarndyce but she has met a nice young doctor, Allan Woodcourt, and they are to be married.

At length the cause of *Jarndyce v Jarndyce* comes into the list again. Hopes were high that there might be judgment favourable to Richard and Ada.

Charles Dickens lets Esther Summerson tell the story in her own words. It was term-time. So the case was to be heard in Westminster Hall.

ii *'Over for good'*

This (delay) made us some quarter of an hour late, and when we (Allan and Esther) came to Westminster Hall we found that the day's business was begun. Worse than that, we found such an unusual crowd in the Court of Chancery that it was full to the door, and we could neither see nor hear what was passing within. It appeared to be something droll, for occasionally there was a laugh, and a cry of 'Silence!' It appeared to be something interesting, for every one was pushing and striving to get nearer. It appeared to be something that made the professional gentlemen very merry, for there were several young counsellors in wigs and whiskers on the outside of the crowd, and when one of them told the others about it, they put their hands in their pockets, and quite doubled themselves up with laughter, and went stamping about the pavement of the hall.

We asked a gentleman by us, if he knew what cause was on? He told us Jarndyce and Jarndyce. We asked him if he knew what was doing in it? He said, really no he did not, nobody ever did; but as well as he could make out, it was over. Over for the day? we asked him. No, he said; over for good.

iii *For whose good?*

But it was not over for the good of Richard and Ada. It was only over for the good of the lawyers:

Over for good!

When we heard this unaccountable answer, we looked at one another quite lost in amazement. Could it be possible that the Will had set things right at last, and that Richard and Ada were going to be rich? It seemed too good to be true. Alas it was!

Our suspense was short; for a break-up soon took place in the crowd, and the people came streaming out looking flushed and hot, and bringing a quantity of bad air with them. Still they were all exceedingly amused, and were more like people coming out from a Farce or a Juggler than from a court of Justice. We stood aside, watching for any countenance we knew; and presently great bundles of papers began to be carried out – bundles in bags, bundles too large to be got into any bags, immense masses of papers of all shapes and no shapes, which the bearers staggered under, and threw down for the time being, anyhow, on the Hall pavement, while they went back to bring out more. Even these clerks were laughing. We glanced at the papers, and seeing Jarndyce and Jarndyce everywhere, asked an official-looking person who was standing in the midst of them, whether the cause was over. 'Yes,' he said; 'it was all up with it at last!' and burst out laughing too.

iv *'A Monument of Chancery practice'*

The bad news was broken to Allan and Esther by Mr Kenge, using his silver trowel. He was there with Mr Vholes who was Richard's solicitor. Allan asked for the result of the case:

'Is this Will considered a genuine document, sir?' said Allan; 'will you tell us that?'

'Most certainly, if I could,' said Mr Kenge; 'but we have not gone into that, we have not gone into that.'

'We have not gone into that,' repeated Mr Vholes, as if his low inward voice were an echo.

'You are to reflect, Mr Woodcourt,' observed Mr Kenge, using his silver trowel, persuasively and smoothingly, 'that this has been a great cause, that this has been a protracted cause, that this has been a complex cause. Jarndyce and Jarndyce has been termed, not inaptly, a Monument of Chancery practice.'

v *'Patience has sat upon it'*

That reference to 'Monument' prompts Dickens to use Shakespeare's simile in *Twelfth Night* (Act II, sc. 4) of a woman disappointed in love:

She sat like patience on a monument,
Smiling at grief.

'And Patience has sat upon it a long time,' said Allan.

'Very well indeed, sir,' returned Mr Kenge, with a certain condescending laugh he had. 'Very well! You are further to reflect, Mr Woodcourt,' becoming dignified to severity, 'that on the numerous difficulties, contingencies, masterly fictions, and forms of procedure in this great cause, there has been expended study, ability, eloquence, knowledge, intellect, Mr Woodcourt, high intellect. For many years, the – a – I would say the flower of the Bar, and the – a – I would presume to add, the matured autumnal fruits of the Woolsack – have been lavished upon Jarndyce and Jarndyce. If the public have the benefit, and if the country have the adornment, of this great Grasp, it must be paid for, in money or money's worth, sir.'

vi *The curtain*

At length, as the phrase goes, 'the penny dropped.' The truth was out.

'Mr Kenge,' said Allan, appearing enlightened all in a moment. 'Excuse me, our time presses. Do I understand that the whole estate is found to have been absorbed in costs?'

'Hem! I believe so,' returned Mr Kenge. 'Mr Vholes, what do *you* say?'

'I believe so,' said Mr Vholes.

'And that thus the suit lapses and melts away?'

'Probably,' returned Mr Kenge. 'Mr Vholes?'

'Probably,' said Mr Vholes.

'My dearest life,' whispered Allan, 'this will break Richard's heart!'

It did.

12 The middle-aged lady

In contrast with *Bleak House*, Charles Dickens could be very amusing. I cannot resist telling you of his little masterpiece. It is about the middle-aged lady in the double-bedded room. It comes from *The Pickwick Papers*. The incident takes place at the Great White Horse at Ipswich which Dickens describes:

> The Great White Horse is famous in the neighbourhood, in the same degree as a prize ox, or county paper-chronicled turnip, or unwieldy pig -- for its enormous size. Never were such labyrinths of uncarpeted passages, such clusters of mouldy, ill-lighted rooms, such huge numbers of small dens for eating or sleeping in, beneath any one roof, as are collected together between the four walls of the Great White Horse at Ipswich.

Mr Pickwick had gone to Ipswich by coach and had booked in at the Great White Horse. He had got settled into his room – a double-bedded room with a fire – sat down in a chair and fallen asleep. Then he remembered that he had left his watch on the table downstairs. He went down and got it. Then going back he lost his way, but eventually opened a door, saw it had two bedsteads in it. 'This is right,' he said to himself. He took off his coat, waistcoat and neckcloth, and tied his night-cap securely on his head, by tying the strings tightly beneath his chin. He was about to continue undressing when the door opened.

i *A person with a candle*

His happiness turned into dismay:

> Here Mr Pickwick smiled again, a broader smile than before, and was about to continue the process of undressing, in the best possible humour, when he was suddenly stopped by a most unexpected interruption; to wit, the entrance into the room of some person with a candle, who, after locking the door, advanced to the dressing table, and set down the light upon it.
>
> The smile that played on Mr Pickwick's features was instantaneously lost in a look of the most unbounded and wonder-stricken surprise. The person, whoever it was, had come in so suddenly and with so little noise, that Mr Pickwick had had no time to call out, or oppose their entrance. Who could it be? A robber? Some

evil-minded person who had seen him come up stairs with a handsome watch in his hand, perhaps. What was he to do!

To appreciate the situation, you must remember that in 1836 when Dickens wrote *Pickwick Papers*, every bedstead was a four-poster with curtains all round which could be pulled to keep out the draught. Also that everyone used to wear a night-cap for the same reason. Some, perhaps, had also the other kind of night-cap which the *Shorter Oxford Dictionary* describes as 'an alcoholic drink taken immediately before going to bed to induce sleep'.

The only way in which Mr Pickwick could catch a glimpse of his mysterious visitor with the least danger of being seen himself, was by creeping on to the bed, and peeping out from between the curtains on the opposite side. To this manoeuvre he accordingly resorted. Keeping the curtains carefully closed with his hand, so that nothing more of him could be seen than his face and night-cap and putting on his spectacles, he mustered up courage, and looked out.

ii *Horror and dismay*

It turned out to be a lady who had come in. As well as the candle which she had placed on the dressing table, she had brought in a rushlight and shade and placed it on the floor in the basin. A 'rushlight' was a candle of feeble power made by dipping the pith of a rush in grease. The scene was delightfully drawn by 'Phiz' (Hablot K Browne) and is reproduced in all the editions of *Pickwick Papers*.

Mr Pickwick almost fainted with horror and dismay. Standing before the dressing-glass was a middle-aged lady, in yellow curl-papers, busily engaged in brushing what ladies call their 'back-hair.' However the unconscious middle-aged lady came into that room, it was quite clear that she contemplated remaining there for the night; for she had brought a rushlight and shade with her, which, with praiseworthy precaution against fire, she had stationed in a basin on the floor, where it was glimmering away, like a gigantic lighthouse in a particularly small piece of water.

'Bless my soul,' thought Mr Pickwick, 'what a dreadful thing!'

'Hem!' said the lady; and in went Mr Pickwick's head with automaton-like rapidity.

'I never met with anything as awful as this,' thought poor Mr Pickwick, the cold perspiration starting in drops upon his night-cap. 'Never, this is fearful.'

iii *The night-cap won't come off*

Mr Pickwick had a night-cap with a tassel. The lady had a muslin one with a plaited border.

It was quite impossible to resist the urgent desire to see what was going forward. So out went Mr Pickwick's head again. The prospect was worse than before. The middle-aged lady had finished arranging her hair; had carefully enveloped it in a muslin night-cap with a small plaited border; and was gazing pensively on the fire.

'This matter is growing alarming,' reasoned Mr Pickwick with himself. 'I can't allow things to go on in this way. By the self-possession of that lady it is clear to me that I must have come into the wrong room. If I call out she'll alarm the house; but if I remain here the consequences will be still more frightful.'

Mr Pickwick, it is quite unnecessary to say, was one of the most modest and delicate-minded of mortals. The very idea of exhibiting his night-cap to a lady overpowered him, but he had tied those confounded strings in a knot, and, do what he would, he couldn't get it off. The disclosure must be made.

iv *'Ha-hum!'*

Then there came a noise from behind the curtains:

There was only one other way of doing it. He shrank behind the curtains, and called out very loudly:

'Ha-hum!'

That the lady started at this unexpected sound was evident, by her falling up against the rushlight shade; that she persuaded herself it must have been the effect of imagination was equally clear, for when Mr Pickwick, under the impression that she had fainted away stone-dead from fright, ventured to peep out again, she was gazing pensively on the fire as before.

'Most extraordinary female this,' thought Mr Pickwick, popping in again. 'Ha-hum!'

These last sounds, so like those in which, as legends inform us, the ferocious giant Blunderbore was in the habit of expressing his opinion that it was time to lay the cloth, were too distinctly audible to be again mistaken for the workings of fancy.

I do not suppose the children of today know about Blunderbore. He comes into a nursery tale of Jack the Giant Killer. He was one of the giants killed by Jack. He demanded breakfast by roaring out:

Ha-hum!
Fe, Fi, Fo, Fum,
I smell the blood of an Englishman.
Be he alive or be he dead,
I'll grind his bones to make my bread.

He was induced by Jack to overeat and cut his own throat to relieve 'the gorge'.

v *'Only a gentleman'*

The lady screamed with fright.

'Gracious Heaven!' said the middle-aged lady, 'what's that?'

'It's – it's – only a gentleman, Ma'am,' said Mr Pickwick from behind the curtains.

'A gentleman!' said the lady with a terrific scream.

'It's all over!' thought Mr Pickwick.

'A strange man!' shrieked the lady. Another instant and the house would be alarmed. Her garments rustled as she rushed towards the door.

'Ma'am,' said Mr Pickwick, thrusting out his head in the extremity of his desperation, 'Ma'am!'

Now, although Mr Pickwick was not actuated by any definite object in putting out his head, it was instantaneously productive of a good effect. The lady, as we have already stated, was near the door. She must pass it, to reach the staircase and she would most undoubtedly have done so by this time, had not the sudden apparition of Mr Pickwick's night-cap driven her back into the remotest corner of the apartment, where she stood staring wildly at Mr Pickwick, while Mr Pickwick in his turn stared wildly at her.

vi *'What do you want?'*

Mr Pickwick tried to explain and said he had mistaken her bedroom for his own:

'Wretch,' said the lady covering her eyes with her hands, 'what do you want here?'

'Nothing, Ma'am; nothing, whatever, Ma'am;' said Mr Pickwick earnestly.

'Nothing!' said the lady, looking up.

'Nothing, Ma'am, upon my honour,' said Mr Pickwick, nodding his head so energetically that the tassel of his night-cap danced again. 'I am almost ready to sink, Ma'am, beneath the confusion of addressing a lady in my night-cap (here the lady hastily snatched off hers), but I can't get it off, Ma'am (here Mr Pickwick gave it a tremendous tug, in proof of his statement). It is evident to me, Ma'am, now, that I have mistaken this bedroom for my own. I had not been here five minutes, Ma'am, when you suddenly entered it.'

'If this improbable story be really true, sir,' said the lady, sobbing violently, 'you will leave it instantly.'

'I will, Ma'am, with greatest pleasure,' replied Mr Pickwick.

'Instantly, sir,' said the lady.

'Certainly, Ma'am,' interposed Mr Pickwick very quickly. 'Certainly, Ma'am. I – I – am very sorry, Ma'am,' said Mr Pickwick, making his appearance at the bottom of the bed, 'to have been the innocent occasion of this alarm and emotion; deeply sorry, Ma'am.'

vii *Dropping both his shoes*

Mr Pickwick was fortunately spared the most extreme embarrassment. He had not taken off his shirt, breeches or stockings. But he had taken off everything else. And he had to carry them off. Including his hat, which he put on over his night-cap. It made him look like one of the 'old patrol'. They were the watchmen who, before the Police Act of 1839, patrolled the streets to safeguard life and property.

The lady pointed to the door. One excellent quality of Mr Pickwick's character was beautifully displayed at this moment, under the most trying circumstances. Although he had hastily put on his hat over his night-cap, after the manner of the old patrol; although he carried his shoes and gaiters in his hand, and his coat and waistcoat over his arm; nothing could subdue his native politeness.

'I am exceedingly sorry, Ma'am,' said Mr Pickwick, bowing very low.

'If you are, sir, you will at once leave the room,' said the lady.

'Immediately, Ma'am; this instant, Ma'am,' said Mr Pickwick, opening the door, and dropping both his shoes with a crash in so doing.

'I trust, Ma'am,' resumed Mr Pickwick, gathering up his shoes, and turning round to bow again: 'I trust, Ma'am, that my unblemished character, and the devoted respect I entertain for your sex, will plead as some slight excuse for this' – but before Mr Pickwick could conclude the sentence the lady had thrust him into the passage, and locked and bolted the door behind him.

Outside in the dark, Mr Pickwick groped his way along the passage, stumbling over several pairs of boots in so doing. He was rescued, however, by his faithful attendant, Sam Weller:

It was indeed Mr Samuel Weller, who after sitting up thus late, in conversation with the Boots, who was sitting up for the mail, was now about to retire to rest.

'Sam,' said Mr Pickwick, suddenly appearing before him, 'Where's my bedroom?'

Mr Weller stared at his master with the most emphatic surprise; and it was not until the question had been repeated three several times, that he turned round, and led the way to the long-sought apartment.

'Sam,' said Mr Pickwick as he got into bed. 'I have made one of the most extraordinary mistakes tonight, that ever were heard of.'

'Wery likely, sir,' replied Mr Weller drily.

'But of this I am determined, Sam,' said Mr Pickwick; 'that if I were to stop in this house for six months, I would never trust myself about it, alone, again.'

'That's the wery prudentest resolution as you could come to, sir,' replied Mr Weller. 'You rayther want somebody to look arter you, sir, wen your judgment goes out a wisitin'.'

13 The power of the press

Introduction

Anthony Trollope is read nowadays for his charming style. But he has a lesson to teach. In his first successful novel, *The Warden*, he exposes the power of the press. He shows that it on some occasions exercises its vast power without responsibility. It claims freedom and independence for itself but abuses it wholesale. In *The Warden* Trollope tells how *The Times* forces a good man to resign his appointment and destroys a charitable institution. I venture to repeat here what I said in *British Steel Corporation v Granada Television* [1981] AC 1096 at 1130:

> In order to be deserving of freedom, the press must show itself worthy of it. A free press must be a responsible press. The power of the press is great. It must not abuse its power. If a newspaper should act irresponsibly, then it forfeits its claim to . . . freedom.

Anthony Trollope writes in 1852 – in the middle of the 19th Century.

He gives a contemporary picture of a typical cathedral city and the clergy in it. He tells of the grave abuses that existed there – especially in the distribution of incomes. Some church dignitaries received far too much. Others far too little. Some lived like lords. Others like paupers. The scandals were exposed in the press and in Parliament. In time they were remedied. But looking back now, after over 130 years, the remedy has been made at a great price. The incomes of the clergy have been levelled down – right down – to the bottom. The clergy are the most poorly paid of all educated men. Yet they retain the respect and affection of all good people.

1 Saint Cross

i *An ancient charity*

At the time when Trollope wrote *The Warden*, there was a great case pending in the law courts. It gave him the idea for the novel. It is called *Attorney-General v St Cross Hospital* (1853) 17 Beav 435. St Cross was an ancient charity. It was established for the relief of the poor. But for the best part of 700 years the Master had been guilty of scandalous conduct. He had diverted the revenues to his own use. He had put them into his own pocket for his own benefit.

All of us in Hampshire know St Cross. It has a lovely church a mile from the centre of Winchester. It has its brethren who live in their comfortable dwellings – with long tall chimneys reaching to the sky. It stands in a magnificent quadrangle round a grassy sward. Each of the brethren wears his mediaeval cap and gown, and on his breast a silver cross. Eighteen wear the black gowns of the original St Cross: and eight wear the claret coloured gowns of the Order of Noble Poverty. You would never think that anything had ever gone amiss there. To this day if you go to the gate of St Cross, you can ask for the Wayfarer's Dole. The porter gives you a little piece of bread and a small glass of beer.

ii *The Times attacks it*

In the 1820s a retired clergyman went through the deeds in the muniment room. He discovered much discreditable conduct and started a campaign against the then master. He was The Reverend Francis North, Earl of Guilford. (He was a direct descendant of the Lord Keeper in the time of Charles II.) *The Times* took it up. It launched its thunderbolts against the Earl. He had received the revenues. The monies ought to have been used for the support of the poor. Instead, they were used by the Earl for his own purposes.

iii *The Attorney-General wakes up*

The outcry made the Attorney-General wake up. He is in law the guardian angel of all charities. In the lawyer's phrase, the Crown is *parens patriae.* In September 1849 the Attorney-General filed an information against the Earl of Guilford and the Bishop of Winchester. In August 1853 the Master of the Rolls (Sir John Romilly) held that the Earl had acted very wrongly. He summarised the history over the last 700 years. He said that the Master 'had succeeded in diverting the charity property from its legitimate purpose for one hundred and fifty years.' He made a decree appointing new trustees to manage the charity.

iv *All is well now*

It is now over 130 years since that case was decided. No similar scandal has since broken over the Trustees of St Cross. They keep the lovely church in good repair. They look after the brethren well. They own estates still. These include our cricket ground at Whitchurch and the tithe barn. We pay them an appropriate rent. No doubt it is properly applied. The house next door to us was for many years the vicarage and is still called St Cross House.

2 Hiram's Hospital

i *A different story*

Many times in *The Warden*, Trollope refers to the *St Cross* case. It was much in his mind. But he made a very different story of it. Instead of placing the hospital in Winchester, he places it in Salisbury which he calls Barchester. Instead of calling it St Cross, he calls it Hiram's Hospital. Instead of having Henry de Blois as founder in 1136 AD, he has a wealthy wool-stapler called John Hiram who made a will in 1434 giving his money to the poor. Instead of having a rapacious master, Hiram's Hospital has a dear lovable warden at a comfortable (but not excessive) salary. Instead of old brethren, he has twelve old pensioners called bedesmen.

ii *Mr Harding is the Warden*

Mr Harding, the warden, is a widower with two daughters. He has a substantial income of £800 a year from Hiram's charity and a salary of £80 from his office as precentor of the cathedral. His elder daughter, Susan, is married to the Archdeacon of Barchester, Dr Grantly. He is a sleek, opulent, overbearing churchman, determined to defend all the revenues of the Church, including those of Hiram's Hospital. He is the very embodiment of the Church Militant. The younger daughter, Eleanor, is in love with a young surgeon, John Bold. His passion is the reform of all abuses in Church and State.

iii *He is cultured and musical*

Trollope gives this picture of the good Mr Harding who is cultured and musical:

Since his appointment to his precentorship, he has published, with all possible additions of vellum, typography, and gilding, a collection of our ancient church music, with some correct dissertations on Purcell, Crotch, and Nares. He has greatly improved the choir of Barchester, which, under his dominion, now rivals that of any cathedral in England. He has taken something more than his fair share in the cathedral services, and has played the violoncello daily to such audiences as he could collect, or, *faute de mieux*, to no audience at all.

He is also sufficiently well off to be generous to many:

Then he is generous to his daughter, for whose service he keeps a small carriage and pair of ponies. He is, indeed, generous to all, but especially to the twelve old men who are in a peculiar manner under his care.

iv *Murmurs of dissent*

But murmurs are arising which will in time disturb the peace and comfort of Mr Harding. They are that he gets too much and the twelve old men too little:

Mr Harding has been now precentor of Barchester for ten years; and, alas, the murmurs respecting the proceeds of Hiram's estate are again becoming audible. It is not that any one begrudges to Mr Harding the income which he enjoys, and the comfortable place which so well becomes him; but such matters have begun to be talked of in various parts of England. Eager pushing politicians have asserted in the House of Commons, with very telling indignation, that the grasping priests of the Church of England are gorged with the wealth which the charity of former times has left for the solace of the aged, or the education of the young. The well-known case of the Hospital of St Cross, has even come before the law courts of the country. . . . Men are beginning to say that these things must be looked into.

Mr Harding, whose conscience in the matter is clear, and who has never felt that he had received a pound from Hiram's will to which he was not entitled, has naturally taken the part of the church in talking over these matters with his friend, the bishop, and his son-in-law, the archdeacon.

v *Mr Harding in uneasy*

These murmurs make Mr Harding uneasy. He is the warden and Mr Chadwick is the steward of the estate. Some of the old men are saying that they ought to have £100 a year:

Nevertheless, Mr Harding is becoming uneasy at the rumour which he knows to prevail in Barchester on the subject. He is aware that, at any rate, two of his old men have been heard to say, that if every one had his own, they might each have their hundred pounds a year, and live like gentlemen, instead of a beggarly one shilling and sixpence a day; and that they had slender cause to be thankful for a miserable dole of twopence, when Mr Harding and Mr Chadwick, between them, ran away with thousands of pounds which good old John Hiram never intended for the like of them. It is the ingratitude of this which stings Mr Harding.

3 The protagonists

i *Mr Harding in between*

The murmurs soon become a roar. On the one side is John Bold (who loves Mr Harding's younger daughter). He says that Mr Harding gets too much and that each of the twelve bedesmen should get £100 a year out of the charity. On the other side is Dr Grantly, the Archdeacon (who is married to Mr Harding's elder daughter). He is determined that Mr Harding's income shall not be touched or diminished in any way. The unfortunate Mr Harding comes in between.

ii *The Archdeacon's wealth*

The Archdeacon gets his wealth, not from his archdeaconry, but from his living at Plumstead Episcopi which is one of the richest livings in the diocese. His wealth is shown by this delightful description of his breakfast-table which followed a sumptuous dinner the night before:

And now let us observe the well-furnished breakfast-parlour at Plumstead Episcopi, and the comfortable air of all the belongings of the rectory.... The breakfast-service on the table was equally costly and equally plain; the apparent object had been to spend money without obtaining brilliancy or splendour. The urn was of thick and solid silver, as were also the tea-pot, coffee-pot, cream-ewer, and sugar-bowl; the cups were old, dim dragon china, worth about a pound a piece, but very despicable in the eyes of the uninitiated. The silver forks were so heavy as to be disagreeable to the hand, and the bread-basket was of a weight really formidable to any but robust persons. The tea consumed was of the very best, the coffee the very blackest, the cream the very thickest; there was dry toast and buttered toast, muffins and crumpets; hot bread and cold bread, white bread and brown bread, home-made bread and bakers' bread, wheaten bread and oaten bread, and if there be other breads than these, they were there; there were eggs in napkins, and crispy bits of bacon under silver covers; and there were little fishes in a little box, and devilled kidneys frizzling on a hot-water dish; – which, by-the-by, were placed closely contiguous to the plate of the worthy archdeacon himself. Over and above this, on a snow-white napkin, spread upon the sideboard, was a huge ham and a huge sirloin; the latter having laden the dinner-table on the previous evening. Such was the ordinary fare at Plumstead Episcopi.

iii *The secret volume of Rabelais*

Trollope's picture of the opulent Archdeacon would be incomplete unless I mention his secret vice. Trollope gives us this nice touch. He tells of his secret love of Rabelaisian humour, notoriously coarse and immoral.

After breakfast, on the morning of which we are writing, the archdeacon, as usual, retired to his study, intimating that he was going to be very busy, but that he would see Mr Chadwick if he called. On entering this sacred room he carefully opened the paper case on which he was wont to compose his favourite sermons, and spread on it a fair sheet of paper and one partly written on; he then placed his inkstand, looked at his pen, and folded his blotting paper; having done so, he got up again from his seat, stood with his back to the fire-place, and yawned comfortably, stretching out vastly his huge arms, and opening his burly chest. He then walked across the room and locked the door; and having so prepared himself, he threw himself into his easy chair, took from a secret drawer beneath his table a volume of Rabelais, and began to amuse himself with the witty mischief of Panurge; and so passed the archdeacon's morning on that day.

You may not know anything about Panurge. He is a character in Rabelais' satire, *Pantagruel.* He is a cunning, voluble, witty and cowardly buffoon. Rabelais describes him as

a very dissolute and debauched fellow, if there were any in Paris: otherwise and in all matters else, the best and most virtuous man in the world.

No doubt a character very attractive to Dr Grantly.

iv *John Bold is a firebrand*

John Bold is not so colourful a character as the Archdeacon, nor is he so attractive. He is unpleasant indeed, as this description of him shows:

Now I will not say that the archdeacon is strictly correct in stigmatising John Bold as a demagogue, for I hardly know how extreme must be a man's opinions before he can be justly so called; but Bold is a strong reformer. His passion is the reform of all abuses; state abuses, church abuses, corporation abuses (he has got himself elected a town councillor of Barchester, and has so worried three consecutive mayors, that it became somewhat difficult to find a fourth), abuses in medical practice, and general abuses in the world at large. Bold is thoroughly sincere in his patriotic endeavours to mend mankind, and there is something to be admired in the energy with which he devotes himself to remedying evil and stopping injustice; but I fear that he is too much imbued with the idea that he has a special mission for reforming. It would be well if one so young had a little more diffidence himself, and more trust in the honest purposes of others – if he could be brought to believe that old customs need not necessarily be evil, and that changes may possibly be dangerous; but no, Bold has all the ardour, and all the self-assurance of a Danton, and hurls his anathemas against time-honoured practices with the violence of a French Jacobin.

No wonder that Dr Grantly should regard Bold as a firebrand, falling, as he has done, almost in the centre of the quiet ancient close of Barchester Cathedral.

You may not know about Danton. He was a leader in the French Revolution. He came into conflict with Robespierre and was guillotined. The French Jacobins were political reformers of that time.

4 Twelve old men

i *All their wants supplied*

John Bold and his attorney, Finney, go to see the twelve old men in Hiram's Hospital – and try to get them on their side:

It is not to be supposed that Hiram's bedesmen themselves were altogether passive spectators. Finney, the attorney, had been among them, asking sly questions, and raising immoderate hopes, creating a party hostile to the warden, and establishing a corps in the enemy's camp, as he figuratively calls it to himself. Poor old men; whoever may be righted or wronged by this inquiry, they at any rate will assuredly be only injured; to them it can only be an unmixed evil. How can their lot be improved? all their wants are supplied; every comfort is administered; they have warm houses, good clothes, plentiful diet, and rest after a life of labour; and above all, that treasure so inestimable in declining years, a true and kind friend to listen to their sorrows, watch over their sickness, and administer comfort as regards this world and the world to come!

ii *They have their rights*

John Bold sometimes thinks of this, when he is talking loudly of the rights of the bedesmen, whom he has taken under his protection; but he quiets the suggestion within his breast with the high-sounding name of justice – '*fiat justitia ruat coelum.*' These old men should, by rights, have one hundred pounds a year instead of one shilling and sixpence a day, and the warden should have two hundred or three hundred pounds instead of eight hundred pounds. What is unjust must be wrong; what is wrong should be righted; and if he declined the task, who else would do it?

'Each one of you is clearly entitled to one hundred pounds a year by common law:' such had been the important whisper made by Finney into the ears of Abel Handy, and by him retailed to his eleven brethren.

iii *'We wants what's ourn'*

Abel Handy leads the revolt. He says in his attractive dialect:

'We wants what John Hiram left us, we wants what's ourn by law; it don't matter what we expected; what's ourn by law should be ourn, and by goles we'll have it.'

Only one of them supports the warden. He is dear old Mr Bunce who is over eighty years of age.

5 A briefless barrister

i *Tom Towers*

The most influential man is Tom Towers. He is a briefless barrister who turned to journalism and became a leader-writer for *The Jupiter*, the pseudonym by which Trollope calls *The Times* (alias *The*

Thunderer) throughout. He does this because Jupiter (alias Zeus) was, in classical mythology, the greatest of the gods, who destroyed the giants and had his home on the summit of Mount Olympus.

ii *Friendly with John Bold*

Tom Towers and John Bold have been friends for years. Bold tells Towers of all that happens in Barchester. Towers retails it all to the public in *The Jupiter.* This is Trollope's biting satire of Towers and his power:

I have before said that he of the Jupiter and John Bold were intimate. There was no very great difference in their ages, for Towers was still considerably under forty; and when Bold had been attending the London hospitals, Towers, who was not then the great man that he had since become, had been much with him. Then they had often discussed together the objects of their ambition and future prospects: then Tom Towers was struggling hard to maintain himself, as a briefless barrister, by shorthand reporting for any of the papers that would engage him; then he had not dared to dream of writing leaders for the Jupiter, or canvassing the conduct of Cabinet ministers.

iii *His hidden glory*

Things had altered since that time; the briefless barrister was still briefless, but he now despised briefs: could he have been sure of a judge's seat he would hardly have left his present career. It is true he wore no ermine, bore no outward marks of a world's respect; but with what a load of inward importance was he charged! It is true his name appeared in no large capitals; on no wall was chalked up 'Tom Towers for ever;' – 'Freedom of the Press and Tom Towers:' but what member of Parliament had half his power? It is true that in far-off provinces men did not talk daily of Tom Towers but they read the Jupiter, and acknowledged that without the Jupiter life was not worth having. This kind of hidden but still conscious glory suited the nature of the man.

iv *His power*

He loved to sit silent in a corner of his club and listen to the loud chattering of politicians, and to think how they were all in his power – how he could smite the loudest of them, were it worth his while to raise his pen for such a purpose. He loved to watch the great men of whom he daily wrote, and flatter himself that he was greater than any of them. Each of them was responsible to his country, each of them must answer if inquired into, each of them must endure abuse with good humour, and insolence without anger. But to whom was he, Tom Towers, responsible? No one could insult him; no one could inquire into him. He could speak out withering words, and no one could answer him: ministers courted him, though perhaps they knew not his name; bishops feared him; judges doubted their own verdicts unless he confirmed them; and generals, in their councils of war, did not consider more deeply what the enemy would do, than what the Jupiter would say.

v *He is a god*

Tom Towers never boasted of the Jupiter; he scarcely ever named the paper even to the most intimate of his friends; he did not even wish to be spoken of as connected with it; but he did not the less value his privileges, or think the less of his own importance. It is probable that Tom Towers considered himself the most powerful man in Europe; and so he walked on from day to day, studiously striving to look a man, but knowing within his breast that he was a god.

6 Printing House Square

i *'Is this Mount Olympus?'*

The Times was for many years published in Printing House Square in the City of London. (I went there as a young barrister to inspect the documents in a case against *The Times*.) *The Times* has since moved into dreary Gray's Inn Road and more recently – with the new technology – to Wapping in the East End. This is Trollope's description of Printing House Square in a passage of sustained irony, mocking it as Mount Olympus:

Velvet and gilding do not make a throne, nor gold and jewels a sceptre. It is a throne because the most exalted one sits there – and a sceptre because the most mighty one wields it. So it is with Mount Olympus. Should a stranger make his way thither at dull noonday, or during the sleepy hours of the silent afternoon, he would find no acknowledged temple of power and beauty, no fitting fane for the great Thunderer, no proud façades and pillared roofs to support the dignity of this greatest of earthly potentates. To the outward and uninitiated eye, Mount Olympus is a somewhat humble spot – undistinguished, unadorned, – nay, almost mean. It stands alone, as it were, in a mighty city, close to the densest throng of men, but partaking neither of the noise nor the crowd; a small secluded, dreary spot, tenanted, one would say, by quite unambitious people at the easiest rents. 'Is this Mount Olympus?' asks the unbelieving stranger. 'Is it from these small, dark, dingy buildings that those infallible laws proceed which cabinets are called upon to obey; by which bishops are to be guided, lords and commons controlled, – judges instructed in law, generals in strategy, admirals in naval tactics, and orange-women in the management of their barrows?' 'Yes, my friend – from these walls. From here issue the only known infallible bulls for the guidance of British souls and bodies. . . .'

Oh heavens! and this is Mount Olympus!

ii *'The Jupiter is never wrong'*

Trollope goes on with his scornful fulminations against the omniscient *Jupiter* (*Times*):

It is a fact amazing to ordinary mortals that the Jupiter is never wrong. With what endless care, with what unsparing labour, do we not strive to get together for our great national council the men most fitting to compose it. And how we fail! Parliament is always wrong: look at the Jupiter and see how futile are their meetings, how vain their council, how needless all their trouble! With what pride do we regard our chief ministers, the great servants of state, the oligarchs of the nation on whose wisdom we lean, to whom we look for guidance in our difficulties! But what are they to the writers of the Jupiter? They hold council together and with anxious thought painfully elaborate their country's good; but when all is done, the Jupiter declares that all is nought. Why should we look to Lord John Russell – why should we regard Palmerston and Gladstone, when Tom Towers without a struggle can put us right? Look at our generals, what faults they make; at our admirals, how inactive they are. What money, honesty, and science can do, is done; and yet how badly are our troops brought together, fed, conveyed, clothed, armed, and managed. The most excellent of our good men do their best to man our ships, with the assistance of all possible external appliances; but in vain. All, all is wrong – alas! alas! Tom Towers, and he alone, knows all about it. Why, oh why, ye earthly ministers, why have ye not followed more closely this heaven-sent messenger that is amongst us?

Were it not well for us in our ignorance that we confided all things to the Jupiter? Would it not be wise in us to abandon useless talking, idle thinking, and profitless labour? Away with majorities in the House of Commons, with verdicts from judicial bench given after much delay, with doubtful laws, and the fallible attempts of humanity! Does not the Jupiter, coming forth daily with fifty thousand impressions full of unerring decision on every mortal subject, set all matters sufficiently at rest? Is not Tom Towers here, able to guide us and willing?

7 A thunderbolt

i *It strikes Barchester*

Trollope turns to the impact of *The Jupiter* on the affairs of Hiram's Hospital. It is a leading article written, no doubt, by Tom Towers with St Cross in mind, condemning the dear old Mr Harding as if he were a knave:

But above all, it had been mentioned in the daily Jupiter. That all-powerful organ of the press in one of its leading thunderbolts launched at St Cross, had thus remarked: 'Another case, of smaller dimensions indeed, but of similar import, is now likely to come under public notice. We are informed that the warden or master of an old almshouse attached to Barchester Cathedral is in receipt of twenty-five times the annual income appointed for him by the will of the founder, while the sum yearly expended on the absolute purposes of the charity has always remained fixed. In other words, the legatees under the founder's will have received no advantage from the increase in the value of the property during the last four centuries, such increase having been absorbed by the so-called warden. It is impossible to conceive a case of greater injustice. It is no answer to say that some six or nine or twelve old men receive as much of the goods of this world as such old men require.'

ii *The Warden is pilloried*

'On what foundation, moral or divine, traditional or legal, is grounded the warden's claim to the large income he receives for doing nothing? The contentment of these almsmen, if content they be, can give him no title to this wealth! Does he ever ask himself, when he stretches wide his clerical palm to receive the pay of some dozen of the working clergy, for what service he is so remunerated? Does his conscience ever entertain the question of his right to such subsidies? Or is it possible that the subject never so presents itself to his mind; that he has received for many years, and intends, should God spare him, to receive for years to come, these fruits of the industrious piety of past ages, indifferent as to any right on his own part, or of any injustice to others! We must express an opinion that nowhere but in the Church of England, and only there among its priests, could such a state of moral indifference be found.'

iii *The effect on Mr Harding*

That article had a devastating effect on Mr Harding who was helpless to defend himself:

I must for the present leave my readers to imagine the state of Mr Harding's mind after reading the above article. They say that forty thousand copies of the Jupiter are daily sold, and that each copy is read by five persons at the least. Two hundred thousand readers then would hear this accusation against him; two hundred thousand hearts would swell with indignation at the griping injustice, the barefaced robbery of the warden of Barchester Hospital! And how was he to answer this? How was he to open his inmost heart to this multitude, to these thousands, the educated, the polished, the picked men of his own country; how show them that he was no robber, no avaricious lazy priest scrambling for gold, but a retiring humble-spirited man, who had innocently taken what had innocently been offered to him?

8 Legal proceedings

i *John Bold brings an action*

John Bold himself took proceedings at law. Trollope does not tell us their nature. It appears to have been a suit by John Bold himself against Mr Harding, the warden, and Mr Chadwick, the steward of Hiram's Hospital. In those proceedings John Bold claimed that the revenue from John Hiram's estate should be applied for the bedesmen. They caused great distress and worry to Mr Harding.

ii *Eleanor pleads*

The warden's younger daughter, Eleanor, pleads with John Bold, asking him to withdraw the proceedings:

'Promise me, promise me,' said Eleanor; 'say that my father is safe – one word will do. I know how true you are; say one word, and I will let you go.'

She still held him, and looked eagerly into his face, with her hair dishevelled, and her eyes all bloodshot. She had no thought now of herself, no care now for her appearance; and yet he thought he had never seen her half so lovely; he was amazed at the intensity of her beauty, and could hardly believe that it was she whom he had dared to love. 'Promise me,' said she; 'I will not leave you till you have promised me.'

'I will,' said he at length; 'I do – all I can do, I will do.'

'Then may God Almighty bless you for ever and ever!'

iii *Advice by Sir Abraham Haphazard*

Dr Grantly is also concerned with the proceedings. He seeks the advice of the Attorney-General, Sir Abraham Haphazard. (In those days the Attorney-General could undertake private work.) Sir Abraham advises that the proceedings are technically wrong because they are against Mr Harding and Mr Chadwick: and those two are not trustees of John Hiram's will. They are only servants. But Sir Abraham does not give any opinion on the merits of the case. He does not say whether, under the will, the warden is entitled to his £800 a year or not. That was what really concerned Mr Harding. He did not wish to have the money if it was not really his.

9 Another thunderbolt

i *In* The Jupiter *again*

At this point there was still hope that the storm would subside: that John Bold would withdraw his action. Eleanor told her father of her successful plea: but he was not impressed. All was set to naught by another article by Tom Towers in *The Jupiter*:

'Oh, papa!' she exclaimed, all but crying with vexation – 'I thought you would have been so happy – I thought all would have been right now.'

'Mr Bold,' continued he, 'has set great people to work; so great that I doubt they are now beyond his control. Read that, my dear:' and the warden, doubling up a number of the Jupiter, pointed to the peculiar article which she was to read. It was to the last of the three leaders, which are generally furnished daily for the support of the nation, that Mr Harding directed her attention. It dealt some heavy blows on various clerical delinquents; on families who received their tens of thousands yearly for doing nothing; on men who, as the article stated, rolled in wealth which they had neither earned nor inherited, and which was in fact stolen from the poorer clergy. It named some sons of bishops, and grandsons of archbishops; men great in their way, who had redeemed their disgrace in the eyes of many by the enormity of their plunder; and then, having disposed of these leviathans, it descended to Mr Harding.

ii *It scoffs at the legal plea*

The article scoffs at the legal plea set up by the Archdeacon on behalf of the warden:

'We allude to the question of the Barchester almshouse at the present moment, because we understand that a plea has been set up which will be peculiarly revolting to the minds of English churchmen. An action has been taken against Mr Warden Harding, on behalf of the almsmen, by a gentleman acting solely on public grounds, and it is to be argued that Mr Harding takes nothing but what he receives as a servant of the hospital, and that he is not himself responsible for the amount of stipend given to him for his work. Such a plea would doubtless be fair, if any one questioned the daily wages of a bricklayer employed on the building, or the fee of the charwoman who cleans it; but we cannot envy the feeling of a clergyman of the Church of England who could allow such an argument to be put into his mouth.

If this plea be put forward we trust Mr Harding will be forced as a witness to state the nature of his employment; the amount of work that he does; the income which he receives; and the source from whence he obtained his appointment. We do not think he will receive much public sympathy to atone for the annoyance of such an examination.'

As Eleanor read the article her face flushed with indignation, and when she had finished it, she almost feared to look up at her father.

'Well, my dear,' said he; 'what do you think of that – is it worth while to be a warden at that price?'

'Oh, papa; – dear papa!'

iii *It is the last straw*

That article was the last straw that broke the warden's heart. He decided to resign:

'They shall not put forward this plea on my behalf,' continued the warden. 'Whatever may be the truth of the matter, that at any rate is not true; and the man who wrote that article is right in saying that such a plea is revolting to an honest mind. I will go up to London, my dear, and see these lawyers myself, and if no better excuse can be made for me than that, I and the hospital will part.'

'But the archdeacon, papa?'

'I can't help it, my dear; there are some things which a man cannot bear, – I cannot bear that' – and he put his hand upon the newspaper.

10 Resignation

i *An interview with the Attorney-General*

Mr Harding spent a long day in London. The Attorney-General did not see him till ten o'clock at night. Sir Abraham tells him that the action by Bold against him is to be abandoned. But Mr Harding is not satisfied. He wants Sir Abraham's opinion on the merits of the case:

'What I want you, Sir Abraham, to tell me, is this – am I, as warden, legally and distinctly entitled to the proceeds of the property, after the due maintenance of the twelve bedesmen?'

Sir Abraham declared that he couldn't exactly say in so many words that Mr Harding was legally entitled, to, &c., &c., &c., and ended in expressing a strong opinion that it would be madness to raise any further question on the matter, as the suit was to be, – nay, was, abandoned.

ii *Mr Harding decides to resign*

'But if this income be not justly mine, what if she and I have both to beg?' said the warden at last, sharply, and in a voice so different from that he had hitherto used, that Sir Abraham was startled. 'If so, it would be better to beg.'

'My dear sir, nobody now questions its justness.'

'Yes, Sir Abraham, one does question it, – the most important of all witnesses against me – I question it myself. My God knows whether or no I love my daughter; but I would sooner that she and I should both beg, than that she should live in comfort on money which is truly the property of the poor. It may seem strange to you, Sir Abraham, it is strange to myself, that I should have been ten years in that happy home, and not have thought of these things, till they were so roughly dinned into my ears. I cannot boast of my conscience, when it required the violence of a public newspaper to awaken it; but, now that it is awake, I must obey it. When I came here I did not know that the suit was withdrawn by Mr Bold, and my object was to beg you to abandon my defence. As there is no action, there can be no defence. But it is, at any rate, as well that you should know that from tomorrow I shall cease to be the warden of the hospital. My friends and I differ on this subject, Sir Abraham, and that adds much to my sorrow: but it cannot be helped.'

iii *'Sleep upon it'*

. . . 'You'll sleep on this, Mr Harding, and tomorrow –'

'I have done more than sleep upon it,' said the warden; 'I have laid awake upon it, and that night after night. I found I could not sleep upon it. Now I hope to do so.'

The Attorney-General had no answer to make to this; so he expressed a quiet hope that whatever settlement was finally made would be satisfactory; and Mr Harding withdrew, thanking the great man for his kind attention.

iv *The vacancy is not filled*

So Mr Harding resigned the wardenship. The Bishop did not appoint any new warden in his place. He did not fill the vacancy. He did not want any successor to be as troubled as Mr Harding had been. The twelve old men did not get their anticipated one hundred pounds a year. They fared badly with no one to visit them or care for them. They died off one by one. Their places were not filled. As to the building, Trollope describes it:

The building of the hospital itself has not been allowed to go to ruins. Mr Chadwick, who still holds his stewardship, and pays the accruing rents into an account opened at a bank for the purpose, sees to that; but the whole place has become disordered and ugly. The warden's garden is a wretched wilderness, the drive and paths are covered with weeds, the flower-beds are bare, and the unshorn lawn is now a mass of long damp grass and unwholesome moss. The beauty of the place is gone; its attractions have withered. Alas! a very few years since it was the prettiest spot in Barchester, and now it is a disgrace to the city.

Happily, Trollope's picture of Hiram's Hospital does not apply to St Cross at Winchester. As I have told you earlier, it is kept in delightful order, with many visitors admiring it and receiving, if they ask, the Wayfarer's Dole.

11 Retirement

i *Mr Harding's last post*

Trollope gives the warden a peaceful retirement. He draws a picture of a little church at Winchester. He calls it St Cuthbert's at Barchester. But it is obviously St Swithun's-upon-Kingsgate at Winchester. You can go there today and see it for yourself. Trollope tells us that Mr Harding was

put into possession of a small living within the walls of the city. It is the smallest possible parish, containing a part of the Cathedral Close, and a few old houses adjoining. The church is a singular little Gothic building, perched over a gateway, through which the Close is entered, and is approached by a flight of stone steps which leads down under the archway of the gate. It is no bigger than an ordinary room, – perhaps twenty-seven feet long by eighteen wide, – but still it is a perfect church. It contains an old carved pulpit and reading-desk, a tiny altar under a window filled with dark old-coloured glass, a font, some half-dozen pews, and perhaps a dozen seats for the poor, and also a vestry. The roof is high pitched, and of black old oak, and the three large beams which support it run down to the side walls, and terminate in grotesquely carved faces – two devils and an angel on one side, two angels and a devil on the other. Such is the church of St Cuthbert at Barchester, of which Mr Harding became rector, with a clear income of seventy-five pounds a year.

ii *A charming end*

Then there is this charming end to the story of *The Warden*:

Here he performs afternoon service every Sunday, and administers the Sacrament once in every three months. His audience is not large; and, had they been so, he could not have accommodated them; but enough come to fill his six pews, and, on the front seat of those devoted to the poor is always to be seen our old friend Mr Bunce, decently arrayed in his bedesman's gown.

Mr Harding is still precentor of Barchester, and it is very rarely the case that those who attend the Sunday morning service miss the gratification of hearing him chant the Litany, as no other man in England can do it. . . .

It was long before the people of Barchester forgot to call Mr Harding by his long well-known name of Warden. It had become so customary to say Mr Warden, that it was not easily dropped. 'No, no,' he always says when so addressed, 'not warden now, only precentor.'

A footnote

Now will you please turn to my book, *The Closing Chapter*, at pages 8 to 10. There is a close parallel which may interest you.

14 The impudent impostor

Introduction

The *Tichborne case* was the table talk of everyone for eight years from 1866 to 1874. The newspapers of England and Australia were full of it. Supporters were ranged on either side. The costs were enormous. The case is celebrated – not for any legal interest – but for its popular interest. It comprised two trials. One a civil case in ejectment. The other a criminal case for perjury. Together they make it the longest case ever tried in our courts.

Seventy years later, in 1936, Lord Maugham wrote a book about the case. He became Lord Chancellor and made me a silk. He was a brother of Somerset Maugham and our dear friend, Honor, is his daughter. He did much research on it and got help from our friends in the libraries. If you read his book, you will realise that truth is indeed stranger than fiction. It outdoes any novel.

The Tichborne family have for many years held vast estates. In 1854 the expectant heir was Roger Charles Tichborne, a young man of 25. He was lost at sea: 'missing, presumed dead.' On his death his younger brother, Alfred, became the expectant heir. Twelve years later, in 1866, an impudent impostor in Australia claimed that he was Roger, the 'missing' heir and entitled to the estates. He came to England and swore on oath that he was Roger. Eight years later, in 1874, he was found guilty of perjury and sentenced to fourteen years' penal servitude.

1 The succession

i *The Tichborne heritage*

Tichborne is a small village near Alresford in Hampshire. Its name is taken from the stream there called the Itchen (De Itchen Bourne). The family was there before the Norman Conquest. It has long been Roman Catholic. Many years ago one of them was made a baronet.

The title and estates descended down the male line until in the early 1800s there were three brothers who succeeded one after the other – Henry, Edward and James.

ii *The Dowager Lady Tichborne*

The youngest of the three brothers, James Tichborne, married a Frenchwoman, Henriette. She is the evil genius of the story. I had thought of calling her a bastard. Because she was. She was the illegitimate daughter of an English Gentleman and a French Lady. (I have used capital G and capital L because they were both high-born.) And it was she, in her distorted mind, who supported the claim of the impudent impostor.

iii *Her two sons*

James and Henriette Tichborne were married in 1827 in Paris. Their elder son, Roger, was born there in 1829. Their younger son, Alfred, in 1839. No one thought at that time that there was any chance of either of the two boys succeeding to the title and estates. Their two uncles (Henry and Edward) might have had sons to succeed them. But they had none. And thereby hangs this tale.

iv *Kate, their first cousin*

In 1845, Roger's elder uncle, Henry, died, leaving six daughters but no sons. He was succeeded by Roger's next uncle, Edward. (Edward assumed the surname, Doughty, so as to benefit under a will. So he became Sir Edward Doughty and lived at Tichborne.) Edward had a daughter, Katherine (Kate) Doughty but no sons. (She comes vividly into the story.) So there was every chance that James, Roger's father, would succeed to the title and estates, and, after him, Roger.

2 Roger Tichborne

i *Roger as a French boy*

Roger's parents had their home in Paris. Roger was brought up as a French boy, speaking French, with a French mother, French nurses and French teachers. But when in 1845 his uncle Henry died and his uncle Edward succeeded him, his father James became the expectant heir and Roger was thus close to the succession. So his father brought him to England and he was thenceforward brought up as an English boy.

ii *Roger as an English boy*

Roger was sent to the Roman Catholic school called Stonyhurst in Lancashire. He learnt English there and could speak it reasonably well – with a French accent. He went for his holidays to his uncle, Sir Edward Doughty (né Tichborne), where Lady Doughty treated him as a son. There he met their daughter, his first cousin, Kate. In 1845 he was 16 and she was 11. He was at Stonyhurst and she was at a convent school. They got on well together – and afterwards fell in love. By which, too, hangs this tale.

iii *Roger is tattooed*

At this time there was a craze among schoolboys for tattooing one another. A boy called Bellew tattooed on Roger's arm the letters R.C.T. (representing Roger Charles Tichborne). His evidence became of vital importance in the case: because the impudent impostor had no tattoo marks on his arm. He tried to get over it by saying that he had had the letters R.C.T. tattooed but had had them removed.

3 The love story

i *Roger falls in love with Kate*

After leaving Stonyhurst, Roger got a commission in the 6th Dragoon Guards, better known at that time as the Carabineers. This was done by pulling strings in the right quarters. On his leaves, he went back to Tichborne where his uncle (Sir Edward) lived. There he again met his first cousin, Kate. She was now a lovely girl who had just left her convent school. He was 22. She was 17. They fell in love. This is what Lord Maugham tells us:

> Roger's affection for his cousin Katherine grew steadily till it became a passion, but it is not necessary to give a detailed account of its course – which did not run smooth. . . . He refrained for a long time from telling his love, but like a well conducted Victorian young man he thought it right to confide in the mother. Nor did she discourage the idea; for she was genuinely fond of Roger, and of course in the matrimonial pool he was a magnificent fish. There were however serious difficulties. On the one hand the Catholic Church does not generally allow the marriage of first cousins, and a dispensation would be necessary. On the other hand

kind friends in Ireland had been giving Lady Doughty terrible accounts of the dissipations of the young Carabineer. Roger she was told was not only an excessive smoker but a deep drinker.

ii *Her Victorian father refuses*

Uncle Edward was blind to all this love-making, but when he got to know about it, he was furious. Like a typical Victorian father, he put his foot down. His daughter Kate was not to marry her first cousin. He called the young officer into his library and told him to take the first train back to London:

At Christmas 1851 Roger was on leave and staying at Tichborne. Sir Edward Doughty was not well, but on Sunday the 11th January 1852 he saw the young couple walking together before breakfast and the scales fell from his eyes. During breakfast Roger was asked to see Sir Edward in the library. He did not return to finish his meal, for the skies had fallen on poor Roger's dream of happiness. Sir Edward was resolutely set against the match. Roger was allowed to say goodbye that evening, and was obliged to leave on the Monday by the first train for London.

iii *Roger's promise to her*

He wrote to his cousin, at her request, an account of his distracted feelings and his intentions. . . . After expressing his intention to go to India he added, – 'I promise to my own dearest Kate, on my word and honour, that I will be back in England if she is not married or engaged, towards the end of the autumn of 1854 or the month of January 1855 and then will marry her.'

That love affair was passionate but innocent. Roger did not seduce Kate – as the impudent impostor afterwards alleged. His allegation played a prominent part in the trial – and in the newspapers.

iv *The final parting*

Roger did see Kate once more. He was posted to India and was given embarkation leave. He wrote a letter to the steward of the Tichborne estates, Mr Gosford, whom he knew well. Roger handed him a 'sealed packet' (which the impudent impostor later made use of) for him to keep. He also wrote a memorandum which he gave to his cousin Kate. This is how Lord Maugham describes it:

On the 22nd June 1852 Roger, who had been allowed to return to Tichborne for the purpose, said a last goodbye to his cousin. . . . The two cousins went for a walk along the charming river side and, whilst (as we may fairly suppose) the birds were singing and the trout were rising, Roger produced from his pocket a memorandum which he had previously written out and with a sigh he gave it to Katherine.

22nd June 1852.

I make this day a promise that if I marry my cousin Catherine Doughty this year, or before three years are over at the latest, to build a church or chapel at Tichborne to the Holy Virgin, in thanksgiving for the protection which she has thrown over us, and in praying God that our wishes may be fulfilled.

R.C. Tichborne.

Kate afterwards wrote on the back:

'This was written the last day I ever saw Roger.'

And thus the young lovers parted, Roger being twenty-three and Katherine eighteen.

4 The last of Roger

i *Roger travels to South America*

The regiment did not go to India. Roger decided to leave the army and travel. He sailed round Cape Horn to Valparaiso. Whilst there in June 1853, he got a letter from his aunt, telling him that his uncle, Sir Edward Doughty, had died on the 5 March 1853. So his father, James, inherited the title and the vast estates. And Roger was his immediate heir. He did not come home. He stayed on in South America. He rode on horseback or mule from Valparaiso across the Andes to Buenos Ayres. He did it very quickly.

ii *Roger is lost at sea*

Now we come to the last days of Roger. Lord Maugham tells us of the evidence:

Roger sailed from Buenos Ayres to Rio de Janeiro in March and stayed there some little time. He booked a passage in an English three masted sailing ship the *Bella* of between 300 and 400 tons burden belonging to Liverpool which was sailing to Kingston, Jamaica, and thence to New York.

There was ample evidence that Roger sailed in the *Bella*. She left Rio on the morning of the 20 April 1854:

The *Bella* was never seen again. On the third or fourth day out she foundered. Her longboat was picked up some 400 miles from land floating bottom upwards close to the spot where it was presumed the ship had capsized in a squall, since some wreckage which came from the ship was found close by. No other boat was found. No person who sailed on the ill-fated ship (unless it was the claimant!) ever was seen again or made any claim for salary or wages. Everything that was possible was done under the circumstances. A vessel was sent out by the British Admiral on the station to search for a boat if one was afloat, but nothing was found. The insurance money was paid. The Tichborne family did not too speedily abandon hope. Time was allowed to permit of survivors who reached any part of the globe to communicate with England. At length the death of Roger Charles Tichborne was presumed and his Will was proved in July 1855.

You will remember that Roger had left a 'sealed packet' with Mr Gosford. Some time after Roger's death, Mr Gosford destroyed it. So no one knew what it contained. The impudent impostor invented his own version of it.

iii *A baby succeeds to the title and estates*

So ends the life of Roger Charles Tichborne. He was presumed to have died on the 23 April 1854. His younger brother, Alfred, became the expectant heir. His father, Sir James (10th bart.), lived on for eight years until he died on the 11 June 1862. Alfred then succeeded to the title and estates. He became Sir Alfred (11th bart.), but he died in 1866, and was the father of a posthumous son, Henry. This baby became the 12th Baronet and succeeded to the title and estates.

5 The claimant

In the very next year, 1867, a man arrived in England and claimed that he was the lost Roger. He described himself as 'Sir Roger Tichborne Bart.' He claimed that he was the true successor to the title and estates: and that the baby was not entitled at all.

i *Very different from Roger*

It is amazing that anyone should have given any credence to the claimant. He was an impudent impostor. He was very different from Roger Tichborne. This is Lord Maugham's description of Roger Tichborne:

> He was about 5 feet 8½ inches in height, but exceedingly thin and spare in form, a man of considerable physical energy, delighting in riding, fishing and hunting; . . . He smoked a great deal and drank more than was good for him; . . . but not more than an ordinary fox-hunting squire of the fifties. . . . He uniformly behaved with the tact, good manners, and discretion of a Victorian gentleman.

Roger had the letters R.C.T. tattooed on his arm. But the claimant was a big fat man weighing over 20 stone – with no tattoo marks on his arm. He was not a gentleman but a low-down butcher. He could speak Spanish but did not know a word of French. Yet as events show he had a remarkable memory. He had much self-assurance. He was a good actor. He got a lot of detail from a lot of people about Roger. He pieced it together and was able to convince many that he was truly Roger Tichborne but had grown stout over the years. He passed himself off as 'The Baronet' with much aplomb.

ii *The early life of the claimant*

As a result of the two trials it was found that the claimant was in truth Arthur Orton, the son of a butcher who lived in the High Street, Wapping, in the East End of London. He was born in March 1834 (so he was five years younger than Roger Tichborne). Young Arthur Orton in his boyhood suffered from St Vitus' dance and was sent to sea as a cure for it. He sailed to South America and round Cape Horn to Valparaiso. He there deserted his ship and made his way to the Chilean town of Melipilla. He was then 15, and stayed there for nineteen months. It was in the house of Don Tomas Castro. He learnt Spanish. He came back home to Wapping in 1851 at the age of 17. He helped his father in the butcher's shop. But in 1853 he went out to Tasmania. Then in 1855 to Australia. He was suspected of murder and disappeared in 1859. His whereabouts were not known until in 1862 he was found settled in a small Australian town called Wagga Wagga. He said that his name was Tom Castro. (You will remember that he stayed with a Castro in Chile.) He set up business as a butcher. He weighed 20 stone. He was in debt and read an advertisement in the local paper. That started him on his career as the Impudent Impostor.

6 An advertisement in Australia

i *The Dowager believed Roger to be alive*

Now we come back to the Dowager Lady Tichborne. As I have said, her husband Sir James (10th bart.) had died on the 11 June 1862. She never accepted that her son Roger was dead. This is how Lord Maugham describes her state of mind:

> Lady Tichborne however had always clung to the hope that her eldest son would return. While Sir James Tichborne was alive every idle tale told by a wandering sailor was readily swallowed by her. Beggars at Tichborne used to wait till Sir James had gone out, and used then to make their way up to the house with tales of the missing heir. When Sir James died she began, greatly contrary to the interests of her son Alfred, to advertise for news of Roger in various papers in three languages.

But she had no success from her own advertisements.

ii *The Missing Friends' Agency*

Now there was in Sydney, Australia, a Mr Cubitt who ran an agency which he called 'The Missing Friends' Agency.' He specialised in finding the whereabouts of missing people. He did a good business: because of the number of convicts who had been transported to Botany Bay – and whose relatives had lost track of them. (It was Sir Robert Menzies who once said to me, 'You must remember that the first people in Australia were picked by the best judges of England.')

To further his business, Mr Cubitt in 1865 put an advertisement in *The Times* in England. He invited people here to use his good offices to find missing persons. Lady Tichborne saw his advertisement on the 19 May 1865. She wrote him a long letter telling him about the missing Roger and that he was heir to a very large property. Mr Cubitt took it up keenly. He saw that he might get something out of it himself. So he drafted an advertisement based on her letter and put it in the Australian papers.

iii *Mr Cubitt's advertisement*

A handsome reward will be given to any person who can furnish such information as will discover the fate of Roger Charles Tichborne. He sailed from the port of Rio de Janeiro on the 20th of April 1854, in the ship *La Bella*, and has never been heard of since, but a report reached England to the effect that a portion of the crew and passengers of a vessel of that name was picked up by a vessel bound to Australia – Melbourne it is believed – it is not known whether the said Roger Charles Tichborne was amongst the drowned or saved. He would at the present time be about thirty-two years of age; is of a delicate constitution; rather tall; with very light brown hair, and blue eyes. Mr Tichborne is the son of Sir James Tichborne, Bart. now deceased, and is heir to all his estates. . . . All replies to be addressed to Mr Arthur Cubitt, etc.

7 The claimant's response

i *His clay pipe*

Arthur Orton (who now called himself Tom Castro and became the claimant) saw that advertisement. He saw a chance of bettering himself. He determined to put himself forward as being Roger Charles Tichborne. He got out his clay pipe, and cut on it the letters 'R.C.T.' meaning to use it as evidence of his identity. He went along to a solicitor in Wagga Wagga named William Gibbes. He told the solicitor that he was Tom Castro, that he was a married man, was in need of money and could not pay a debt of six pounds. But he went on (pretending to be ignorant of the advertisement):

I have a little property in England if only I could get hold of it. I am heir to a title but I was shipwrecked and have lost touch.

Mr Gibbes quickly jumped to a conclusion. He had himself read Mr

Cubitt's advertisement. He called his wife in. She said, 'That must be the man who is advertised for!' Together they decided to break the good news to Tom Castro. Lord Maugham describes the scene:

> 'Oh, I know who you are; and I know your name.'
> 'Is that it?' asked the coy and unwilling baronet, holding up his pipe (a common clay) on which he had carefully cut the letters 'R.C.T.' 'Are those the initials?' 'Yes,' answered the triumphant Gibbes.
> The claimant was thus started on his long and tortuous career.

ii *On to a good thing!*

Gibbes at once wrote to Cubitt saying that he thought he had found the missing heir. Cubitt took it up avidly. The two of them were on to a good thing!

iii *The Dowager is told*

It was Cubitt who told the Dowager of the finding of her 'missing' son. She was delighted and replied accepting him as her long-lost son:

> 25th February 1866
>
> My dearest and beloved Roger,
> I hope you will not refuse to come back to your poor mother who is still living. I have never lost the hope of seeing you again in this world. . . .

iv *She arranged for him to have money*

> . . . I trust my beloved roger, that you will come back immediately and all the money required to pay your expenses will be soon found, only write to me and give me some detail about yourself, you know that if you let a banker know that you are *Sir roger tichborne*, they will advance you the money necessary. . . .
>
> Your own mother
> H. F. Tichborne.

v *The 'Baronet' goes to Sydney*

From that time onwards Castro described himself as 'Sir Roger Charles Tichborne Baronet.' On that pretence he got money from 'supporters' who hoped to share in the reward. He went to Sydney and stayed with his wife at the Metropolitan Hotel, using the name and title of 'Sir Roger Tichborne Baronet.' The newspapers in Australia and Sydney were full of it.

vi *The old negro Bogle*

This gave the 'Baronet' an introduction to an old negro called Bogle who was living in Sydney. He had been a servant to Roger's uncle Edward at Tichborne and had known the real Roger well. Bogle had taken Roger fishing and shooting. Bogle was only too ready to jump on the band-wagon of the baronet – also hoping to share in the reward. He told the 'Baronet' that he recognised him at once as the long-lost Roger. He gave him a full description of the life of Roger at Tichborne. The 'Baronet' had a good memory and personified himself in the part with great ability and agility.

That recognition was a god-send to the 'Baronet.' He took Bogle into his service. Bogle and his family moved into the hotel at Sydney. They went with him to England and were with him throughout. Bogle was a dishonest old rogue, like his master the 'Baronet.'

8 At Alresford

i *The 'Baronet' comes to England*

On the 22 September 1866 the claimant, under the name and title of Sir Roger Tichborne Bart., left Sydney for England. Lord Maugham tells us:

> The distinguished gentleman was naturally well attended. He took with him his wife and two children, an English nursemaid Miss Rosina McArthur, the faithful Bogle and his son, and finally young Butts his secretary.

They all arrived safely on Christmas Eve 1866. Bogle suggested to the claimant that he should go to Ford's Hotel in Manchester Square, that being the hotel 'where the family always stay.' The fires were burning brightly in Ford's Hotel, and his wife and children were there with him to enjoy the rest and comfort of a first-class hotel.

ii *He visits Tichborne*

After a short visit to Wapping (incognito) to see his family (where he found them dead or gone) the 'Baronet' went to Tichborne. It was his first visit in his life. Lord Maugham gives us this entertaining description:

> It must be mentioned that various Australian journals, including the *Melbourne Argus*, had reached England with the news that 'Sir Roger Tichborne' had sailed for England to claim his estates, and the family, and the inhabitants of Tichborne and Alresford were anxiously awaiting his arrival.

iii *A cart-horse*

On Sunday the 29th December, the churchgoers were interested to see an enormous man (weighing at that time some 20 stone) wrapped in great coats, muffled with a large shawl, with a peaked cap on his head, walking along the road. He stopped an old blacksmith called Etheridge and asked him the way to Tichborne. 'Why,' said Etheridge, pointing it out, 'there's the Church.' . . .

Later, Etheridge was returning home when he met the same stout man again and the following dialogue is said to have ensued:

'They say Roger Tichborne has come back.'
'Oh! no, he has not. He was drowned.'
'Do you believe I am Roger Tichborne?'
'No, I'll be d——d if you are. If you are, you've turned from a race-horse into a cart-horse.'

iv *He puts up at the Swan*

On all his visits, the 'Baronet' stayed at the Swan Inn at Alresford. It was kept at that time by a Mr Rous who had been a clerk to the solicitor to the Tichborne family. He saw that it was good for business for him to support the 'Baronet.' So he got the 'Baronet' to telegraph to Bogle to come down immediately to Alresford.

The negro was well known and liked in the neighbourhood, and he found when he arrived that evening some four hundred people assembled at the station to welcome him back. The faithful black had come to acknowledge the stranger as his master! He was naturally received with acclamations.

The bells rang out in the churches of Alresford and Tichborne to greet the triumphant reappearance of the 'Baronet' at his ancestral home.

The Swan at Alresford used to be crowded when the Baronet and his friends were known to be there. The local villagers used to be given refreshment under the hospitable direction of Mr Rous the landlord before they were ushered one by one into the sanctum where the genial claimant, playing with distinction his part of the rightful heir, was seated.

9 Recognition by the Dowager

i *In a Paris hotel*

It was necessary for the 'Baronet' to see his 'mother' so as to get her to support his claim. He got hold of an acquaintance, Mr Leet, and a solicitor, Mr Holmes. Together they went to Paris. There the Dowager Lady Tichborne is said to have recognised the 'Baronet' as her long-lost son Roger. Lord Maugham is very scathing about it:

The party arrived in Paris rather late that night and went to the Hotel de Lille et d'Albion in the Rue St Honoré. The Dowager Lady Tichborne was staying not far off in the Place de la Madeleine. . . . Next morning she sent her Irish servant, one Coyne, to fetch her son.

After two unsuccessful attempts Coyne reported to the Dowager that he would not come. She told Coyne

to go back and either bring her son in a cab or to make his two companions come to see her. On Coyne's third visit to the hotel he found the three men breakfasting together. After they had finished Holmes and Leet locked the claimant in the dining-room, – apparently regardless of his title, his dignity, and his ancient lineage, – and went with Coyne to see Lady Tichborne.

ii *She goes to him*

So the 'Baronet' never did go to her hotel. She had to go to his. She was taken in the afternoon to see her son. Coyne's evidence (at the criminal trial) as to what happened was this:

'I showed her up to the room where the claimant was. I went in myself, and saw the claimant. Lady Tichborne walked in first, and I and Mr Holmes walked in afterwards. He was lying on the bed with his clothes on. He was lying with his face towards the wall. She stood over him and kissed him, and he stopped so, with his face to the wall. She said. "He looks like his father, and his ears look like his uncle's." As soon as she said that she turned round and told me to take his clothes off, as he was nearly stifled. I managed to turn him over and took his coat off. He told me to put some coals on the fire. Mr Holmes said, "You witness that; you hear how she has identified him?" and I said, "So do you." . . . He said nothing but remained lying on the bed.'

iii *A worthless recognition*

Lord Maugham makes this comment:

The reader will very likely ask himself the question: Was ever son after so long and strange an absence so recognised by a mother?
I am quite confident that the recognition by Lady Tichborne in the circumstances above briefly stated was little better than worthless. . . . It is equally certain that but for that recognition the Tichborne Case would never have occupied the Courts at all, at any rate not for many hours.

iv *The old family solicitor*

In addition to the Dowager, the 'Baronet' got a useful supporter in Mr Hopkins. He was the old family solicitor who had long retired from practice and still felt aggrieved that the management of

Tichborne legal affairs had been taken away from him. Perhaps this grievance made him ready to accept the 'Baronet.'

10 At Croydon

i *The 'Baronet' holds court*

On returning from Paris the 'Baronet' set up house at Essex Lodge, Croydon. He was apparently well supplied with money from supporters. He had a very expensive establishment – such as befitted a baronet. He had his wife and children with him and also the invaluable Bogle. He got his 'mother' the Dowager Lady Tichborne to join him there. He got ex-soldiers from the Carabineers (Roger's regiment) to come there – so that they should tell him of Roger's life in the army. This is Lord Maugham's description of it:

Essex Lodge at this time presented an animated scene and we may fancy that a visit to it was as amusing as a play. There was of course the claimant, a genial and I think, strange as it may seem, a dignified representative of the baronetage. He had not allowed constant worry to affect his weight and he now turned the scale at twenty-five stone. There were ex-troopers smoking and drinking in the principal rooms, and from time to time some of them would be sleeping in the attics. Anyone who had ever met, or said he had met, Roger Tichborne was a welcome visitor and he was naturally offered free beer before he made an affidavit. . . . Bogle, Carter and McCann were there as servants or at any rate they lived with the servants. The wife of the claimant and her two children and their attractive nurse were in the background.

ii *The frail old Dowager*

And finally there was the gently nurtured Dowager, a very small, frail, white-haired lady with big dark eyes and the remains of beauty, who shrank from the noise, and the drink, and the rough language of the troopers. She became progressively more unhappy, and by the end of April (1867) she could stand the Croydon household no longer. There is evidence from the nurse that she used to weep alone in her room. But she seems seldom or never to have admitted to feeling any doubt as to whether the claimant was really her son.

11 Kate is accused

i *The 'sealed packet'*

Although the Dowager had – or was said to have – recognised the 'Baronet' as her son Roger, the trustees of the Tichborne estates had not done so. In order to get hold of the estates, the 'Baronet' had to take legal proceedings. These were started in Chancery. The 'Baronet' made an affidavit in support of his claim. He was cross-examined on it in 1867 before a special examiner. So was Mr Gosford, the steward of the Tichborne estates. He was asked about the 'sealed packet' (of which I have told you). He said he had destroyed it after Roger's death. This gave the 'Baronet' a great opportunity, because (according to him) he, as Roger Tichborne, had alleged in it that he had seduced his cousin Kate. This is what it said according to the 'Baronet':

'November 1852

> If it be true that my cousin Kate Doughty should prove to be *enciente* [sic], you are to make the necessary arrangements. . . . You are to show great kindness to her, and let her have everything she requires. . . .'

ii *The forgery*

It was a palpable forgery. He could not spell '*enceinte*' which means 'with child.' His allegation was investigated at length during the subsequent trials. The newspapers were full of it.

iii *The perjury*

Lord Maugham describes the cross-examination:

> Question: 'Do you mean to swear before the Judge and jury that you seduced this lady?' To which the claimant made the amazing reply, 'I most solemnly to my God swear I did.' Even those adherents who believed that the witness was guilty of this misdeed appear to have been a little shocked at the invocation of God in such a connection.

The comment of an independent observer was:

> 'A blacker lie was never committed to paper, and a more diabolical plot was never framed by the heart of man.'

It was one of the principal charges of perjury on which the 'Baronet' was convicted.

iv *Disaster befalls the 'Baronet'*

Soon afterwards disaster befell the claim of the 'Baronet.' On the 12 March 1868 the Dowager died. The 'Baronet' attended the funeral as chief mourner. No doubt he was deeply moved. He had lost the trump card in his hand. In the next October the other buttress of the 'Baronet's' case – Mr Hopkins, the old family solicitor – also died. To add to these disasters a number of relatives and friends of Roger

Tichborne were convinced that the 'Baronet' was an impudent impostor and would give evidence against him.

12 The civil action

i *The action of ejectment*

Eventually the Court of Chancery gave leave to the claimant to bring an action at law in 'ejectment.' He brought it in the name of 'Sir Roger Tichborne Bart.' He claimed that he was entitled to the Tichborne estates and asked for an order to eject the trustees from those estates. It was ordered to be tried by a jury. The case was heard before Sir William Bovill, the Chief Justice of the Common Pleas. The leading counsel for the claimant were Serjeant Ballantine (of the highest repute) and Mr Hardinge Giffard QC (afterwards Lord Halsbury, thrice Lord Chancellor). The trustees were represented by Sir John Duke Coleridge, the Solicitor-General (afterwards Lord Chief Justice) and Mr Hawkins QC (afterwards Lord Brampton). Lord Maugham gives the speeches and evidence at length, covering 160 pages.

ii *The jury stop the case*

I go straight to the end. The jury were much influenced by the evidence of Lord Bellew (about the tattoo marks) and Mrs Radcliffe, née Kate Doughty (showing her innocence). On the 102nd day of the trial, the 5 March 1872, the foreman of the jury rose and said:

> 'We have heard the evidence regarding the tattoo marks; and subject to your Lordship's directions, and to the hearing of any further evidence that counsel may desire to place before them, the jury do not require any further evidence.'

iii *Non-suit*

On the next Wednesday:

> Ballantine asked whether the jury by their interposition had meant that they had satisfied themselves solely upon that portion of the case which related to the tattoo marks, or whether they had formed their opinion on the whole case. The jury asked leave to retire, and after an absence of half an hour they returned to state that their decision was based upon the entire evidence as well as upon that which concerned the tattoo marks. Upon this Ballantine in a short and dignified speech said that with the consent of his client and the approval of his learned friends (which of course included Giffard) he elected to be non-suited.

You may wonder what that means – a non-suit! It means that the claimant withdraws his claim and elects not to proceed further with it. But it is not a judgment against him. He can start again if he wishes! This is how Lord Maugham puts it:

The non-suit was a peculiar feature of our laws. It put an end to an action without either a verdict of a jury or a decision of the Judge: it was little more than a formal record of the fact that the plaintiff elected not to proceed with his action and submitted to pay the defendant's costs. Ballantine perhaps thought that, at the worst, time would elapse before criminal proceedings could be launched against the claimant, who in the meantime would have an opportunity of disappearing.

iv *The Lord Chief Justice acts*

The Lord Chief Justice however considered that the case required an exceptional step. After expressing his complete approval of the course taken by the jury, he observed that in his opinion the claimant had been guilty of wilful and corrupt perjury, and that there was reasonable ground for directing him to be prosecuted on that charge. He accordingly committed the claimant to be detained in the Common Gaol until the next session of the Central Criminal Court unless he should find bail to the amount of £10,000. He also added that he thought it right to express his entire belief in the evidence given by Mrs Radcliffe, depending not on her testimony alone, but confirmed by letters, correspondence, and all the other evidence in the case.

v *Off to Newgate*

Until now the 'Baronet' had been staying at an expensive hotel in Jermyn Street. Now he was arrested and taken to Newgate:

During the latter days of the trial the claimant had been absent from the Court. He was staying at the Waterloo Hotel, Jermyn Street, where he had resided throughout the case. He was arrested there without any difficulty by three police officers in the afternoon of the conclusion of the case. He received them with great composure and remarked that his arrest at that time would put him to considerable inconvenience. The brougham which he had used daily for a year to go to and from the Court was now employed to take him to Newgate; and it is interesting to note that he was cheered when he entered the walls of that magnificent, but gloomy, prison.

13 The criminal case

i *A true bill*

On the 9th April the grand jury at the Central Criminal Court returned a true bill on all the indictments of perjury and forgery, and shortly afterwards the case was removed on *certiorari* to the Court of Queen's Bench on the application of the Attorney-General.

ii *The charge of perjury*

So he was indicted for perjury. The case was regarded as of so great importance that it was ordered to be a 'trial at Bar,' that is, before three Judges. It was presided over by Sir Alexander Cockburn, Lord Chief Justice of the Queen's Bench. It took some time to come on. The claimant was on bail. Lord Maugham describes vividly what went on during the interval:

The steps the claimant took in the interval may not unfairly be described as involving methods of systematic agitation. There was hardly a large town in England in which he did not appear on a public platform and address a crowded meeting, supported either by Mr Guildford Onslow M.P. and Mr Whalley M.P. or some other fervid supporters. Appeals for money to conduct Sir Roger's defence were made in harangues which contained violent attacks on the witnesses hostile to the claimant. The audiences appear to have been unanimous in their belief that he was a greatly ill-used man, and at theatres, music-halls, pigeon-shooting matches and open-air fêtes he was treated as a national hero. His prowess as a shot at the Gun Club and elsewhere was regarded as strong proof of his identity. A journal called *The Tichborne Gazette* was started, (a copy lies before me, price one penny), to exploit the imaginary wrongs of Sir Roger, and to publish long lists of subscribers to his defence fund. When the claimant visited Alresford with Mr Guildford Onslow, with whom he happened to be staying, the horses were taken from the wagonette and the carriage was drawn by the crowd into the yard of the Swan Hotel where fiery speeches were of course delivered. The claimant began his oration with the words 'Friends, tenants and neighbours,' a fine Caesarean allocution. These proceedings were very disturbing to those in charge of the prosecution, and various applications were made to commit some of the speakers for contempt of Court.

iii *The trial*

The trial took place in one of the several Courts on the right hand side of Westminster Hall looking from Palace Yard. The indictment being confined to misdemeanours, there was no right to challenge jurymen.

Serjeant Ballantine did not appear for the defendant. He had lost all faith in him. He was defended by Dr Kenealy who was so rude and insulting to the Judges – and made such unfounded charges – that he was severely rebuked by the Lord Chief Justice. He was later disbenched and disbarred.

iv *The jury's verdict*

The jury retired at three minutes past twelve and they returned into the crowded Court in thirty minutes. They found the defendant guilty on both counts, and in answer to the Lord Chief Justice, the foreman read the following paper:

'We find, first, that the defendant is not Roger Charles Doughty Tichborne; secondly, we find that the defendant did not seduce Miss Katharine Doughty, now

Lady Radcliffe; and we further believe that there is not the slightest evidence that Roger ever was guilty of undue familiarity with Miss Katharine Doughty on any occasion whatever. Thirdly, we find that the defendant is Arthur Orton.'

They added as the opinion of them all:

'That the charges of bribery, conspiracy, and undue influence made against the prosecution in this case are entirely devoid of foundation, and we regret extremely the violent language and demeanour of the leading counsel for the defendant, and his attacks on the counsel for the prosecution, and on several of the witnesses produced in the cause.'

You see from their statement that they had been much influenced by the claimant's wicked assertion that he, as Roger Tichborne, had seduced Kate Doughty. He was sentenced to fourteen years' penal servitude.

Thus ended on Saturday the 28th February 1874, the 188th day of the trial, one of the most remarkable and certainly the longest criminal trial which up to that date had ever occupied an English Court of Justice.

In modern times the criminal trial should have been finished in a few days. Blood tests, handwriting experts, and medical evidence about tattoo marks should have made short work of it.

15 The Empire-Builder

Introduction

You may think it odd that I should have a chapter on *Cecil Rhodes.* It is a little known book by a Professor of History, Basil Williams. He was well qualified to write because, as a young clerk to Parliament, he attended the Committee of Inquiry on the Jameson Raid.

I have chosen the book because in 1921 when I was aged twenty-two I was much influenced by it. I have written in it, 'A T Denning, Feb 1921'. I wonder why it influenced me. I bought it when I was first employed. I was a 'don' – as they call them – teaching at Winchester College. My salary was £350 a year. But I did not want to be a schoolmaster all my life. The book on Rhodes influenced me in two ways: first, it showed what ambition and enterprise could achieve; second, it showed the value of Oxford life. At any rate I decided to give up teaching and return to Oxford and read law. I cannot rate Basil Williams as a great writer of prose, but this chapter has enabled me to introduce to you samples of the prose of Edward Gibbon, John Ruskin and Samuel Johnson – each relevant to the topic in hand.

1 Life at Oxford

I value greatly my time at Oxford just as Rhodes did. He regarded it so highly that he founded the Rhodes Scholarships available only at Oxford. He regarded it very differently from Edward Gibbon whose own *Life* is widely recognised as the best autobiography in the English language. He was at my own college, Magdalen, and tells of his going there. It is a good example of his stately prose:

i *Edward Gibbon at Magdalen*

My own introduction to the university of Oxford forms a new era in my life; and at the distance of forty years I still remember my first emotions of surprise and satisfaction. In my fifteenth year I felt myself suddenly raised from a boy to a man: the persons, whom I respected as my superiors in age and academical rank, entertained me with every mark of attention and civility; and my vanity was flattered by the velvet cap and silk gown, which distinguish a gentleman commoner from a plebeian student. A decent allowance, more money than a schoolboy had ever seen, was at my own disposal; and I might command, among the tradesmen of Oxford, an indefinite and dangerous latitude of credit. A key was delivered into my hands, which gave me the free use of a numerous and learned library, my apartment consisted of three elegant and well-furnished rooms in the new building, a stately pile, of Magdalen College, and the adjacent walks, had they been frequented by Plato's disciples, might have been compared to the Attic shade on the banks of the Ilissus. Such was the fair prospect of my entrance (April 3, 1752) into the university of Oxford.

The new buildings of 1752 are still there and still called in 1985 'the new buildings', recently restored. The adjacent walks are still there, called 'Addison's Walk' after Joseph Addison who was a Fellow there in 1700.

ii *He was sent down*

But Edward Gibbon was sent down for not doing any work:

To the university of Oxford I acknowledge no obligation; and she will as cheerfully renounce me for a son, as I am willing to disclaim her for a mother. I spent fourteen months at Magdalen College; they proved the fourteen months the most idle and unprofitable of my whole life: the reader will pronounce between the school and the scholar; but I cannot affect to believe that Nature had disqualified me for all literary pursuits.

He goes on to say that if he had been properly taught:

. . . my hours would have been occupied by useful and agreeable studies, the wanderings of fancy would have been restrained, and I should have escaped the temptations of idleness, which finally precipitated my departure from Oxford.

iii *Cecil Rhodes at Oriel*

But to return from the historian Gibbon to the man of action Rhodes. He matriculated at Oxford in 1873 – 120 years after Gibbon. So he went to Oriel as a passman. (His statue there overlooks the High.) There – with no knowledge of Greek or Latin – he became inspired with the philosophy of the ancients:

iv *The Oxford spirit*

But though he was so different from most of his undergraduate contemporaries, the Oxford spirit, so hard to define and yet so easy to recognize, sank into his nature. Aristotle's Ethics, the groundwork and the special glory of the Oxford system, with its virile appeal to young men to exercise their best faculties to the full, in order to attain a life of happiness and virtue, became to him a lasting source of inspiration: Gibbon, too, most characteristic, if most ungrateful, of Oxford's sons, gave him a basis for his political creed, that Rome's burden of governing the world had now fallen on England's shoulders.

v *John Ruskin at Oxford*

But it was not Aristotle's Ethics that influenced Rhodes. It was the teaching of John Ruskin – not in the school of painting or art – but in the school of empire-building. Ruskin gave his Inaugural Lecture in 1873 – the same year as Rhodes matriculated:

There, too, during Rhodes's years at Oxford, was John Ruskin, preaching a new gospel of beauty and of public service to an age wearied of ugliness and commercial self-interest; the whole university thronged to his lectures; at his bidding dons and undergraduates went out daily to Hinksey and took off their coats to labour at Ruskin's road and learn the meaning of hard, unselfish toil; in language rarely surpassed for eloquence and burning conviction he was setting before them their duty as citizens of no mean city.

vi *A call to 'young Oxford'*

Ruskin's style was florid but effective. It inspired the young:

'There is a destiny now possible to us,' so spake the prophet in words yet ringing in the ears of young Oxford, when Rhodes came up, 'the highest ever set before a nation to be accepted or refused. We are still undegenerate in race; a race mingled of the best northern blood. We are not yet dissolute in temper, but still have the firmness to govern and the grace to obey. . . . Will you youths of England make your country again a royal throne of kings; a sceptred isle, for all the world a source of light, a centre of peace; mistress of learning and of the Arts, faithful guardian of time-tried principles, under temptation from fond experiments and licentious desires; and amidst the cruel and clamorous jealousies of the nations, worshipped in her strange valour, of goodwill towards men?'

vii *Colonisation*

Ruskin preached colonisation in a manner which was popular in those days but utterly discredited now:

'This is what England must either do, or perish: she must found colonies as fast and as far as she is able, formed of her most energetic and worthiest men; seizing every piece of fruitful waste ground she can set her foot on, and there teaching these her colonists that their chief virtue is to be fidelity to their country, and that their first aim is to be to advance the power of England by land and sea: and that, though they live on a distant plot of ground, they are no more to consider themselves therefore disfranchised from their native land than the sailors of her fleets do, because they float on distant seas.'

viii *'An impossible ideal'*

Ruskin went on to proclaim his ideal:

'. . . If we can get men, for little pay, to cast themselves against cannon-mouths for love of England, we may find men also who will plough and sow for her, who will behave kindly and righteously for her, and who will bring up their children to love her, and who will gladden themselves in the brightness of her glory, more than in all the light of tropical skies. . . . You think that an impossible ideal. Be it so; refuse to accept it, if you will; but see that you form your own in its stead. All that I ask of you is to have a fixed purpose of some kind for your country and for yourselves, no matter how restricted, so that it be fixed and unselfish.'

It was for words such as those that Rhodes ever afterwards held the Inaugural Lecture as one of his greatest possessions. He jotted down his own thoughts on it, but it was more the Oxford spirit that influenced him.

ix *The most valuable part*

But to Rhodes, as to most university men, teachers however inspired and lectures however sublime were not the most valuable part of Oxford life. The freedom and unconventionality of the undergraduate, untrammelled as he is by pompous precedents, yet insensibly moulded by a tradition of fastidious scholarship and exact research of truth, the interminable discussions wherein generation after generation of Oxford men renew the investigation of common beliefs in politics, religion and morals, and constantly bring currents of fresh air into the nation's creeds – all this delighted and impressed him.

2 Life in South Africa

i *Diamonds and gold*

Oxford was one great influence on Rhodes. The other was his life amongst the diamond-seekers and gold-diggers in South Africa. He was born in 1853, the son of the Vicar of Bishops Stortford. He went to the grammar school there. Leaving at sixteen, he was weakly – fearing consumption – and was sent to South Africa for his health. Whilst still only a lad of eighteen or nineteen, he grew cotton, he found diamonds, he dug for gold, he made money. At the age of twenty, he went up to Oxford. He did not stay his three years straight off. He went to and from South Africa, keeping terms in between. He did not take his degree until 1881 when he was twenty-eight. But by that time he had amassed huge wealth. He did it by great energy and acute business sense, acquiring diamond-mines and gold-mines and dealing in stocks and shares. He formed the De Beers Mining Company and entered politics. In a few years he became Prime Minister of the Cape Province.

ii *Rhodesia named*

In 1889 at the age of thirty-six, he got a Charter incorporating the British South Africa Company. He became its managing director with almost absolute power. It had control over a vast territory which was given the name Rhodesia. He said to one of his friends:

> Well, you know, to have a bit of country named after one is one of the things a man might be proud of.

His pride, however, was mistaken. The march of time has overtaken it. It is now called Zimbabwe.

iii *At the topmost round*

By 1895 when he was only forty-two, Rhodes had reached the height of his fame. Basil Williams describes it:

> By 1895 Rhodes was at the pinnacle of success and glory. A life-time's thought, no doubt, but only six years' ostensible work had enabled him to 'paint the map of Africa red' to a greater extent than had been accomplished by the labours of previous centuries. And it was no mere painting of the map. Over a large part of this great dominion, 750,000 square miles in extent, larger than Spain, France and the former German Empire put together, order and settled government had been established; no internal or external danger to its peace gave cause for apprehension.... The climate had been proved healthy and fit for white men to work in and rear families. Already Rhodes's wish, 'Homes, more homes, that is what I want,' formulated as he looked over the uplands of Rhodesia....

iv *His wealth is not all*

Rhodes's great wealth was no doubt a large factor in his success; and there was an element of truth in the critic's envious comment that it was easy for him to attain his objects 'with your armies and your gold and with all the quiet, majestic, resistless advance of an elephant through brushwood.' He himself never underestimated this factor. 'If we have imaginative ideas, we must have pounds, shillings and pence to carry them out,' he said.

v *The feeling of the people*

Rhodes himself knew that even with wealth and public spirit he could never have succeeded without the feeling of the people and his own persistence. In this matter of the feeling of the people he had the true instinct of the great statesman. 'We went far to the north,' he told a Cape Town audience; 'we occupied all short of the Zambesi; we did it by the feeling of the people. For after all, even if you have the wealth, it is impossible to carry out a conception unless you have the feeling of the people with you; . . . and I have found out one thing,' he added, 'and that is, if you have an idea and it is a good idea, if you will only stick to it, you will come out all right. . . . In those early days everyone was against me. When I pointed out to the House, as an individual member, that the hinterland must be preserved, I could not get a vote, I could not get a single vote; and one had to continue at the question in spite of every difficulty. I made the seizure of the interior a paramount thing in my politics and made everything else subordinate. . . . My paramount object weighed with me as supreme.'

vi *A Colossus*

His ambition was achieved. He was a Colossus bestriding Southern Africa from Cape Town in the south to the Zambesi in the north.

You will see that I use the same simile as Shakespeare:

> He doth bestride the narrow world
> Like a Colossus.[1]

The Colossus of Rhodes was one of the Seven Wonders of the World. It was completed about 280 BC and stood 105 feet high. There is nothing to support the story which arose in the 16th Century that it was built 'bestriding' the harbour – with tall ships sailing between the legs.

vii *He never married*

Whenever we read about a great man, we want to know about his wife: because she is so important in helping or hindering his achievements. That was important for Rhodes. He had no wife.

He himself indeed once contemplated marriage, but later he came to the conclusion that he could never marry: his reason being that he had so much to do in the world that he could not give a wife as much of his thought and care as she was entitled to get. Possibly, had he met the right woman, he would have changed his mind. It would certainly have been happier for him to have had a good wife: she might have saved him from many mistakes of his later years and calmed the fiery outbursts that did him and his cause no good: and there is no doubt that she would have had a most considerate husband.

3 Decline of Rhodes

i *Spoilt by success*

Basil Williams gives a vivid picture of the decline of Cecil Rhodes. He had a lovely house and garden at Groote Schuur near Cape Town:

[1] *Julius Caesar*, Act I, sc 2.

and in London he had a permanent suite at the Burlington Hotel. But his wealth and his success had spoilt him. In 1895, aged forty-two, he felt he might die at forty-five. He lived till 1902 and died at forty-nine.

By 1895 a subtle change was coming over him: he was losing some of his powers of self-restraint and of waiting upon the occasion. His health was partly to blame. Although his big burly form seemed to have overcome the early disposition to consumption, he had recently had warnings of the heart trouble which in the end was to prove fatal . . . he used often to say that he would not live beyond forty-five, and that, within his few remaining years, he must accomplish all he still had left unfinished. With this obsession upon him, he began to feel that the time for patient and laborious methods was past and to give rein to his natural impatience. Power, too, and success had begun to spoil him. He became strangely arrogant: old friends noted with pain the change from his former simple and boyish good-fellowship to the almost pompous and overweening attitude of the later Rhodes. 'Newspapers,' he once roared out; 'do you think I care a continental fig what the newspapers may say? I am strong enough to do what I choose in spite of the whole pack of them.' He was beginning to say in his heart that he was not as other men, but like a god, and that he had only to say, it shall be so, and it was so. This arrogant spirit was encouraged and pampered by his surroundings. He had turned away or lost many of his old friends, and in their place had come a horde of flatterers, secretaries and second-rate Dutchmen, who lived on him and treated him as Canute was treated by his courtiers. At the Burlington his ante-chamber was thronged, like my Lord Chesterfield's, with needy parasites in search of a favour; and the Dr Johnsons too rarely found access.

The references are so apt that I would expand on them.

ii *Canute and his courtiers*

This story is often misunderstood. Canute was King of England from 1016–1035 AD. His courtiers had flattered him by telling him that he was all-powerful. To show that they were wrong, he sat by the rising tide in Southampton Water and bade the water to go back. When it rose and wetted his feet, he turned to the courtiers, saying, 'Look how little power I have. I cannot by my command stop so much as this small portion of water.'

ii *Dr Johnson's letter to Lord Chesterfield*

When Samuel Johnson was struggling for a living, he approached the prominent politician Lord Chesterfield for his support as patron. But Lord Chesterfield ignored him. Then when Johnson was bringing out his great *Dictionary*, Lord Chesterfield wrote articles commending it. Thereupon Johnson wrote a letter to Lord Chesterfield, of which Boswell afterwards managed to get 'a perfect transcript of what the world had so eagerly desired to see.' It is a superb irony on the role of a patron:

My Lord,

. . .

When, upon some slight encouragement, I first visited your lordship, I was overpowered, like the rest of mankind, by the enchantment of your address, and could not forbear to wish that I might boast myself *le vainqueur du vainqueur de la terre* – that I might obtain that regard for which I saw the world contending; but I found my attendance so little encouraged that neither pride nor modesty would suffer me to continue it. When I had once addressed your lordship in public, I had exhausted all the art of pleasing which a retired and uncourtly scholar can possess. I had done all that I could; and no man is well pleased to have his all neglected, be it ever so little.

. . .

Seven years, my lord, have now passed since I waited in your outward rooms, or was repulsed from your door; during which time I have been pushing on my work through difficulties of which it is useless to complain, and have brought it, at last, to the verge of publication, without one act of assistance, one word of encouragement, or one smile of favour. Such treatment I did not expect, for I never had a patron before.

. . .

Is not a patron, my lord, one who looks with unconcern on a man struggling for life in the water, and, when he has reached ground, encumbers him with help? The notice which you have been pleased to take of my labours, had it been early, had been kind: but it has been delayed till I am indifferent, and cannot enjoy it; till I am solitary, and cannot impart it; till I am known, and do not want it. I hope it is no very cynical asperity not to confess obligations where no benefit has been received, or to be unwilling that the public should consider me as owing that to a patron which Providence has enabled me to do for myself.

. . .

Sam. Johnson.

4 The fall of Rhodes

i *Dr Jameson – his close friend*

The fall of Cecil Rhodes was due to the failure of the Jameson Raid. To understand it, you must know that the Cape Province (based on Cape Town under Rhodes) was predominantly British: and that the Transvaal (based on Johannesburg under Kruger) was predominantly Dutch. Rhodes had the idea of bringing the Transvaal into the orbit of the British Empire. But he was opposed by the formidable old man, Kruger, of the Transvaal. Kruger was supported by the Germans who wanted to make it part of the German Empire. This roused Rhodes's apprehensions. So much so that he took part in a plot to invade the Transvaal. He chose as its leader Dr Jameson.

Starr Jameson, a young Scottish doctor, was of the same age as Rhodes. He had gone out to South Africa, like Rhodes, because of a weak lung. They became close friends. Jameson was a brilliant man. Rhodes had advanced him to be Administrator of Southern Rhodesia.

ii *The English rebels*

Now there were in the Transvaal a group of men called the 'Uitlanders', mostly men of British descent. They had been badly treated by Kruger. A large number at Johannesburg were so indignant that they contemplated rebelling against Kruger. They were, however, as sheep without a shepherd and had neither arms nor plans for a successful revolt. Rhodes became convinced that if the rising was to be a success, he himself must take a hand in it. So he became party to the plot which was to become his downfall.

iii *The plot*

The plot was that 5,000 rifles and a million rounds of ammunition were to be smuggled into the Transvaal to help the rebels: that, at a given signal, Jameson should cross the border at the head of 1,500 men, with guns and Maxims. The date tentatively fixed for the rising was 28 December 1895. All was to be paid for by Rhodes.

iv *Difficulties arise*

All sorts of difficulties arose, about which I will not write in detail. Jameson did not get 1,500 men together. He only got 600. Many of these were regular officers seconded from the British army under Sir John Willoughby, Major of the Horse Guards. They were a high-spirited lot, keen to show their mettle:

> If Jameson himself was rash, these regular officers gave him very little ballast; all seem to have regarded the success of the expedition as a foregone conclusion and to have undertaken it with the light-hearted carelessness of cheery schoolboys.

Arms had been smuggled into Johannesburg but nowhere near the 5,000 rifles. And the English rebels themselves were quarrelling about the flag and all sorts of things.

v *Rhodes orders postponement*

In view of these difficulties, Rhodes decided that the rising should not take place then. It was to be postponed until the Johannesburg rebels were readier. Throughout 26, 27 and 28 December telegrams were being sent to Jameson bidding him stand fast.

vi *Jameson does not obey*

Jameson was restless. He thought he would be like Nelson. He turned a blind eye or a deaf ear to the messages from Rhodes. He was tired of delays and of the excuses put forward for postponement. He thought they were simply signs of oozing courage. And his 600 young cavalrymen – impetuous and rash – were all for rushing in. Moreover, there were signs that the secret was leaking out:

> For all these reasons he (Jameson) decided he must act at once if at all: 'You may say what you like,' he is reported to have exclaimed, as he rose from reading Macaulay's essay, 'but Clive would have done it!' So, in spite of Rhodes's direct and reiterated orders, he prepared to 'do the best he could as circumstances arise.'

vii *A repeat performance*

It is almost a repeat performance of the difference when the over-confident Brutus overruled the reluctant Cassius and in consequence suffered defeat at Philippi:[1]

> There is a tide in the affairs of men,
> Which taken at the flood, leads on to fortune;
> Omitted, all the voyage of their life
> Is bound in shallows, and in miseries.
> On such a full sea are we now afloat;
> And we must take the current when it serves,
> Or lose our ventures.

viii *Jameson risks it*

On the morning of Sunday 29 December Jameson sent a telegram to Rhodes saying that he was starting that night. Rhodes at once drafted a telegram ordering him on no account to move. But the telegram never got to Jameson. The telegraph offices were shut for the rest of the day; and by the evening the lines to Cape Town had been cut by troopers. So the telegram was never sent off.

But Rhodes did not know this. He hoped the telegram had gone, and that Jameson had not ridden in. On that fateful Sunday 29 December, a senior Minister and one of his oldest friends, W P Schreiner (who had heard rumours of the plot) went to Groote Schuur and warned Rhodes against having anything to do with it. Rhodes appeared unconcerned:

> 'Oh, that's all right,' said Rhodes, shrugging his shoulders: he then still hoped his telegram would recall Jameson.

(We are most interested in Schreiner because his son, Oliver Schreiner, was a dear friend of ours. He was a Justice of the Supreme Court of South Africa and took us to the Kruger Game Reserve.)

But on Monday 30 December, a despatch rider reached Schreiner with telegrams saying that Jameson had ridden into the Transvaal.

[1] Shakespeare, *Julius Caesar*, Act IV, sc 3.

Schreiner at once went to console Rhodes. Basil Williams gives Schreiner's own account:

ix *'Old Jameson has upset my apple-cart'*

Rhodes was out riding with a friend, so Schreiner left a message and went home to dinner. Hardly had he finished when Rhodes's boy came with a lantern to guide him through the woods to Groote Schuur. Schreiner came into Rhodes's study with the telegrams in his hand: 'The moment I saw him,' is Schreiner's own account, 'I saw a man I had never seen before. His appearance was utterly dejected and different. Before I could say a word, he said, "Yes, yes, it is true. Old Jameson has upset my apple-cart. It is all true." I said I had some telegrams. He said, "Never mind, it is all true. Old Jameson has upset my apple-cart."... I was staggered,' continues Schreiner; 'I said, "What do you mean, what can you mean?...Why did you not say anything to me yesterday when I was here?" and he said then at once, "I thought I had stopped him. I sent messages to stop him and did not want to say anything about it if I stopped him."... "Why do you not stop him now? Although he has ridden in you can still stop him." He said, "Poor old Jameson. Twenty years we have been friends, and now he goes in and ruins me. I cannot hinder him. I cannot go in and destroy him."' Then for three hours the two friends talked about this tragic ending to their partnership, for both at once saw that Rhodes's Ministry was doomed. 'During the entire interview,' says Schreiner, 'Mr Rhodes was really broken down. He was broken down. He was not the man who could be playing that part. Whatever the reason may have been, when I spoke to him he was broken down.... He was absolutely broken down in spirit, ruined ... I left in very great distress.' That one may well believe; for Schreiner was one of Rhodes's most faithful followers.

x *Jameson surrenders*

On Thursday 2 January 1896, Jameson and his whole party surrendered to the Boers at Doornkop, near Krugersdorp, twenty miles short of their goal.

At that very moment the Kaiser, the German Emperor, sent a telegram of congratulation to Kruger. The British nation were furious. We were not going to stand any German interference in South Africa. We promptly ordered out the fleet as a warning. (Eighteen years later we had to deal with that self-same Kaiser – at a great cost to ourselves in lives.)

xi *Sentence on Jameson*

Jameson and his officers were handed over by Kruger to the British authorities and, after a trial at bar, were sentenced to terms of imprisonment. The rebels in Johannesburg were put on trial in the Transvaal and the leaders sentenced to death but those sentences were commuted for fines. Rhodes paid all the fines, costs and expenses.

There was a Committee of Inquiry in Cape Town. But far more serious was the inquiry by a Committee of the House of Commons in 1897. This is Basil Williams' description of it:

5 The trial of Rhodes

i *A dull committee-room*

No such scene greeted him at the inquiry in London as that immortalized by Macaulay in his description of the trial of Warren Hastings.... The setting was not Rufus's Hall, but a dull committee-room adjoining. No beauty, rank or eminence graced the proceedings, for all but those connected in some way with the case were rigidly excluded. Dramatic moments, indeed, there were: ... but there was no eager crowd, swayed by divergent feelings, to share in and murmur at the exciting moments.

ii *Rhodes is nervous*

... Rhodes took the inquiry very seriously, and on his voyage to England spent two hours every day on ship-board rehearsing his evidence with a friend: the friend had to ask the sort of questions he imagined Labouchère or Harcourt would put. 'Yes, that is a very fair question,' Rhodes would say, and carefully consider how he would answer it. In spite of all this preparation he was evidently nervous when he really found himself walking up to the little table placed in the centre of the horseshoe round which the Committee were sitting. He came in looking, as to features, very much like a Roman Emperor – massive head, masterful nose, and sleepy eyes, yet with a veiled fire in them – but in gait and gesture very unlike any Roman Emperor: ill-fitting clothes huddled on to an awkward body, a rather shambling walk and a half-dazed appearance. The first unfavourable impression was confirmed when he began to speak. His voice was squeaky and staccato, he sat humped up in his chair and was obviously ill at ease before his inquisitors. The answers he gave seemed involved and sometimes off the point. One began to wonder if this were really the great Colossus who bestrode half a continent. He seemed heavy, even stupid.

Here Basil Williams uses the same phrase as Shakespeare did about 'bestriding'.

iii *Rhodes takes the floor*

Then came the hour for luncheon, which, with characteristic disregard of ceremony, the Committee and witnesses ate off little trays brought in by a waiter, so that the proceedings were not interrupted. Rhodes murmured his order to the waiter and then went on as before. The luncheons were brought in; and before Rhodes was set a solitary sandwich and a large tankard of stout. One bite of the sandwich, one long draught from the tankard; and then, as if suddenly aroused by this diversion, he shook himself together, like a lion just awaking, pulled straight his coat, sat up square to his tormentors, sent forth a gleam from that hitherto sleepy eye, and then – he just took that Committee in hand. Hitherto they had seemed to play with him, henceforward the roles were reversed. There was no longer any question of examining Rhodes on his misdeeds; Rhodes himself took the floor and began examining the Committee on their knowledge of South Africa and lecturing them on things he thought it good for their souls to know. He enjoyed himself vastly. He dragged them away from the Raid, not because he wished to conceal his own part in the business – he stated quite frankly at the outset that he accepted full responsibility for it – but he brushed it aside as irrelevant, because he wanted to make that Committee, and through them the British public, understand their own mistakes and responsibility in South Africa and the policy for which he stood. Germany's part in Transvaal affairs? Oh, Germany's susceptibilities must be considered, and we must observe the correct diplomatic reticence, was the attitude of most of the Committee. Diplomacy go hang, said Rhodes in effect; you've got to know what I believe to be the facts: and these facts he proceeded to tell them. He had five days in that witness chair; but once he was on his mettle he never let that Committee go.

iv *The verdict*

The verdict of this Committee was very much the same as that of the Cape inquiry. The Raid was condemned, and Rhodes was severely censured for the misuse of his office as Prime Minister of the Cape and managing director of the Chartered Company; that was the least which the national honour demanded, especially in view of assertions, such as Jameson's, 'I know, if I had succeeded, I should have been forgiven.'

v *The debate*

There was a debate in the Commons on the report. Some urged that the name of Rhodes should be removed from the list of Privy Councillors but the House would not listen to the suggestion. Most sympathised with him. All knew that if the Raid had succeeded he would have been received with acclaim.

The fact is that in many quarters in England there was little condemnation of the Raid. Rhodes was aware of this when he said, 'I found all the busmen smiling at me when I came to London; so I knew it was all right.'

6 His last years

At the time of his downfall in 1896 Rhodes was only forty-three. As I have said he suffered from heart trouble. It got progressively worse. He lived only six more years and died in 1902 at the age of forty-nine. But during that time he made his plans for his most enduring memorial – the Rhodes Scholarships at Oxford.

i *The Rhodes Scholarships*

His plan was to provide scholarships for students to come to Oxford from all the self-governing colonies and the United States of America.

In the final will of 1899, however, he laid down explicitly his central notion of a great educational scheme to apply to all the English-speaking portions of the globe. The plan he adopted, after long consultations with his friends Stead and Hawkesley, was to provide scholarships for young students from all the self-governing colonies and from the States of America of sufficient value to enable them to have courses at his own university of Oxford.

ii *His plan succeeds*

His founding of these scholarships places him in the same class as the great men of the past like William of Wykeham and Thomas Wolsey. This was the view of Basil Williams in 1921 – nearly twenty years after the death of Rhodes. It is equally true today – over eighty years after his death. The Rhodes Scholars from Oxford have played and still fill important roles all the world over. Many of them have been my friends.

These provisions for the 'Rhodes Scholarships' are those that attracted most attention in Rhodes's will: with these he was himself most happy. Lord Rosebery relates his saying to him: 'When I find myself in uncongenial company, or when people are playing their games, or when I am alone in a railway carriage, I shut my eyes and think of my great idea. I turn it over in my mind and try to get new light on it. It is the pleasantest companion I have.' The scheme has now been working for nearly twenty years, and it has proved at least as great a success as the founder hoped. At Oxford, chosen for his experiment *quia multum dilexit*, young men, from every corner of the British Empire and from every State of the great Republic our fathers founded, come yearly to be taught and to teach the common interests of good government, and to put into practice the Aristotelian theory of virtue, which Rhodes looked on as one of the great precepts of life, 'the exercise of the human faculties in such ways as to develop the highest excellence in the best circumstances.'

iii *His dominating personality*

Basil Williams gives this fascinating description of the force of Rhodes's dominating personality:

He was one of those rare beings of whom one can say that, whatever he turned his hand to, he would have been a master; and, like all such beings, he seemed to have his star, his aura of success, which fascinated the world and made it yield him even more success than he had asked for. Yet, as with Caesar on the Ides of March, or with Napoleon at Waterloo, the star suddenly failed him at a crucial moment, because in his pride he presumed on success and forgot that the strongest may become intolerable. It is this gift of dominating personality which is most elusive to describe and yet which most interests the world, regardless of whether its owner succeeds or fails; the gift which makes all eyes turn to the man who has it, wherever he appears, though there may be others present who have achieved more or been greater benefactors to humanity. Who would turn to look at Brutus, who overcame Caesar, could he behold Caesar himself, or even Wellington, were Napoleon with him? A Gibbon, maybe, raised a monument to the Roman Empire and to himself greater than any single achievement of a Chatham: yet still Gibbon remains merely a man who wrote a great book, while Chatham, apart from any action, is a supreme personality. And so it was with Rhodes: you might hate him, you might loathe all he did, you might even think meanly of his actual achievement, but you could not ignore him any more than you could ignore a flash of lightning that suddenly blazes forth across a murky night.

iv *His memorial*

Rhodes was buried in his chosen resting-place – the View of the World in the Matoppos. His burial was attended by his close friends and a huge concourse of settlers and natives who were devoted to him. He was their great protector.

We have been to Cape Town and to the memorial on Table Mountain, designed by Herbert Baker. There is the impressive statue by F G Watts of 'Physical Energy' which symbolises Rhodes. It is of a horseman with his eyes fixed on the distant horizon, and his mount straining at the bit, leaping into the future. Inside the memorial there is a bust of Rhodes by J M Swan. On the pedestal there are Kipling's lines:

> The immense and brooding spirit still shall quicken and control.
> Living he was the land and dead his soul shall be her soul.

7 The future

In ten years from 1885 to 1895, from his age of thirty-two to forty-two, Cecil Rhodes built a great Empire – a British Empire – stretching far across Southern Africa. It was his dream come true. He painted it red on the map.

Now, a hundred years later, all is changed. Most countries of Southern Africa have become independent. Only Zimbabwe remains in our Commonwealth.

It was my task in 1960 to preside over a Conference on *The Future of Law in Africa*. I wrote a foreword for it. It is as appropriate today as it was in 1960. This is the last paragraph of it:

> Now is the time to think and do. Africa, like some great giant awaking out of centuries of slumber, stretches its limbs, stands up and looks at the dawn. It is the dawn of its own day it is looking at. We in the older civilisations have almost forgotten what that kind of dawn can be. We no longer expect to see the dew on the grass. But Africa sees it now and will soon be on the march. Can we not help it gird on its coat for the journey – it is a coat of many colours – the coat of African Law?

16 A country gentleman's recreation

Introduction

Izaak Walton is the patron saint of fishing, or as he would describe it, of angling. He published a book on it in 1653 which he called, felicitously, *The Compleat Angler, or the Contemplative Man's Recreation*. He was an ironmonger in London and, in his leisure, fished on the river Lea in Hertfordshire. But on his retirement, in the last ten years of his life, he made his home in or near our county of Hampshire. He praises highly the fine waters of Hampshire 'which I think exceeds all England for swift, shallow, clear, pleasant brooks, and store of trouts.' He often fished the upper reaches of the Itchen on his way to Winchester. He took a lease of 'Norington farme' at Overton, three miles up from us, 'near the head waters of the finest trout stream in England.' That is, of our river Test which runs through our garden and where we delight to have our friends to fish. Izaak is commemorated by a lovely stained glass window in our cathedral at Winchester. It shows him with a friend on the bank of the river Itchen, with St Catherine's Hill in the background.

1 *The Compleat Angler*

i *The feeling of happiness*

The Compleat Angler is held in high esteem, in part for its description of angling, in part for its quaint style, but above all for the feeling of happiness which it conveys to the reader.

It takes the form of a discourse between the author, Izaak, as 'Piscator' (a fisherman), 'Auceps' (a falconer) and 'Venator' (a hunter). 'Venator' is sometimes called the 'Scholar' because he is being taught fishing by the 'Master' Piscator. Each commends his own recreation. The Falconer praises his, and afterwards goes off. The Hunter stays on. He is persuaded to try angling and becomes the pupil of the Fisherman. But before doing so he takes the Fisherman for a short spell with the otter-hounds. Afterwards the Fisherman instructs the Hunter in the mode of catching all the various kinds of fresh-water fish, with instructions for dressing some of them for the table. They meet a milkmaid and her mother who sing songs for them. They go to the Inn for dinner and enjoy a freshly-caught trout. Happiness always. Never a word of discord or difference.

ii *The road to Ware*

In the first chapter, Izaak Walton sets the scene on the road from London to Ware. He (Piscator) overtakes the two others (Venator and Auceps) on the road and they start their discourse. Is is a road made famous a hundred years later by William Cowper in his poem about John Gilpin. I am sure you will have heard of it, but you may like to have it again. It always amazes me that that melancholy poet should have written such a diverting poem. It is very long with sixty-three verses, so I will shorten it to fifteen.

John Gilpin was 'a citizen of credit and renown' with his business in Cheapside. He and his wife decided to celebrate their twentieth wedding anniversary by going to dinner at 'The Bell' at Edmonton. His wife and her sister and four children filled the chaise. So John had to go separately on horseback. He borrowed a horse from a friend and got on it. But three customers came in and he had to dismount to serve them. He then found that his wife had left the wine behind. So he got two stone bottles, filled them with wine, and slung them across his shoulders, one on each side, like weights in a horse-race. He threw his long red cloak around him and got on the horse again. The horse started quietly enough on the stones of Cheapside, but when he got on to smooth road, the trouble began – and a story which delights young and old.

> But finding soon a smoother road
> Beneath his well-shod feet,
> The snorting beast began to trot,
> Which galled him in his seat.
>
> So 'Fair and softly,' John he cried,
> But John he cried in vain;
> That trot became a gallop soon,
> In spite of curb and rein.

So stooping down, as needs he must
   Who cannot sit upright,
He grasped the mane with both his hands
   And eke with all his might.

His horse, who never in that sort
   Had handled been before,
What thing upon his back had got
   Did wonder more and more.

Away went Gilpin, neck or naught;
   Away went hat and wig;
He little dreamt, when he set out,
   Of running such a rig....

The dogs did bark, the children screamed,
   Up flew the windows all;
And every soul cried out, 'Well done!'
   As loud as he could bawl.

Away went Gilpin – who but he?
   His fame soon spread around;
'He carries weight!' 'He rides a race!'
   ''Tis for a thousand pound!'

And still as fast as he drew near,
   'Twas wonderful to view,
How in a trice the turnpike men
   Their gates wide open threw....

He lost his cloak, the bottles shattered, he passed his wife at Edmonton and galloped on to Ware.

At Edmonton, his loving wife
   From the balcony espied
Her tender husband, wondering much
   To see how he did ride.

'Stop, stop, John Gilpin! – Here's the house!'
   They all at once did cry;
'The dinner waits, and we are tired:' –
   Said Gilpin – 'So am I!'

But yet his horse was not a whit
   Inclined to tarry there;
For why? – his owner had a house
   Full ten miles off, at Ware....

At Ware John decided that he must go back to Edmonton.

Said John – 'It is my wedding day,
   And all the world would stare,
If wife should dine at Edmonton,
   And I should dine at Ware.',...

The horse took him back, passed his wife at Edmonton and finished up at Cheapside again.

And now the turnpike gates again
Flew open in short space;
The tollmen thinking as before
That Gilpin rode a race.

And so he did, and won it too,
For he got first to town;
Nor stopped till where he had got up
He did again get down.

Now let us sing long live the King,
And Gilpin, long live he;
And when he next doth ride abroad,
May I be there to see!

2 Their Discourse

i *A fine May morning*

After that diversion, I return to the road to Ware as walked by Izaak Walton on a fine May morning. He (Piscator) overtakes Venator and Auceps.

Piscator. You are well overtaken, Gentlemen, a good morning to you both; I have stretched my legs up *Tottenham-hill* to overtake you, hoping your business may occasion you towards *Ware* whether I am going this fine, fresh *May* morning.

Venator. Sir, I for my part shall almost answer your hopes, for my purpose is to drink my mornings draught at the *Thatcht House* in *Hodsden*, and I think not to rest till I come thither, where I have appointed a friend or two to meet me: but for this Gentleman (the Falconer) that you see with me, I know not how far he intends his journey; he came so lately into my company, that I have scarce had time to ask him the question.

Auceps. Sir, I shall by your favour bear you company as far as *Theobalds*, and there leave you, for then I turn up to a friends house who mews[1] a Hawk for me, which I now long to see.

Venator. Sir, we are all so happy as to have a fine, fresh, cool morning, and I hope we shall each be the happier in the others company. And Gentlemen, that I may not lose yours, I shall either abate or amend my pace to enjoy it; knowing that (as the Italians say) *Good company in a Journey makes the way to seem the shorter.*

Auceps. It may do so Sir, with the help of good discourse, which methinks we may promise from you that both look and speak so chearfully: and for my part I

[1] 'Mews' means 'keeps in a cage or coop.'

promise you, as an invitation to it, that I will be as free and openhearted, as discretion will allow me to be with strangers.

Venator. and Sir, I promise the like.

3 The Otter

i *Hunting the otter*

The Hunter says he is going to hunt the otter. The Fisherman says he will help because otters can be destructive of fish.

Piscator. I am right glad to hear your answers, and in confidence you speak the truth, I shall put on a boldness to ask you Sir, Whether business or pleasure caused you to be so early up, and walk so fast, for this other Gentleman hath declared he is going to see a Hawk, that a friend mews for him.

Venator. Sir mine is a mixture of both, a little business and more pleasure, for I intend this day to do all my business, and then bestow another day or two in hunting the *Otter*, which a friend that I go to meet, tells me, is much pleasanter than any other chase whatsoever; howsoever I mean to try it; for to morrow morning we shall meet a pack of Otter dogs of *noble Mr Sadlers* upon *Amwell hill*, who will be there so early, that they intend to prevent[1] the Sun-rising.

Piscator. Sir, my fortune has answered my desires, and my purpose is to bestow a day or two in helping to destroy some of those villanous vermin, for I hate them perfectly, because they love fish so well, or rather, because they destroy so much; indeed so much, that in my judgment all men that keep *Otter-dogs* ought to have pensions from the King to encourage them to destroy the very breed of those base *Otters*, they do so much mischief.

4 Birds of the air

i *The hawk in his element*

The Falconer, as he has said, is on his way to see a friend who is mewing a hawk for him. The Falconer says that the air is his element and gives this ecstatic description of the falcon or hawk which obeys his command and eats out of his hand:

Auceps. ... In the Air my troops of Hawks soar up on high, and when they are lost in the sight of men, then they attend upon and converse with the gods, therefore I think my *Eagle* is so justly styled, *Joves servant in Ordinary*: and that very *Falcon*, that I am now going to see deserves no meaner a title, for she usually in her flight endangers herself, (like the son of *Daedalus*) to have her wings scorch'd by the Suns heat, she flyes so near it, but her mettle makes her careless of danger, for she then heeds nothing, but makes her nimble Pinions cut the fluid air, and so makes her

[1] 'Prevent,' in its old sense, meant 'to get there before.'

high way over the steepest mountains and deepest rivers, and in her glorious carere looks with contempt upon those high Steeples and magnificent Palaces which we adore and wonder at; from which height I can make her to descend by a word from my mouth (which she both knows and obeys) to accept of meat from my hand, to own me for her Master, to go home with me, and be willing the next day to afford me the like recreation.

ii *The songsters*

The Falconer goes on to pass by all other birds until he comes to the songsters. He tells most pleasingly of them.

... These I will pass by, but not those little nimble Musicians of the air, that warble forth their curious Ditties, with which Nature hath furnished them to the shame of Art.

As first the *Lark*, when she means to rejoyce; to chear her self and those that hear her, she then quits the earth, and sings as she ascends higher into the air, and having ended her Heavenly imployment, grows then mute and sad to think she must descend to the dull earth, which she would not touch but for necessity.

How do the *Black-bird* and *Thrassel* with their melodious voices bid welcome to the chearful Spring, and in their fixed Months warble forth such ditties, as no art or instrument can reach to?

Nay, the smaller birds also do the like in their particular seasons, as namely the *Leverock*, the *Tit-lark*, the little *Linnet*, and the honest *Robin*, that loves mankind both alive and dead.

But the *Nightingale* (another of my Airy Creatures) breathes such sweet loud musick out of her little instrumental throat, that it might make mankind to think Miracles are not ceased. He that at midnight (when the very labourer sleeps securely) should hear (as I have very often) the clear airs, the sweet descants, the natural rising and falling, the doubling and redoubling of her voice, might well be lifted above earth, and say; Lord, what Musick hast thou provided for the Saints in Heaven, when thou affordest bad men such musick on Earth!

5 The Milkmaid and her mother

As they were coming back from their fishing, they came upon a Milkmaid and her mother. The maid's name was *Maudlin* which was the common way then of pronouncing *Magdalen*. (Like my college at Oxford which is still always called *Maudlin* though spelt *Magdalen*.) Piscator had come upon them a few days before and they had sung songs for him. He decides to ask them to sing again: and in return to give them a chub they had just caught.

Piscator. God speed you, good woman, I have been a Fishing ... and having caught more Fish than will sup my self and my friend, I will bestow this upon you and your Daughter.

The Milkwoman thanks him, using good old-fashioned English words like Sillybub (a drink made of milk or cream, curdled with wine, cider or other acid), Verjuice (the acid juice of green crab-apples) and a Hay-cock (heap of hay) for it. (Has Hay-cock a different meaning here?)

Milkwoman. Marry God requite you Sir, and we'll eat it chearfully: and if you come this way a Fishing two months hence, a grace of God I'le give you a Sillybub of new Verjuice in a new made Hay-cock for it, and my *Maudlin* shall sing you one of her best *Ballads*; for she and I both love all *Anglers*, they be such honest, civil, quiet men; in the mean time will you drink a draught of *Red-Cows milk*, you shall have it freely.

Piscator. ...Sing us a song that was sung by your daughter when I last passed over this meadow, about eight or nine days since.

Milkwoman. What song was it, I pray? Was it '*Come shepherds, deck your herds*?' or '*As at noon Dulcina rested*?' or '*Phillida flouts me*?' or '*Chevy Chace*?' or '*Johnny Armstrong*?' or '*Troy Town*?'

Piscator. No, it is none of those; it is a song that your daughter sung the first part, and you sung the answer to it.

Milkwoman. ... Come, *Maudlin*, sing the first part to the Gentlemen with a merry heart; and I'll sing the second when you have done.

She sings the poem by Christopher Marlowe.

The Milkmaid's Song

Come live with me and be my Love,
And we will all the pleasures prove
That hills and valleys, dales and fields,
Or woods or steepy mountain yields.

...

The shepherd swains shall dance and sing
For thy delight each May morning:
If these delights thy mind may move,
Then live with me and be my Love.

Venator (the Scholar) then tells how the first Queen Elizabeth often wished to be a milkmaid.

Venator. Trust me, Master, it is a choice Song, and sweetly sung by honest *Maudlin*. I now see it was not without cause, that our good Queen *Elizabeth* did so often wish her self a Milkmaid all the month of *May*, because they are not troubled with fears and cares, but sing sweetly all the day, and sleep securely all the night: and without doubt, honest, innocent, pretty *Maudlin* does so.

The mother sings the reply by Sir Walter Raleigh.

The Milkmaid's Mother's Answer

If all the world and love were young,
And truth in every shepherd's tongue,
These pretty pleasures might me move
To live with thee, and be thy Love.

. . .

But could youth last, and love still breed,
Had joys no date, nor age no need,
Then these delights my mind might move
To live with thee and be thy Love.

Piscator. Well sung good Woman I thank you, I'le give you another dish of fish one of these days; and then, beg another Song of you. Come Scholar, let *Maudlin* alone: do not offer to spoil her voice.

As a postscript to that delightful picture, I will quote for you a letter by that charming girl, Dorothy Osborne, of June 1653:

You ask me how I pass my time here. . . . The heat of the day is spent in reading or working, and about six or seven o'clock I walk out into a common that lies hard by the house where a great many young wenches keep sheep and cows and sit in the shade singing of ballads. I talk to them and find they want nothing to make them the happiest people in the world, but the knowledge that they are so. Most commonly when we are in the midst of our discourse, one looks about her and spies her cows going into the corn, and then away they all run as if they had wings at their heels.

6 They go to the inn

i *They meet Brother Peter and Coridon*

After hearing the songs, Piscator and Venator (the Scholar) go to the inn, where they meet Peter, Piscator's brother, and his friend Coridon who are going to fish next morning.

Piscator. Well met Brother *Peter*, I heard you and a friend would lodge here to night, and that hath made me to bring my Friend to lodge here too. . . .

Peter. Brother *Piscator*, my friend is an honest *Country-man*, and his name is *Coridon*, and he is a downright witty companion that met me here purposely to be pleasant and eat a *Trout*. And I have not yet wetted my Line since we met together? but I hope to fit him with a *Trout* for his breakfast, for I'le be early up.

ii *They order supper*

Piscator says they have already caught a fine trout.

Piscator. Nay Brother you shall not stay so long: for look you here is a Trout will fill six reasonable bellies. Come Hostess, dress it presently, and get us what other meat the house will afford, and give us some of your best *Barly-wine*, the good liquor that our honest Fore-fathers did use to drink of; the drink which preserved their health, and made them live so long, and to do so many good deeds.

Peter. O' my word this *Trout* is perfect in season. Come, I thank you, and here is a hearty draught to you, and to all the brothers of the Angle wheresoever they be, and to my young brothers good fortune to morrow: I will furnish him with a Rod, if you will furnish him with the rest of the Tackling; we will set him up and make him a Fisher.

And I will tell him one thing for his encouragement, that his fortune hath made him happy to be Scholar to such a Master; a Master that knows as much both of the nature and breeding of fish as any man: and can also tell him as well how to catch and cook them, from the *Minnow* to the *Salmon*, as any that I ever met withall.

iii *A lovely trout with sauce*

It is a lovely trout and well seasoned with a good sauce.

Piscator. 'Tis enough, honest Scholar, come lets to supper. Come my friend *Coridon* this *Trout* looks lovely, it was twentie two inches when it was taken, and the belly of it looked some part of it as yellow as a Marigold, and part of it as white as a lilly, and yet methinks it looks better in this good sawce.

Coridon. Indeed honest friend, it looks well, and tastes well, I thank you for it, and so doth my friend *Peter*, or else he is to blame.

Peter. Yes, and so I do, we all thank you, and when we have supt, I will get my friend *Coridon* to sing you a Song for requital.

Coridon. I will sing a song, if any body will sing another; else, to be plain with you, *I will sing none*: I am none of those that sing for meat, but for company: I say, *'Tis merry in Hall, when men sing all.*

iv *Sheets smelling of lavender*

After the song by Coridon and some merriment, they go to bed – in nice sheets smelling of lavender.

Coridon. . . . And now lets every one go to bed that we may rise early; but first lets pay our reckoning, for I will have nothing to hinder me in the morning for my purpose is to prevent the Sun-rising.

Peter. A match; Come *Coridon*, you are to be my Bed-fellow: I know, brother, you and your Scholar will lie together; but where shall we meet to morrow night? for my friend *Coridon* and I will go up the water towards *Ware.*

Piscator. And my Scholar and I will go down towards *Waltham.*

Coridon. Then lets meet here, for here are fresh sheets that smell of *Lavender*, and I am sure we cannot expect better meat, or better usage in any place.

Peter. 'Tis a match. Good night to every body.

Piscator. And so say I.

Venator. And so say I.

7 Next day

i *Up early to fish*

Next morning they are up early and go off to the river to fish for trout.

Piscator. Good morrow good Hostess, I see my brother *Peter* is still in bed: Come give my Scholar and me a Morning-drink, and a bit of meat to breakfast, and be sure to get a good dish of meat or two against supper, for we shall come home as hungry as Hawks. Come Scholar, lets be going.

Venator. Well now, good Master, as we walk towards the River give me direction, according to your promise, how I shall fish for a *Trout.*

Piscator. My honest Scholar, I will take this very convenient opportunity to do it.

ii *A happy walk back*

After fishing and discourse, they have a happy walk back.

Piscator. Well, Scholar, having now taught you to paint your rod, and we having still a mile to Totnam High-Cross, I will, as we walk towards it, in the cool shade of this sweet honeysuckle hedge, mention to you some of the thoughts and joys that have possessed my soul since we two met together.

17 A curate's observations

Introduction

Now I jump a hundred years from Izaak Walton to Gilbert White. Selborne is one of the best known villages in England. There is nothing very special about it. But it has become famous because Gilbert White wrote about the district and the birds and animals that he saw there. He studied their habits and wrote letters about them to two of his friends. These were published in 1788 under the title of *The Natural History of Selborne.*

Gilbert White was a curate at Selborne. He was born there in 1720 and lived there for most of his life. His duties as curate were so light that he had time for his studies of natural history. His work is remarkable for his keenness of observation: but it has many passages of descriptive worth.

I am particularly interested in Gilbert White because he was a Junior Fellow of my own college, Magdalen College, Oxford. The living is in the gift of the college. One of my closest friends there was John Darlington. I was his best man. He was Rector of Selborne for many years and we visited him there. So we know the village well.

The Selborne country

This is Gilbert White's description of the situation of Selborne:

The parish of Selborne lies in the extreme eastern corner of the county of Hampshire, bordering on the county of Sussex, and not far from the county of Surrey. . . . The soils of this district are almost as various and diversified as the views and aspects. The high part of the south-west consists of a vast hill of chalk, rising three hundred feet above the village, and is divided into a sheep down, the high wood, and a long hanging wood, called The Hanger. The covert of this eminence is altogether *beech*, the most lovely of all forest trees, whether we consider its smooth rind or bark, its glossy foliage, or graceful pendulous boughs. The down, or sheep walk, is a pleasing parklike spot, of about one mile by half that space, jutting out on the verge of the hill country, where it begins to break down into the plains, and commanding a very engaging view, being an assemblage of hill, dale, woodlands, heath, and water. The prospect is bounded to the south-east and east by the vast range of mountains called the Sussex Downs. . . .

At the foot of this hill, one stage or step from the uplands, lies the village, which consists of one single straggling street, three quarters of a mile in length, in a sheltered vale, and running parallel with The Hanger.

i *The Raven Tree*

Here is the sad story of the raven which suffered death protecting its young:

In the centre of this grove there stood an oak, which, though shapely and tall on the whole, bulged out into a large excrescence about the middle of the stem. On this a pair of ravens had fixed their residence for such a series of years that the oak was distinguished by the title of the Raven Tree. Many were the attempts of the neighbouring youths to get at this eyry: the difficulty whetted their inclinations, and each was ambitious of surmounting the arduous task. But when they arrived at the swelling, it jutted out so in their way, and was so far beyond their grasp, that the most daring lads were awed, and acknowledged the undertaking to be too hazardous. So the ravens built on, nest upon nest, in perfect security, till the fatal day arrived in which the wood was to be levelled. It was in the month of February, when those birds usually sit. The saw was applied to the butt, the wedges were inserted into the opening, the woods echoed to the heavy blows of the beetle or mallet, the tree nodded to its fall; but still the dam sat on. At last, when it gave way, the bird was flung from her nest; and, though her parental affection deserved a better fate, was whipped down by the twigs, which brought her dead to the ground.

ii *The red deer*

Next there is the extinction of the red deer – a fine species of huge red deer with great antlers. They used to live in Wolmer Forest – a tract of land of seven miles by two and a half miles – mostly in the parish of Selborne. Gilbert White tells of the end of them.

. . . I mean the red-deer, which toward the beginning of this century amounted to about five hundred head, and made a stately appearance. There is an old keeper, now alive, named Adams, whose great-grandfather (mentioned in a perambulation taken in 1635), grandfather, father and self, enjoyed the head keepership of Wolmer Forest in succession for more than a hundred years. This person assures me, that his father has often told him, that Queen Anne, as she was journeying on the Portsmouth road, did not think the forest of Wolmer beneath her royal regard. For she came out of the great road at Lippock, which is just by, and, reposing herself on a bank smoothed for that purpose, lying about half a mile to the east of Wolmer Pond, and still called Queen's Bank, saw with great complacency and satisfaction the whole herd of red-deer brought by the keepers along the vale before her, consisting then of about five hundred head. A sight this worthy the attention of the greatest sovereign! But he farther adds that, by means of the Waltham blacks, or, to use his own expression, as soon as they began blacking, they were reduced to about fifty head, and so continued decreasing till the time of the late Duke of Cumberland. About the year 1737, his highness sent down a huntsman, and six yeomen-prickers, in scarlet jackets laced with gold, attended by the stag-hounds; ordering them to take every deer in this forest alive, and to convey them in carts to Windsor. In the course of the summer they caught every stag, some of which showed extraordinary diversion: but, in the following winter, when the hinds were also carried off, such fine chases were exhibited as served the country people for matter of talk and wonder for years afterwards. I saw myself one of the yeomen-prickers single out a stag from the herd, and must confess it was the most curious feat of activity I ever beheld. The exertions made by the horse and deer much exceeded all my expectations; though the former greatly excelled the latter in speed. When the devoted deer was separated from his companions, they gave him, by their watches, law, as they called it, for twenty minutes; when, sounding their horns, the stop-dogs were permitted to pursue, and a most gallant scene ensued.

It would seem that Gilbert White was not against hunting.

iii *Deer stealing*

He tells how prevalent deer stealing was by poachers until stopped by the Waltham 'Black Act.'

Our old race of deer stealers is hardly extinct yet: it was but a little while ago that, over their ale, they used to recount the exploits of their youth; such as watching the pregnant hind to her lair, and, when the calf was dropped, paring its feet with a penknife to the quick to prevent its escape, till it was large and fat enough to be killed; the shooting at one of their neighbors with a bullet in a turnip field by moonshine, mistaking him for a deer; and the losing a dog in the following extraordinary manner. Some fellows, suspecting that a calf new-fallen was deposited in a certain spot of thick fern, went, with a lurcher, to surprise it; when the parent hind rushed out of the brake, and, taking a vast spring with all her feet close together, pitched upon the neck of the dog, and broke it short in two.

iv *The swallows*

It is remarkable that Gilbert White thought that many of the swallow kind did not migrate to Africa but lived here for the winter in holes and caverns: but we all know that they fly off in September to pass the winter in the warmth of Africa, and come back in April. How nice it would be if we could all do the same! It is a familiar sight for us here when each year huge flocks of them gather together and fill the skies on their way south. But Gilbert White thought they stayed here:

As a gentleman and myself were walking on the 4th of last November (1771) round the sea-banks at Newhaven, near the mouth of the Lewes river, in pursuit of natural knowledge, we were surprised to see three house-swallows gliding very swiftly by it. That morning was rather chilly, with the wind at north-west; but the tenor of the weather for some time before had been delicate, and the noons remarkably warm. From this incident, and from repeated accounts which I meet with, I am more and more induced to believe that many of the swallow kind do not depart from this island; but lay themselves up in holes and caverns; and do, insect-like and bat-like, come forth at mild times, and then retire again to their *latebrae*. Nor make I the least doubt but that, if I lived at Newhaven, Seaford, Brighthelmstone, or any of those towns near the chalk-cliffs of the Sussex coast, I should by proper observations, see swallows stirring at periods of the winter when the noons were soft and inviting and the sun warm and invigorating. And I am the more of this opinion from what I have remarked during some of our late springs, that though some swallows did make their appearance about the usual time, namely, the 13th or 14th of April, yet meeting with a harsh reception, and blustering cold north-east winds, they immediately withdrew, absconding for several days, till the weather gave them better encouragement.

So Gilbert White was wrong about swallows, but right about everything else.

18 Set in our North Downs

Introduction

When I was at school, one of our set pieces was Sir Walter Scott's *Lay of the Last Minstrel.* I could recite it straight off. But the lines which have stuck in my mind are those in which he endorses the love of each one of us for his own countryside

> Breathes there the man with soul so dead,
> Who never to himself hath said,
> 'This is my own, my native land!'
> Whose heart hath ne'er within him burn'd
> As home his footsteps he hath turn'd
> From wandering on a foreign strand?
> If such there breathe, go, mark him well;
> For him no Minstrel raptures swell.

He goes down 'Unwept, unhonour'd, and unsung.'

I have often said those words to myself on returning from overseas – on an ocean liner up Southampton Water – or in an aircraft coming into Heathrow. Whilst enjoying the lands abroad, I have always been glad to get back home.

A little later I will tell you of two writers about our part of Hampshire, but I venture to try my own hand first.

1 Where we live

i *The River Test*

We are set amidst the North Downs in the valley of the River Test. We have blessings from heaven above. The rain from the clouds falls on the high hills to the north of us. It filters through the chalk downland. It goes deep down into the earth and forms reservoirs far below the ground. It comes out into the valley: in springs of living water – bright, clear and pure – fit for everyone to drink. The springs become rivulets and the rivulets become the river, bordered with watercress, bulrushes and flags. Its source is three miles up from us. When it gets here, it is about thirty feet wide and eighteen inches deep. It flows southward, fed by springs all the way, getting wider and deeper till it reaches the sea in Southampton Water.

ii *The villages*

Every two or three miles along the river, there is a lovely village built by our forefathers. Fifteen hundred years ago the valley was a low-lying marsh, with a narrow cartway on higher ground curling along, skirting the edge of the swamp. Our forefathers transformed it by harnessing the water to their use. They made hatches to control the flow. They turned the marshland into fertile water-meadows. They built mills every half-mile or so to grind the corn and make the cloth. They metalled the cartway with stones of flint from the fields. They kept sheep on the uplands and cows in the meadows. They grew corn in the fields. They built isolated cottages in the downlands. They built groups of cottages near the river: all made with chalk and wattle. They thatched them with straw. They dug wells for water. In every village they built a church. Each has a name giving a clue to its origin: Free Folk, White Church, Long Parish, Wher Well.

iii *The people*

Many of our families have been here from the beginning. They tell us of their parents and grandparents from one generation to another, working on the land. Our good Dolly, now aged 89, remembers her girlhood in a remote cottage on the downlands. Her father was a head carter with his two fine horses – and his wife and their six children. His wages were fourteen shillings a week – working every day except Sundays, Good Friday and Christmas Day. He received a much valued five pounds at Michaelmas which was used to buy their clothes. Her mother gathered stones from the fields at sixpence a day. The children walked three miles to school and three miles back every day. Her brother at twelve left school and carried hurdles on his back for the sheepfolds. But they were happy. The words of Thomas Gray fit them well:

> Far from the madding crowd's ignoble strife
> Their sober wishes never learn'd to stray;
> Along the cool sequester'd vale of life
> They kept the noiseless tenor of their way.

How different from the mechanised life of today. One man with a tractor can do twice the work of three carters and six horses in half the time.

iv *The changing character*

The farm workers get fewer and fewer. Their cottages are taken up by week-enders or commuters. New housing estates are built. They are occupied by newcomers who go to work in the neighbouring new towns like Basingstoke and Andover. We old folk regret the change. It is not the place we knew.

2 *Rural Rides*

i *William Cobbett*

I turn now to William Cobbett who filled the national scene from 1800 to 1835. His *Rural Rides* contain some of the best, the most vivid and vigorous writing that has ever appeared in the English language. He was a politician with extreme views in favour of the working classes and against the new rich of the Industrial Revolution. As a side-line he published *Parliamentary Debates*, afterwards taken over by *Hansard*, and also a complete collection of *State Trials* – to which I have often been indebted. And I value a rare copy of his *Rural Rides* which my son gave me for Christmas 1973. Cobbett often rode our own countryside in north Hampshire. He rated it best of all places in which to live, as I do: for in my schooldays it was still much as he describes it here. He says there is nothing to compare

> . . . with a country where high downs prevail, with here and there a large wood on the top or the side of a hill, and where you see, in the deep dells, here and there a farm-house, and here and there a village, the buildings sheltered by a group of lofty trees.
>
> This is my taste, and here, in the north of Hampshire, it has its full gratification. I like to look at the winding side of a great down, with two or three numerous flocks of sheep on it, belonging to different farms; and to see, lower down, the folds, in the fields, ready to receive them for the night. We had, when we got upon the downs, after leaving Winchester, this sort of country all the way to Whitchurch. Our point of destination was this village of Burghclere, which lies close under the north side of the lofty hill at Highclere, which is called Beacon-hill, and on the top of which there are still the marks of a Roman encampment. We saw this hill as soon as we got on Winchester downs; and without any regard to *roads*, we *steered* for it, as sailors do for a land-mark. Of these 13 miles (from Winchester to Whitchurch) we rode about eight or nine upon the *greensward*, or over fields equally smooth. And, here is one great pleasure of living in countries of this sort: no sloughs, no ditches, no nasty dirty lanes, and the hedges, where there are any, are more for boundary marks than for fences. Fine for hunting and coursing: no

impediments; no gates to open; nothing to impede the dogs, the horses or the view. The water is not *seen running*; but the great bed of chalk *holds it*, and the sun draws it up for the benefit of the grass and the corn; and, whatever inconvenience is experienced from the necessity of *deep wells*, and of driving sheep and cattle far to water, is amply made up for by the *goodness of the water*, and by the complete absence of floods, of drains, of ditches and of water-furrows.

That was in 1830. Now in 1985 some parts of the great downs are cultivated for corn and other crops, interspersed with woods and copses.

ii *Sussex clay*

Then Cobbett makes a comparison between the economy of the chalk downs of north Hampshire and the heavy clay of the Sussex weald (which we also know well).

As things now are, however, these countries have one great draw-back: the poor day-labourers suffer from the want of fuel, and they have nothing but their *bare pay*. For these reasons they are greatly worse off than those of the *woodland countries*; and it is really surprising what a difference there is between the faces that you see here, and the round, red faces that you see in the *wealds* and the *forests*, particularly in *Sussex*, where the labourers *will* have a *meat-pudding* of some sort or other; and where they *will* have a *fire* to sit by in the winter.

That comparison is no longer true. In Cobbett's day the Sussex weald was heavily wooded and rich in iron ore. Oaks grew well there. They were cut down to stoke the furnaces for the iron ovens. Ponds were dug out to provide a head of water for the hammers. Now this iron has been worked out. And we are on a par with them. The faces of our farm labourers are just as healthy as theirs!

3 The Bright Waters

i *Plunket Greene*

Now I come to a fishing book which is a favourite. It is called *Where the Bright Waters meet*. The bright waters are our little streams, the Test and the Bourne. They meet a mile below us at the place which we call the Cleeves. We used to drive there in a pony-trap and have picnics. The book was written in 1924 by a great singer of his day,

Harry Plunket Greene. I remember him – tall and handsome and friendly with everyone. The book has a happiness about it which is equal to that of Izaak Walton. It also describes our countryside as I knew it when I was a boy. There was a deer park belonging to the Earl of Portsmouth in which there were many deer and Highland cattle. Plunket Greene tells how he discovered, in the year 1900, the Hampshire village of Hurstbourne Priors where he later came to live.

ii *A lovely village*

I took the Whitchurch mill fishing. I cannot remember much about it now except that it was a very small triangular beat, and that I got some very nice fish. We stayed at the White Hart and whenever the water wanted a rest we went off on walking expeditions.

One Sunday morning we determined that we would follow the Test down the valley and see what the country was like. The road ran round a deer-park which lay on the high ground on our right, with the river some way below on our other side, and after following this for a couple of miles we came round a corner on top of a village and fell over head and ears in love with it on the spot. It lay facing us in a broad hollow at the foot of a steep hill. It was a gorgeous day without a breath of wind, and the smoke from the thatched cottages rose up in straight blue lines against the dark elms of the hill behind. The valley ran at right angles to the one we had come through, and in the middle of it lay the village in a golden sheet of buttercups, and through the buttercups under the beechwoods of the deer park there ran a little chalk stream clear as crystal and singing like a lark.

There was a church half hidden in the trees and the people were just coming out after service, and there was an indescribable feeling of peace over the whole scene. It was a typical picture of English country life which Constable might have painted or Gray have sung. We followed the stream up through the meadows past the church. We sat in the buttercups and watched the deer and the black sheep and the Highland cattle in the park above, and the wild duck on the broadwater by our side, and we vowed that if ever we wanted to live in the country this would be the one and only village in the world for us.

iii *The little river Bourne*

It rises generally – for its beginnings vary by miles according to the winter rainfall and its outbreak of springs – in St Mary Bourne, about a mile above the viaduct, and flows into the Test two miles below. Only three miles in all, but those three miles the dry-fly fisherman's paradise! Except in the hatch-holes and the broad water below the park it could be waded anywhere in short waders; the water was crystal-clear – the true chalk stream – and never got discoloured to any extent; it grew the right weed and the weed was alive with shrimp; there was, providentially, no May-fly, and the grayling – the grey squirrel of the trout stream – had not yet put in an appearance; it was full of two- and three-pounders, often with scarcely enough water to cover their backs, and it ran, and runs, through one of the fairest valleys and one of the prettiest villages in the South of England. Nothing could stale its infinite variety. It had hatch-holes, water-cress beds, broad waters, saw-mill shallows, waterfalls and long stretches through meadows of golden buttercups. It twisted and turned, it ran fast and smooth, under trees and in the open, chaffing and laughing itself into your very heart, for if ever there was a happy river in this world it was the little Hampshire Bourne.

iv *The finest trout*

He tells of the finest trout in the river in a story which all of you who are fishermen will like.

I began on him with a shorter line this time, and he took the fly at the very first cast like a lamb. If he was a lamb as he took it he was a lion when he had it. Instead of running up-stream, as I hoped and expected he would do, he gave one swish with his tail and bolted down through the bridge, bending the rod double and dragging the point right under. It was done with such lightning speed I had no time to remonstrate. I threw myself flat on my stomach and got the rod sideways over the bridge, and then the fight began. I was on one side of the bridge and he was half way to Southampton on the other. He got further and further down stream, going from one patch of weeds to the next, and digging and burrowing his nose into the middle of it, while I just hung on, helpless, waiting for the end. He quieted down after a bit, and finding that he could not rub the annoying thing out of his nose on the south side he determined to explore the north, and he began to swim up towards me. I must have been a ridiculous sight, spread-eagled on the rotting planks with splinters digging into my legs and ants and spiders crawling down my neck, vainly endeavouring to hold the rod over the side with one hand, to wind in the line with the other, and to watch him over my shoulder all at the same time. Fortunately I must have been invisible from below, but the moment he got under the bridge he saw the rod and tore past me up-stream with the reel screaming. But now we were on even terms and there was a clear stretch of water ahead, and I was able to play him to a finish. I was really proud of that fight, for, in addition to the cramped style which I was compelled to adopt, it took place in a stream ten feet wide, half-choked with weeds, and I got him on a OOO Iron-blue at the end of a 4x point. He weighed 3¾ lb when I got him home, and I have always bitterly regretted that I did not get him set up, for . . . he was the most beautiful river-trout in shape, colour and proportion I ever saw.

4 *The Brook*

I sometimes wonder whether Tennyson had our brooks and river Test in his mind's eye when he wrote *The Brook*. Most of you will know it. I have quoted from it elsewhere and I make no apology for doing so again. It is so lovely and so expressive and fits our Hampshire scene so well, except for the word 'thorp' (meaning village) which is more like Tennyson's native Lincolnshire.

I come from haunts of coot and hern,
I make a sudden sally
And sparkle out among the fern,
To bicker down a valley.

By thirty hills I hurry down,
Or slip between the ridges,
By twenty thorps, a little town,
And half a hundred bridges. . . .

The little town might well be Whitchurch.

I chatter over stony ways,
In little sharps and trebles,
I bubble into eddying bays,
I babble on the pebbles.

With many a curve my banks I fret
By many a field and fallow,
And many a fairy foreland set
With willow-weed and mallow.

I chatter, chatter, as I flow
To join the brimming river,
For men may come and men may go,
But I go on for ever.

I wind about, and in and out,
With here a blossom sailing
And here and there a lusty trout,
And here and there a grayling,

Here in our river we have our native brown trout. We get rid of the grayling and the 'rainbow' trout as much as we can.

And here and there a foamy flake
Upon me, as I travel
With many a silvery waterbreak
Above the golden gravel,

And draw them all along, and flow
To join the brimming river,
For men may come and men may go,
But I go on for ever.

I steal by lawns and grassy plots,
I slide by hazel covers;
I move the sweet forget-me-nots
That grow for happy lovers.

Here we have the lawns on this side and the hazel covers on the opposite side, and forget-me-nots everywhere.

I slip, I slide, I gloom, I glance,
Among my skimming swallows;
I make the netted sunbeam dance
Against my sandy shallows.

I murmur under moon and stars
In brambly wildernesses;
I linger by my shingly bars;
I loiter round my cresses;

And out again I curve and flow
To join the brimming river,
For men may come and men may go,
But I go on for ever.

It is a happy thought that the brook goes on for ever: but we come and go.

Postscript

At heart I am a countryman. But I do not hunt, or fish, or shoot. I prefer to see the fox, the fish, and the birds in their natural surroundings – without being done down by man. I would not have you think that I am against these activities. The love of them is a natural follow-up of the time when it was necessary for a man to kill to provide food for the family. I would not agree with those kind-hearted folk who would stop the blood sports, as they are called.

19 Sisters and suitors

Introduction

Away from the countryside itself, I turn to a delicate Hampshire lady who wrote the most charming descriptions of social life in the country that have ever been written. She is Jane Austen who was born in 1775 near us at Steventon where her father was the rector. She lived for some years at Chawton near Alton. She died in 1817 – only 41 – and was buried in the Cathedral at Winchester where there is a tablet to her memory. We have in our drawingroom two lovely engravings given as a wedding present to my first wife and me. They are dated 1787 and show a gentleman in the costume of the period paying court to a lady. These contemporary engravings prompt me to tell you something of the social structure of her time. She takes it for granted, but I would tell you of it.

i *Stately homes*

Country life was dominated by great houses occupied by great families. They were set in great parks studded with great trees and roamed by herds of deer. Several of these great houses survive today. They are called the 'Stately Homes of England.' They are sometimes open for the public to see for a small charge – to help pay for the upkeep. A few of them are still in the hands of the original families. Some have been handed over to the National Trust. Others have been turned into schools and conference centres. When I was a boy, we were surrounded by great estates of this kind: The Earls of Portsmouth at Hurstbourne Park; the Portals at Laverstoke House; The Earls of Carnarvon at Highclere Castle. We looked up to them with awe and respect but did not move in their society.

These great estates were communities in themselves. There were scores of servants, inside and out. There were stable blocks filled with horses and carriages. There were cottages for estate workers. There was a home farm and also land let out to tenant farmers.

The whole estate was often 'entailed.' It was settled so that it descended from one eldest son to the next. The younger sons were put into the Law, the Church or the Army – not into trade because that was looked down upon. The daughters stayed at home, doing the needlework or cutting the flowers – until they were married. It was considered beneath them to do housework. That was for the domestic staff.

The owner of the estate often had the patronage of the village church. It was called the 'advowson.' He could present any ordained man to the living – giving him a useful income from the tithes paid by the farmers.

The owner sometimes had a town house as well – where he went with his wife and daughters for the London season – and back to his estate for the rest of the year.

This elegant manner of life was common throughout the higher ranks of society but gradually descending in grandeur and scale from the great estates of the rich or noble families to the modest estates of the country gentlemen.

ii *The characters*

Such was the setting in which Jane Austen placed her characters in her novel *Pride and Prejudice*. She puts Mr Darcy as the owner of a great house and estate at Pemberley in Derbyshire: and Lady Catherine de Bourgh of Rosings Park in Kent with the patronage of the neighbouring church. She puts Mr Bennet as the gentleman owner of a modest house and estate at Longbourn in Hertfordshire.

She brings out the formalities current in speech and address. Thus, Mr and Mrs Bennet address one another as 'Mr' and 'Mrs.' Even Mr Darcy is addressed by his lady love as 'Mr.' We are not told their Christian names.

She also tells of the snobbery which was prevalent to the nth degree. The 'upper ten' looked down on Mrs Bennet because she was the daughter of an attorney in a country town and her sister had married his clerk. Her lack of breeding affected her daughters too. It diminished their chances in the marriage market. The servants were beyond the pale. They come in and out of the story without a word of recognition, even from Jane Austen.

'Pride' is personified by young Mr Darcy. 'Prejudice' is personified by Miss Elizabeth Bennet, the second daughter of Mr and Mrs Bennet. Their characters are brought out skilfully by Jane Austen by means of their conversations and in letters. In the end Mr Darcy sheds his pride and Miss Elizabeth overcomes her prejudice. They get married. We are left to suppose that they live happily ever after.

1 The Bennet establishment

i *The five sisters*

Mr Bennet was not the owner of Longbourn House. It was entailed. He was only entitled to the benefit of it during his own life. It was settled 'in tail male.' That meant that it descended only through the male line. If Mr Bennet died without a son, it would pass to the nearest male in line.

Mr Bennet had married beneath him twenty-three years ago. His wife, Mrs Bennet, was pretty but vulgar and silly. When Mr Bennet married her, they confidently expected to be able to break the entail in this way:

> Of course, they were to have a son. This son was to join in cutting off the entail, as soon as he should be of age, and the widow and younger children would by that means be provided for.

But instead of a son, five daughters entered the world, one after another in quick succession every eighteen months. They were Jane, Elizabeth, Mary, Kitty and Lydia, aged from twenty-two to fifteen. Being girls, they took nothing of the estate. Mr and Mrs Bennet hoped for another child, but none arrived. So, when Mr Bennet died, the estate would go to his remote cousin, Mr Collins. This infuriated Mrs Bennet as appears when Mr Collins wrote a letter to Mr Bennet which he read at breakfast to the family:

> 'It (the letter) is from my cousin, Mr Collins, who, when I am dead, may turn you all out of this house as soon as he pleases.'
> 'Oh! my dear,' cried his wife, 'I cannot bear to hear that mentioned. Pray do not talk of that odious man. I do think it is the hardest thing in the world, that your estate should be entailed away from your own children; and I am sure, if I had been you, I should have tried long ago to do something or other about it.'

Jane and Elizabeth attempted to explain to her the nature of an entail. They had often attempted it before, but it was a subject on which Mrs Bennet was beyond the reach of reason, and she continued to rail bitterly against the cruelty of settling an estate away from a family of five daughters, in favour of a man whom nobody cared anything about.

> 'It certainly is a most iniquitous affair,' said Mr Bennet, 'and nothing can clear Mr Collins from the guilt of inheriting Longbourn. But if you will listen to his letter, you may perhaps be a little softened by his manner of expressing himself.'
>
> 'No, that I am sure I shall not; and I think it was very impertinent of him to write to you at all, and very hypocritical. I hate such false friends. . . .'

ii *Seeking husbands for daughters*

Near Longbourn, there was a large park called Netherfield Park with a large house called Netherfield Hall. When the story opens, a young man of wealth called Mr Bingley – with a fortune made by his father from trade – had decided to take it and establish himself in society. Mrs Bennet got to hear of it and told Mr Bennet.

'What is his name?'

'Bingley.'

'Is he married or single?'

'Oh! single, my dear, to be sure! A single man of large fortune; four or five thousand a-year. What a fine thing for our girls!'

'How so? how can it affect them?'

'My dear Mr Bennet,' replied his wife, 'how can you be so tiresome! you must know that I am thinking of his marrying one of them.'

'Is that his design in settling here?'

'Design! nonsense, how can you talk so! But it is very likely that he *may* fall in love with one of them, and therefore you must visit him as soon as he comes.'

Jane Austen sums up Mrs Bennet in a sentence or two:

She was a woman of mean understanding, little information, and uncertain temper. When she was discontented, she fancied herself nervous. The business of her life was to get her daughters married; its solace was visiting and news.

2 Their suitors

i *Two rich young men*

The story proceeds with Mr Bingley taking Netherfield Park and bringing down his friend Mr Darcy with him to stay. They go to a dance at the Assembly Rooms in a nearby town and Mr Bingley gives a ball at Netherfield Hall. The Bennet sisters go. Mr Bingley is attracted by the eldest sister, Jane, Mr Darcy looks upon the second sister, Elizabeth. This is the impression they gave:

Mr Bingley was good-looking and gentlemanlike; he had a pleasant countenance, and easy, unaffected manners. . . . His friend Mr Darcy soon drew the attention of the room by his fine, tall person, handsome features, noble mien, and the report which was in general circulation within five minutes after his entrance, of his having ten thousand a-year. The gentlemen pronounced him to be a fine figure of a man, the ladies declared he was much handsomer than Mr Bingley, and he was looked at with great admiration for about half the evening, till his manners gave a disgust which turned the tide of his popularity; for he was discovered to be proud, to be above his company, and above being pleased; and not all his large estate in Derbyshire could then save him from having a most forbidding, disagreeable countenance, and being unworthy to be compared with his friend.

The story develops with a love match between Mr Bingley and Jane: and Miss Elizabeth being prejudiced against Mr Darcy because of his haughty manner.

ii *Another eligible*

At this point there comes another young man on the scene. He is Mr Collins, the remote cousin of Mr Bennet and the heir apparent to the Longbourn estate. He is a young clergyman, aged twenty-five, just ordained. But he has been fortunate in coming to the notice of Mr Darcy's aunt, Lady Catherine de Bourgh. She is a widow with a great house and estate at Rosings Park in Kent. She has the patronage of the neighbouring church. It is a valuable rectory with a nice house. She presents Mr Collins to the living. She tells him he must find a wife. He thinks of the Bennet sisters and invites himself to stay with them for a week at Longbourn.

Having now a good house and very sufficient income, he intended to marry; and in seeking a reconciliation with the Longbourn family he had a wife in view, as he meant to chuse one of the daughters, if he found them as handsome and amiable as they were represented by common report. This was his plan of amends – of atonement – for inheriting their father's estate; and he thought it an excellent one, full of eligibility and suitableness, and excessively generous and disinterested on his own part.

He thinks of the eldest, Jane, but Mrs Bennet puts him off because she hopes that Mr Bingley will marry Jane. So he decides to propose to the second sister, Elizabeth.

iii *He courts Elizabeth*

He solicits a private audience with her and addresses her, giving his reasons as if he was preaching a sermon. She refuses him.

It was absolutely necessary to interrupt him now.

'You are too hasty, sir,' she cried. 'You forget that I have made no answer. Let me do it without further loss of time. Accept my thanks for the compliment you are paying me. I am very sensible of the honour of your proposals, but it is impossible for me to do otherwise than decline them.'

'I am not now to learn,' replied Mr Collins, with a formal wave of the hand, 'that it is usual with young ladies to reject the addresses of the man whom they secretly mean to accept, when he first applies for their favour; and that sometimes the refusal is repeated a second or even a third time. I am therefore by no means discouraged by what you have just said, and shall hope to lead you to the altar ere long.'

'Upon my word, sir,' cried Elizabeth, 'your hope is rather an extraordinary one after my declaration. I do assure you that I am not one of those young ladies (if such young ladies there are) who are so daring as to risk their happiness on the chance of being asked a second time. I am perfectly serious in my refusal. You could not make *me* happy, and I am convinced that I am the last woman in the world who would make *you* so. Nay, were your friend Lady Catherine to know me, I am persuaded she would find me in every respect ill qualified for the situation.'

Mrs Bennet was dawdling outside, awaiting the result. Mr Collins told her that Elizabeth had refused him. Mrs Bennet says that she will see Mr Bennet:

'Lizzy is only headstrong in such matters as these. In everything else she is as good-natured a girl as ever lived. I will go directly to Mr Bennet, and we shall very soon settle it with her, I am sure.'

She would not give him time to reply, but hurrying instantly to her husband, called out as she entered the library, 'Oh! Mr Bennet, you are wanted immediately; we are all in an uproar. You must come and make Lizzy marry Mr Collins, for she vows she will not have him, and if you do not make haste he will change his mind and not have *her*.'

Mr Bennet raised his eyes from his book as she entered, and fixed them on her face with a calm unconcern which was not in the least altered by her communication.

'I have not the pleasure of understanding you,' said he, when she had finished her speech. 'Of what are you talking?'

'Of Mr Collins and Lizzy. Lizzy declares she will not have Mr Collins, and Mr Collins begins to say that he will not have Lizzy.'

'And what am I to do on the occasion? – It seems an hopeless business.'

'Speak to Lizzy about it yourself. Tell her that you insist upon her marrying him.'

'Let her be called down. She shall hear my opinion.'

Mrs Bennet rang the bell, and Miss Elizabeth was summoned to the library.

Mr Bennet supports Elizabeth – by putting an unhappy alternative:

'Come here, child,' cried her father as she appeared. 'I have sent for you on an affair of importance. I understand that Mr Collins has made you an offer of marriage. Is it true?' Elizabeth replied that it was. 'Very well – and this offer of marriage you have refused?'

'I have, sir.'

'Very well. We now come to the point. Your mother insists upon your accepting it. Is it not so, Mrs Bennet?'

'Yes, or I will never see her again.'

'An unhappy alternative is before you, Elizabeth. From this day you must be a stranger to one of your parents. Your mother will never see you again if you do *not* marry Mr Collins, and I will never see you again if you *do*.'

Elizabeth could not but smile at such a conclusion of such a beginning; but Mrs Bennet, who had persuaded herself that her husband regarded the affair as she wished, was excessively disappointed.

'What do you mean, Mr Bennet, by talking in this way? You promised me to *insist* upon her marrying him.'

'My dear,' replied her husband, 'I have two small favours to request. First, that you will allow me the free use of my understanding on the present occasion; and secondly, of my room. I shall be glad to have the library to myself as soon as may be.'

iv *He courts Charlotte*

Mr Collins soon got over the refusal. Two days later, while still at Longbourn, he proposed to Elizabeth's dearest friend, Charlotte Lucas. She accepted him.

In as short a time as Mr Collins's long speeches would allow, everything was settled between them to the satisfaction of both; and as they entered the house he earnestly entreated her to name the day that was to make him the happiest of men; and though such a solicitation must be waived for the present, the lady felt no inclination to trifle with his happiness. The stupidity with which he was favoured by nature must guard his courtship from any charm that could make a woman wish for its continuance; and Miss Lucas, who accepted him solely from the pure and disinterested desire of an establishment, cared not how soon that establishment were gained.

v *A fourth eligible*

Another young man who came to the dance and the balls was Mr Wickham. He was an officer in the militia stationed in the nearby town. He had been closely associated with the Darcy family. His father had been the steward for old Mr Darcy: and the old man, out of friendship, had become his godfather and sent him to Cambridge. He was very handsome and well-mannered – a real ladies' man: but he had lost heavily on the gaming tables. He had tried to elope with young Mr Darcy's fifteen-year-old sister Georgiana, but had been prevented just in time. But he did elope successfully with the Bennet's youngest daughter Lydia when she was only fifteen. He took her to a lodging-house in London and would not have married her – except for the intervention of young Mr Darcy who acted through Mr Gardiner, a brother of Mrs Bennet. Mr Wickham agreed to marry Lydia on condition that all his debts were paid, that he was bought a commission in the regular army, and given a very substantial lump sum. Mrs Bennet was transported with delight.

Her joy burst forth, and every following sentence added to its exuberance. She was now in an irritation as violent from delight, as she had ever been fidgety from alarm and vexation. To know that her daughter would be married was enough. She was disturbed by no fear for her felicity, nor humbled by any remembrance of her misconduct.

'My dear, dear Lydia!' she cried. 'This is delightful indeed! – She will be married! – I shall see her again! – She will be married at sixteen! – My good, kind brother! I knew how it would be. – I knew he would manage everything! How I long to see her! and to see dear Wickham too? But the clothes, the wedding clothes! I will write to my sister Gardiner about them directly. Lizzy, my dear, run down to your father, and ask him how much he will give her. Stay, stay, I will go myself. Ring the bell, Kitty, for Hill. I will put on my things in a moment. My dear, dear Lydia! – How merry we shall be together when we meet!'

3 Happy endings

i *Mr Bingley comes to see the family*

The next to be married was Jane. Mr Bingley had been attracted to her from the beginning, but he was unaccountably away for some months. On his return he asked Mrs Bennet if he might call on the family. She accepted with alacrity and did everything she could to leave him alone with Jane:

He came, and in such very good time, that the ladies were none of them dressed. In ran Mrs Bennet to her daughters' room, in her dressing gown, and with her hair half finished, crying out, 'My dear Jane, make haste and hurry down. He is come – Mr Bingley is come – He is indeed. Make haste, make haste. Here, Sarah, come to Miss Bennet this moment, and help her on with her gown. Never mind Miss Lizzy's hair.'

'We will be down as soon as we can,' said Jane; 'but I dare say Kitty is forwarder than either of us, for she went upstairs half an hour ago.'

'Oh! hang Kitty! what has she to do with it? Come, be quick, be quick! where is your sash, my dear?'

But when her mother was gone, Jane would not be prevailed on to go down without one of her sisters.

ii *Mrs Bennet winks at Kitty to leave*

The same anxiety to get them by themselves, was visible again in the evening. After tea, Mr Bennet retired to the library, as was his custom, and Mary went upstairs to her instrument. Two obstacles of the five being thus removed, Mrs Bennet sat looking and winking at Elizabeth and Catherine for a considerable time, without making any impression on them. Elizabeth would not observe her; and when at last Kitty did, she very innocently said, 'What is the matter, mamma! What do you keep winking at me for? What am I to do?'

'Nothing, child, nothing. I did not wink at you.'

She then sat still five minutes longer; but, unable to waste such a precious occasion, she suddenly got up, and saying to Kitty, 'Come here, my love, I want to speak to you,' took her out of the room. Jane instantly gave a look at Elizabeth, which spoke her distress at such premeditation, and her entreaty that *she* would not give in to it.

iii *Mrs Bennet calls out Lizzy too*

In a few minutes, Mrs Bennet half opened the door, and called out, 'Lizzy, my dear, I want to speak with you.'

Elizabeth was forced to go. 'We may as well leave them by themselves, you know,' said her mother as soon as she was in the hall. 'Kitty and I are going upstairs to sit in my dressing-room.'

Elizabeth made no attempt to reason with her mother, but remained quietly in the hall till she and Kitty were out of sight, then returned into the drawing-room.

So nothing was arranged that evening. But Mr Bingley came again the next morning and Jane and he became engaged.

iv *Lady Catherine drives in style to Longbourn*

Most of the book tells of Mr Darcy and Elizabeth, of their meetings, of his admiration of her and her indifference to him, of his first proposal of marriage and her rejection of it, of their making it up and becoming attached to one another, though not actually engaged. At this point comes the most entertaining passage. Lady Catherine de Bourgh has heard that Elizabeth and Mr Darcy are likely to become engaged. She is determined to stop it if she can, because she has always wanted Mr Darcy to marry her own sickly daughter. The conversation is a classic in literature. Lady Catherine makes a journey in grand style to Longbourn to see Elizabeth. She is driven in a chaise-and-four with a servant in livery to drive the horses and a waiting-woman inside. She asks Elizabeth to take a walk with her. She turns to Elizabeth, saying in an angry tone:

> 'A report of a most alarming nature reached me two days ago. I was told that not only your sister was on the point of being most advantageously married, but that *you*, that Miss Elizabeth Bennet, would, in all likelihood, be soon afterwards united to my nephew – my own nephew – Mr Darcy. Though I *know* it must be a scandalous falsehood – though I would not injure him so much as to suppose the truth of it possible, I instantly resolved on setting off for this place, that I might make my sentiments known to you.'
>
> 'If you believed it impossible to be true,' said Elizabeth, colouring with astonishment and disdain, 'I wonder you took the trouble of coming so far. What could your ladyship propose by it?'
>
> 'At once to insist upon having such a report universally contradicted.'
>
> 'Your coming to Longbourn, to see me and my family,' said Elizabeth coolly, 'will be rather a confirmation of it; if, indeed, such a report is in existence.' . . .
>
> 'Miss Bennet, I insist on being satisfied. Has he, has my nephew, made you an offer of marriage?'
>
> 'Your ladyship has declared it to be impossible.'
>
> 'It ought to be so; it must be so, while he retains the use of his reason. But *your* arts and allurements may, in a moment of infatuation, have made him forget what he owes to himself and to all his family. You may have drawn him in.'
>
> 'If I have, I shall be the last person to confess it.'

Lady Catherine insists that Mr Darcy is engaged to her daughter: and cannot therefore become engaged to Elizabeth:

> 'Miss Bennet, do you know who I am? I have not been accustomed to such language as this. I am almost the nearest relation he has in the world, and am entitled to know all his dearest concerns.'
>
> 'But you are not entitled to know *mine*; nor will such behaviour as this ever induce me to be explicit.'
>
> 'Let me be rightly understood. This match, to which you have the presumption to aspire, can never take place. No, never. Mr Darcy is engaged to *my daughter*. Now, what have you to say?'
>
> 'Only this: that if he is so, you can have no reason to suppose he will make an offer to me.'
>
> Lady Catherine hesitated for a moment, and then replied –
>
> 'The engagement between them is of a peculiar kind. From their infancy, they have been intended for each other. It was the favourite wish of *his* mother, as well as of hers. While in their cradles, we planned the union: and now, at the moment when the wishes of both sisters would be accomplished in their marriage, to be prevented by a young woman of inferior birth, of no importance in the world, and

wholly unallied to the family! Do you pay no regard to the wishes of his friends – to his tacit engagement with Miss de Bourgh? Are you lost to every feeling of propriety and delicacy? Have you not heard me say that from his earliest hours he was destined for his cousin?'

'Yes, and I had heard it before. But what is that to me? If there is no other objection to my marrying your nephew, I shall certainly not be kept from it by knowing that his mother and aunt wished him to marry Miss de Bourgh.' . . .

'Let us sit down. You are to understand, Miss Bennet, that I came here with the determined resolution of carrying my purpose; nor will I be dissuaded from it. I have not been used to submit to any person's whims. I have not been in the habit of brooking disappointment.'

'*That* will make your ladyship's situation at present more pitiable; but it will have no effect on *me*.'

Lady Catherine tells Elizabeth that she should not quit the sphere in which she was brought up. Elizabeth says that she is a gentleman's daughter but Lady Catherine retorts, 'Who was your mother?'

'I will not be interrupted! Hear me in silence. My daughter and my nephew are formed for each other. They are descended, on the maternal side, from the same noble line; and, on the fathers', from respectable, honourable, and ancient, though untitled families. Their fortune on both sides is splendid. They are destined for each other by the voice of every member of their respective houses; and what is to divide them? The upstart pretensions of a young woman without family, connections, or fortune. Is this to be endured! But it must not, shall not be! If you were sensible of your own good, you would not wish to quit the sphere in which you have been brought up.'

'In marrying your nephew I should not consider myself as quitting that sphere. He is a gentleman; I am a gentleman's daughter: so far we are equal.'

'True. You *are* a gentleman's daughter. But who was your mother? Who are your uncles and aunts? Do not imagine me ignorant of their condition.'

'Whatever my connections may be,' said Elizabeth, 'if your nephew does not object to them, they can be nothing to *you*.'

'Tell me, once for all, are you engaged to him?'

Though Elizabeth would not, for the mere purpose of obliging Lady Catherine, have answered this question, she could not but say, after a moment's deliberation, 'I am not.'

Lady Catherine seemed pleased.

'And will you promise me never to enter into such an engagement?'

'I will make no promise of the kind.'

Elizabeth says she will not be intimidated but, as a last throw, Lady Catherine brings up Lydia's 'infamous elopement':

'Miss Bennet, I am shocked and astonished. I expected to find a more reasonable young woman. But do not deceive yourself into a belief that I will ever recede. I shall not go away till you have given me the assurance I require.'

'And I certainly *never* shall give it. I am not to be intimidated into anything so wholly unreasonable. . . .'

'Not so hasty, if you please. I have by no means done. To all the objections I have already urged, I have still another to add. I am no stranger to the particulars of your youngest sister's infamous elopement. I know it all; that the young man's marrying her was a patched-up business, at the expense of your father and uncle. And is *such* a girl to be my nephew's sister? Is *her* husband, who is the son of his late father's steward, to be his brother? Heaven and earth – of what are you thinking! Are the shades of Pemberley to be thus polluted?'

'You can *now* have nothing farther to say,' she resentfully answered. 'You have insulted me, in every possible method. I must beg to return to the house.'

v *Elizabeth is engaged*

After that spirited defiance, things moved rapidly. Mr Darcy and Elizabeth became engaged. Mrs Bennet was excited beyond measure.

'Good gracious! Lord bless me! only think! dear me! Mr Darcy! Who would have thought it? And is it really true? Oh, my sweetest Lizzy! how rich and how great you will be! What pin-money, what jewels, what carriages you will have! Jane's is nothing to it – nothing at all. I am so pleased – so happy! Such a charming man! – so handsome! so tall! – Oh, my dear Lizzy! pray apologise for my having disliked him so much before. I hope he will overlook it. Dear, dear Lizzy! A house in town! Everything that is charming! Three daughters married! Ten thousand a year! Oh, Lord! what will become of me? I shall go distracted.'

Jane Austen leaves the story with everyone very happy. Even Lady Catherine is reconciled and visits Mr and Mrs Darcy in their great house at Pemberley.

Postscript

Jane Austen's novels have given rise to many legal puzzles. My friend, Guenter Treitel (a Magdalen man), the Vinerian Professor at Oxford, has written a most scholarly article on *Jane Austen and the Law*.[1] In *Pride and Prejudice* there is a puzzle about the name of Mr Collins. If the estate at Longbourn was to descend in tail male – on the male line only – surely the successor to it would be a Bennet. Professor Treitel suggests (page 566) as an explanation that 'one of two branches of a family all having the same surname of Collins (might have) changed that name to Bennet on or after succeeding to the Longbourn estate.' Another puzzle is why Mr Bennet could not bar the entail even though he had no son. The Professor gives an explanation (page 563) which is quite beyond me. So I expect it would be for you too. The Professor tells us, moreover, all about the law of marriage as it affected Wickham and Lydia (aged sixteen). The legal age for marriage was then twelve for girls and fourteen for boys, but they could not be married 'privately in town' (page 571) as Jane Austen suggests. So poor Jane Austen would fail in any examination in law set by the Professor, but she would pass top of the class in any examination in English set by me.

[1] 100 LQR 549.

20 Mediaeval characters

Introduction

I have left Chaucer's *Prologue* to *The Canterbury Tales*, till last: because you may find it difficult. Perhaps you may wish to omit it altogether. If so, I shall quite understand. But if you can master it, you will find it fascinating. At least, I have. It takes you right back for 700 years and tells you how people dressed and spoke and behaved in those days – far better than any history book could do. All done with delightful touches of humour.

In the *Prologue* Geoffrey Chaucer tells of the pilgrims who rode on horseback to Canterbury. You may have been along a stretch of the Pilgrims' Way which still exists. But do you know why they went? It was to visit the tomb of Thomas à Becket. He was the first Lord Chancellor of England. He held that office for eight years from 1154 AD to 1162 AD. It was whilst he was Lord Chancellor that King Henry II made great innovations in the law. He started the system of Justices of Assize going on circuit round the counties of England. He introduced trial by jury.

1 Thomas à Becket

i *The old beggar*

His secretary William Fitzstephen tells this nice story of the King and Thomas à Becket riding out on horseback and coming upon an old beggar.

One cold wintry day they were riding together through the streets of London when they saw an old beggar-man coming towards them, wearing a worn-out tattered garment. Said the King to the Chancellor

'Do you see that man?'

Chancellor: 'I see him.'

King: 'How poor! How wretched! How naked he is! Would it not be great charity to give him a thick warm coat?

Chancellor: 'Great indeed; and you, as King, ought to have a disposition and an eye for such things.'

Meanwhile the beggar comes up. The King stops, and the Chancellor along with him. The King in a mild tone addresses the beggar and asks him if he would like to have a good cloak. The beggar, not knowing who they were, thought it was all a joke.

The King to the Chancellor: 'You indeed shall have the grace of this great charity.'

And putting his hands on a very fine new cloak of scarlet and ermine which the Chancellor then wore, he struggled to pull it off, whilst the Chancellor did his best to retain it.

After a certain resistance the Chancellor allowed the King to be victorious – to pull off his cloak – and to give it to the beggar . . .

The old beggar-man walked off with the Chancellor's valuable cloak, enriched beyond his hopes, and giving thanks to God.

ii *This turbulent priest*

Later on Thomas à Becket became Archbishop of Canterbury. In this post he fell out with the King. He disputed the authority of the King over the clergy and claimed that it was subordinate to that of the Pope. The difference was so great that the King turned to the nobles around him and exclaimed

'Who will rid me of this turbulent priest?'

iii *Murder in the cathedral*

Thus encouraged, four knights on 29 December 1170 found their way into the Archbishop's Palace at Canterbury. This is the description by J R Green in his *Short History of England*:

After a stormy parley with him in his chamber they withdrew to arm. Thomas was hurried by his clerks into the cathedral, but as he reached the steps leading from the transept to the choir his pursuers burst in from the cloisters. 'Where,' cried Reginald Fitzurse in the dusk of the dimly-lighted minster, 'where is the traitor, Thomas Beket?' The Primate turned resolutely back: 'Here am I, no traitor, but a priest of God,' he replied, and again descending the steps he placed himself with his back against a pillar and fronted his foes. All the bravery and violence of his old knightly life seemed to revive in Thomas as he tossed back the threats and demands of his assailants. 'You are our prisoner,' shouted Fitzurse, and the four knights seized him to drag him from the church. 'Do not touch me, Reginald,' cried the Primate, 'pander that you are, you owe me fealty'; and availing himself of his personal strength he shook him roughly off. 'Strike, strike,' retorted Fitzurse, and blow after blow struck Thomas to the ground. A retainer of Ranulf de Broc with the point of his sword scattered the Primate's brains on the ground. 'Let us be off,' he cried triumphantly, 'this traitor will never rise again.'

The brutal murder was received with a thrill of horror throughout Christendom; miracles were wrought at the martyr's tomb; he was canonized, and became the most popular of English saints.

Thomas described his assailant as a 'pander'. In those days that was a man who procured women for the gratification of another's lust.

iv *300 years of pilgrimage*

The murder was in the year 1170 AD. For the next 300 years pilgrims made their way to Canterbury to visit the tomb of Saint Thomas à Becket. They believed that miracles of healing were to be had there. (Just as people go to Lourdes now.)

2 At the Tabard Inn

Geoffrey Chaucer tells us of one pilgrimage. He was writing in the year 1387 AD. He wrote it all in his own hand. Caxton did not invent printing till 100 years later.

i *Chaucer's English*

Chaucer is, I believe, next to Shakespeare, the best of our English poets. He introduced a new metre into poetry by writing in couplets of two lines rhyming with each other. They are now famous as the 'heroic couplet'. You will see how attractive they are. But how many of us know of his work? Like me, you may have read a few lines at school, but that is all. His work is difficult for us nowadays because his spelling is so odd and some of his words are out-of-date. In his time no one knew how to spell. (We had no dictionary until Samuel Johnson produced his in 1755.) Everyone spelt as he spoke by the sound of his own voice. Professor Nevill Coghill has made an excellent translation into modern English, but to get the real feel of Chaucer's work, you should read it in the original script with its 'heroic couplets'.

In the *Prologue* Chaucer describes the people of his time. He does it with pathos, a shrewd sense and kindly humour that even Shakespeare has not surpassed. I will give you some extracts in his own spelling. If you find it difficult, just say it quietly to yourself. You will get the meaning by the sound of it. The more you read of him, the easier you will find it to understand. My short introduction will give you the gist of it.

ii *Spring-time*

Chaucer sets the scene in Spring-time. March had been very dry. But April had come in with welcome showers. These had helped the young plants. Chaucer knew that 'April showers bring forth May flowers'.

> Whan that Aprille with his shoures sote
> The droghte of Marche hath perced to the rote,
> And bathed every veyne in swich licour,
> Of which vertu engendred is the flour:

Spring is the time too when the birds sing joyfully at daybreak with their dawn chorus. Chaucer calls them 'smale fowles' and says they sleep with their eyes open. He uses the word 'corages' which is now obsolete. It means 'behaviour', 'disposition'.

> And smale fowles maken melodye,
> That slepen al the night with open yë,
> So priketh hem nature in hir corages:
> Than longen folk to goon on pilgrimages

iii *Canterbury*

The pilgrims come from all over England to go to Canterbury. They are on their way to seek (seke) the tomb of St Thomas à Becket. He was the 'holy blisful martir' who had performed miracles of healing. He had helped them when they were sick, which Chaucer also spells 'seke'.

> And specially, from every shires ende
> Of Engelond, to Caunterbury they wende,
> The holy blisful martir for to seke,
> That hem hath holpen, whan that they were seke.

iv *They gather together*

The pilgrims gather together at the Tabard Inn at Southwark. (It was in the street which we now call the Borough High Street, a little to the south of London Bridge.) They were 29 pilgrims in all. Every one had arrived by night-fall. They had good bedrooms for themselves and good stabling for their horses.

> Bifel that, in that seson on a day,
> In Southwerk at the Tabard as I lay
> Redy to wenden on my pilgrimage
> To Caunterbury with ful devout corage,
> At night was come in-to that hostelrye
> Wel nyne and twenty in a companye,

Of sondry folk, by aventure y-falle
In felawshipe, and pilgrims were they alle,
That toward Caunterbury wolden ryde;
The chambres and the stables weren wyde, . . .

v *The reason for the Prologue*

Chaucer tells why he writes the *Prologue*. It is so as to describe the rank and standing of each of the pilgrims and the clothes they wore. He starts with the Knight:

But natheles, whyl I have tyme and space,
Er that I ferther in this tale pace,
Me thinketh it acordaunt to resoun,
To telle yow al the condicioun
Of ech of hem, so as it semed me,
And whiche they weren, and of what degree;
And eek in what array that they were inne:
And at a knight than wol I first biginne.

3 The Knight and his party

i *The Knight*

The Knight was a military man. Chaucer tells us that he had gone on the Crusades and had fought many battles in many countries. He was modest and unassuming and wore a tunic of coarse cloth. But it is sufficient for me to give Chaucer's eulogy of him.

A Knight ther was, and that a worthy man,
That fro the tyme that he first bigan
To ryden out, he loved chivalrye,
Trouthe and honour, fredom and curteisye.
. . .
He was a verray parfit gentil knight.

ii *The Squire*

The Knight had his son with him. Chaucer gives an enchanting picture of him. You will be able to guess most of his words. Such as that he had locks of hair 'curled as if they been laid in a press'. His coat was 'embroidered as if it were a meadow, full of white and red flowers'. He was singing or 'floytinge' (playing the flute), all the day. He could joust (engage in a tournament) and also dance. And please do look at the delightful couplets about his 'hot love' and 'carving at table'.

With him there was his sone, a yong Squyer,
A lovyere, and a lusty bacheler,
With lokkes crulle, as they were leyd in presse.
Of twenty yeer of age he was, I gesse,
. . .
Embrouded was he, as it were a mede
Al ful of fresshe floures, whyte and rede.
Singinge he was, or floytinge, al the day;
He was fresh as is the month of May.
Short was his goune, with sleves longe and wyde.
Wel coude he sitte on hors, and faire ryde.
He coude songes make and wel endyte,
Juste and eek daunce, and wel purtreye and wryte.
So hote he lovede, that by nightertale
He sleep namore than dooth a nightingale.
Curteys he was, lowly, and servisable,
And carf biforn his fader at the table.

iii *The Yeoman*

The Knight had only one servant with him. He was a Yeoman dressed in green very like the traditional Robin Hood who was contemporary with Chaucer. He was well armed with a mighty bow and a quiver of arrows with peacock feathers which did not droop. He had a decorated arm-guard. On one side he had a sword and buckler and on the other side a sharp dagger with ornamented hilt. He had a silver medal of St Christopher and a hunting-horn with a green baldric (shoulder belt).

And he was clad in cote and hood of grene;
A sheef of pecok-arwes brighte and kene
Under his belt he bar ful thriftily;
(Wel coude he dresse his takel yemanly:
His arwes drouped noght with fetheres lowe),
And in his hand he bar a mighty bowe.
. . .
Upon his arm he bar a gay bracer,
And by his syde a swerd and a bokeler,
And on that other syde a gay daggere,
Harneised wel, and sharp as point of spere;
A Cristofre on his brest of silver shene.
An horn he bar, the bawdrik was of grene;
A forster was he, soothly, as I gesse.

iv *The Prioress*

It is surprising that women should go on pilgrimages, but Chaucer gives a charming account of the Prioress. She was smiling and shy and she swore simply by 'Saint Loy'. She sang divine service well. She spoke French with an English accent after the manner of Stratford at the Bow (near London).

> Ther was also a Nonne, a Prioresse,
> That of hir smyling was ful simple and coy;
> Hir gretteste ooth was but by sëynt Loy;
> And she was cleped madame Eglentyne.
> Ful wel she song the service divyne,
> Entuned in hir nose ful semely;
> And Frensh she spak ful faire and fetisly,
> After the scole of Stratford atte Bowe,
> For Frensh of Paris was to hir unknowe.

Her table manners were beyond reproach. She let no morsel drop on her breast or wet her fingers in the sauce. And she left no grease in the cup (coppe).

> At mete wel y-taught was she with-alle;
> She leet no morsel from hir lippes falle,
> Ne wette hir fingres in hir sauce depe.
> Wel coude she carie a morsel, and wel kepe,
> That no drope ne fille up-on hir brest.
> In curteisye was set ful muche hir lest.
> Hir over lippe wyped she so clene,
> That in hir coppe was no ferthing sene
> Of grece, whan she dronken hadde hir draughte.
> Ful semely after hir mete she raughte,
> And sikerly she was of greet disport,

She was tender-hearted and cried when she saw a mouse caught in a trap. She had little dogs (smale houndes) too and would weep if anyone hit them a smart blow.

> She was so charitable and so pitous,
> She wolde wepe, if that she sawe a mous
> Caught in a trappe, if it were deed or bledde.
> Of smale houndes had she, that she fedde
> With rosted flesh, or milk and wastel-breed.
> But sore weep she if oon of hem were deed,
> Or if men smoot it with a yerde smerte:
> And al was conscience and tendre herte.

She wore a bracelet of coral beads and a gold brooch showing that she put love above all.

> Of smal coral about hir arm she bar
> A peire of bedes, gauded al with grene;
> And ther-on heng a broche of gold ful shene,
> On which ther was first write a crowned A,
> And after, 'Amor vincit omnia'.

Chaucer tells us that another nun was riding with her, as her chaplain, and three priests as well.

v *The Monk*

The Monk was a capable man well fitted to be promoted to be an abbot. He had many dainty horses in his stable. He rode joyfully with his bridle jingling in the wind, as loud as a chapel bell in his monastery (celle). He kept greyhounds – as swift as birds (fowel) and spared no expense on his hunting. Chaucer tells us that

> A Monk ther was . . .
> A manly man, to been an abbot able.
> Ful many a deyntee hors hadde he in stable:
> And, whan he rood, men mighte his brydel here
> Ginglen in a whistling wind as clere,
> And eek as loude as dooth the chapel-belle
> Ther as this lord was keper of the celle.
> . . .
> Grehoundes he hadde, as swifte as fowel in flight;
> Of priking and of hunting for the hare
> Was al his lust, for no cost wolde he spare.

His sleeves were edged at the cuffs with fine grey fur. He fastened his hood under his chin with a gold pin in a lover's knot.

> I seigh his sleves purfiled at the hond
> With grys, and that the fyneste of a lond;
> And, for to festne his hood under his chin,
> He hadde of gold y-wroght a curious pin:
> A love-knotte in the gretter ende there was.

He was bald with a shining pate, rosy face and rolling eyes. He was not pale like a tormented (for-pyned) ghost. He loved roast swan: and his palfrey was as brown as a berry.

> His heed was balled, that shoon as any glas,
> And eek his face, as he had been anoint.
> He was a lord ful fat and in good point;
> His eyen stepe, and rollinge in his heed,
> . . .
> Now certeinly he was a fair prelat;
> He was nat pale as a for-pyned goost.
> A fat swan loved he best of any roost.
> He palfrey was as broun as is a berye.

vi *The Friar*

I will not pause long over the Friar save to say that he knew every tavern in every town and every barmaid (tappestere) too. He had twinkling eyes. He was called Hubert.

A Frere there was, a wantown and merye,
. . .
He knew the tavernes wel in every toun.
And everich hostiler and tappestere
. . .
His eyen twinkled in his heed aright,
As doon the sterres in the frosty night.
This worthy limitour was cleped Huberd.

vii *The Merchant*

Nor will I stay on the Merchant except to notice his forked beard and his beaver hat: and his talk of his capital gains.

A Marchant was ther with a forked berd,
In mottelee, and hye on horse he sat,
Up-on his heed a Flaundrish bever hat;
His botes clasped faire and fetisly.
His resons he spak ful solempnely,
Souninge alway th'encrees of his winning.

viii *The Clerk of Oxford*

Next we come to the poor scholar of Oxford. He was a 'Clerk' which meant in Chaucer's day a cleric of the religious orders. This Clerk had not yet got a living (benefice). This is one of the few pieces I remember from my school days. We used to laugh over his 'twenty bokes, clad in blak or reed'. It is touching about his poverty and strikes a sympathetic note with me, because I had very little to live on when I was there. I had to scrape and to save on meals. There were no government grants in my day. It needs no translation. You can guess the two or three old words. 'Lever' is rather, 'fithele' is fiddle.

A clerk there was of Oxenford also,
That un-to logik hadde longe y-go,
As lene was his hors as is a rake,
And he nas nat right fat, I undertake;
But loked holwe, and there-to soberly.
Ful thredbar was his overest courtepy;
For he had geten him yet no benefyce,
Ne was so worldly for to have offyce.
For him was lever have at his beddes heed
Twenty bokes, clad in blak or reed,
Of Aristotle and his philosophye,
Than robes riche, or fithele, or gay sautrye.
But al be that he was a philosophre,
Yet hadde he but litel gold in cofre;
But al that he mighte of his freendes hente,
On bokes and on lerninge he it spente,

And bisily gan for the soules preye
Of hem that yaf him where-with to scoleye.
Of studie took he most cure and most hede.
Noght o word spak he more than was nede,
And that was seyd in forme and reverence,
And short and quik, and ful of hy sentence.
Souninge in moral vertu was his speche,
And gladly wolde he lerne and gladly teche.

4 The Man of Law and his party

i *The Man of Law*

Chaucer's account is the best account we have of a leading member of the Bar in his day. Rather like an eminent Queen's Counsel in our time. He was a Serjeant of the Law, wary and wise. The rank of Serjeant was in mediaeval times the highest order of the Bar. They had their own Inn called Serjeants' Inn (off Chancery Lane). A Serjeant wore a 'coif' (a close-fitting white lawn or silk cap) as a badge of the order. When wigs came to be worn in about 1725, they had to be made with a space on top so as not wholly to conceal the 'coif'.

The Judges were always appointed from among the Serjeants. To this day a judge's wig has a small space on the top to represent the 'coif'. Thus differing from members of the Bar, whose wigs have no 'coif'.

I give Chaucer's description in full, because I hope that lawyers will be interested. But it needs some explanation of the unusual words. The 'parvys' was the portico of St Paul's Church, or perhaps Westminster Hall where lawyers used to meet for consultations. A Serjeant might be appointed a Commissioner of 'Assize' (legal sittings) to go about on circuit (I was in 1943). 'Purchasour' is now obsolete. It means acquiring land by purchasing and not by inheritance. Nowadays 'conveyancer' might be near enough. You will notice that he pretended to be busier than he really was – so as to impress clients. (It still happens today.) He could also remember well all the cases and judgments (domes) from the time of William the Conqueror, no doubt from the Year Books (which had started about 1270 and had been extant for 100 years). He could quote every statute by heart. You could not do it nowadays when our statutes fill 150 volumes.

A Sergeant of the Lawe, war and wys,
That often hadde been at the parvys,
There was also, ful riche of excellence.
Discreet he was, and of greet reverence:
He seemed swich, his wordes weren so wyse.
Justyce he was ful often in assyse,

By patente, and by pleyn commissioun;
For his science, and for his heigh renoun
Of fees and robes hadde he many oon.
So greet a purchasour was no-wher noon.
Al was fee simple to him in effect,
His purchasing mighte nat been infect.
No-wher so bisy a man as he ther nas,
And yet he semed bisier than he was.
In termes hadde he caas and domes alle,
That from the tyme of king William were falle.
Therto he coude endyte, and make a thing,
Ther coude no wight pinche at his wryting;
And every statut coude he pleyn by rote.
He rood but hoomly in a medlee cote
Girt with a ceint of silk, with barres smale;
Of his array telle I no lenger tale.

ii *The Franklin*

Now we come to a man who has disappeared from our society. He was an important landowner who was prominent in the affairs of the County. He was Knight of the Shire and Chairman of Quarter-Sessions. (Rather like some of them in my young days. But these have all gone now – to the regret of many of us.)

Chaucer's Franklin was a most attractive person with his beard 'as white as a daisy'. His great delight was in his food so that he was 'Epicure's own son'. He had every dish that was in season. And woe betide his cook if the sauce was not tasty and ready at the instant.

A Frankeleyn was in his companye;
Whyt was his berd, as is the dayesye.
. . .
To liven in delyt was ever his wone,
For he was Epicurus owne sone.
. . .
After the sondry sesons of the yeer,
So chaunged he his mete and his soper.
Ful many a fat partrich hadde he in mewe,
And many a breem and many a luce in stewe.
Wo was his cook, but-if his sauce were
Poynaunt and sharp, and redy al his gere.
His table dormant in his halle alway
Stood redy covered al the longe day.
At sessiouns ther was he lord and sire;
Ful ofte tyme he was knight of the shire.

iii *The Haberdasher, Carpenter, Weaver, Dyer and Tapestry-maker*

Each of these tradesmen was well respected in the town. Each was fit to be a burgess and to sit on a dais in the Guildhall (yeldhalle). Each was also so wise as to be an Alderman. They had capital and rents enough. Their wives wanted to be called 'ma dame' and would blame their husbands if they were not.

> Wel semed ech of hem a fair burgeys,
> To sitten in a yeldhalle on a deys.
> Everich, for the wisdom that he can,
> Was shaply for to been an alderman.
> For catel hadde they y-nogh and rente,
> And eek hir wyves wolde it wel assente;
> And elles certein were they to blame.
> It is ful fair to been y-clept 'ma dame',

iv *The Cook*

I must let you have all that Chaucer says about the Cook. But I must first explain that 'poudre-marchant' was a flavouring powder, 'galingale' was spice or flavouring, 'mortreux' was a kind of milk soup and 'mormal' was an ulcer. The last couplet is great fun. It was a pity, indeed, that he had an ulcer (mormal) on his shin but I expect that the blancmange made up for it.

> A Cook they hadde with hem for the nones,
> To boille the chiknes with the marybones,
> And poudre-marchant tart, and galingale.
> Wel coude he knowe a draughte of London ale.
> He coude roste, and sethe, and broille, and frye,
> Maken mortreux, and wel bake a pye.
> But greet harm was it, as it thoughte me,
> That on his shine a mormal hadde he;
> For blankmanger, that made he with the beste.

v *The Shipman*

There was a skipper from Dartmouth who owned a ship called the *Maudelayne*. I like his exploit in Bordeaux whilst the 'chapman' (trader) was asleep.

> And, certeinly, he was a good felawe.
> Ful many a draughte of wyn had he y-drawe
> From Burdeux-ward, whyl that the chapman sleep.
> Of nyce conscience took he no keep.

vi *The Doctor of Physic*

The physician must have been more knowledgeable than those of today: because he knew the cause of every illness. He was careful over money. He earned high fees in times of plague, but kept all that he won. And there is a nice couplet about gold. It stimulated the heart (cordial). So he 'loved gold in special'.

He knew the cause of everich maladye,
Were it of hoot or cold, or moiste, or drye,
And where engendred, and of what humour
He was a verrey parfit practisour.
. . .
And yet he was but esy of dispence;
He kepte that he wan in pestilence.
For gold in phisik is a cordial,
Therefore he lovede gold in special.

vii *The Good Wife of Bath*

Now I come to the most celebrated of all the pilgrims. The good wife from near Bath. You must picture her from Chaucer's description. She was somewhat deaf, which was a pity. But she made cloth better than those of Ypres and Ghent.

A good Wyfe was ther of bisyde Bathe,
But she was som-del deef, and that was scathe.
Of clooth-making she hadde swiche an haunt,
She passed hem of Ypres and of Gaunt.

She was such a formidable lady that if any wife in the parish went to the altar steps before her, she was furious.

In al the parisshe wyf ne was ther noon
That to th'offring bifore hir sholde goon;
And if ther dide, certeyn, so wrooth was she,
That she was out of alle charitee.

On Sundays she wore finely woven kerchiefs on her head. They weighed ten pounds. She wore scarlet red stockings, gartered tight, and soft new shoes. Her face was bold, and fair, and red.

Hir coverchiefs ful fyne were of ground;
I dorste swere they weyeden ten pound
That on a Sonday were upon hir heed.
Hir hosen weren of fyn scarlet reed,
Ful streite y-teyd, and shoes ful moiste and newe.
Bold was hir face, and fair, and reed of hewe.

She had married five husbands in church, not counting other company in youth, about which the less said the better.

She was a worthy womman al hir lyve,
Housbondes at chirche-dore she hadde fyve,
Withouten other companye in youthe;
But thereof nedeth nat to speke as nouthe.

She had been to Jerusalem three times and knew all about 'wandering by the way'.

And thryes hadde she been at Jerusalem;
She hadde passed many a straunge streem;
At Rome she hadde been, and at Boloigne,
In Galice at seint Jame, and at Coloigne.
She coude muche of wandring by the weye:

She had gap-teeth, and sat easily on an ambling horse. She was well wimpled up. On her head a hat as broad as a buckler or shield. She had a flowing mantle covering her large hips and on her feet a pair of sharp spurs.

Gat-tothed was she, soothly for to seye.
Up-on an amblere esily she sat,
Y-wimpled wel, and on hir heed an hat
As brood as is a bokeler or a targe;
A foot-mantel aboute hir hipes large,
And on hir feet a paire of spores sharpe.

She could laugh and chat and she knew the remedies for love's mischances. What were they?

In felawschip wel coude she laughe and carpe.
Of remedyes of love she knew perchaunce,
For she coude of that art the olde daunce.

viii *The Parson*

The Parson was the most esteemed of all. He was a good man and visited all the people high or low, in his large parish, staff in hand, in all weathers, no matter rain or thunder.

A good man was ther of religioun,
And was a povre Persoun of a toun;
But riche he was of holy thoght and werk.
He was also a lerned man, a clerk,
That Cristes gospel trewely wolde preche;
. . .
Wyde was his parisshe, and houses fer a-sonder,
But he ne lafte nat, for reyn ne thonder,
In siknes nor in meschief, to visyte
The ferreste in his parisshe, muche and lyte,
Up-on his feet, and in his hand a staf.
This noble ensample to his sheep he yaf,

He did not let out his benefice on hire and leave his flock in the mud. Nor did he run off to London and get money for saying masses for the departed. 'Chaunterie' or chantry means an endowment for the maintenance of priests to say masses, usually for the souls of the dead.

He sette nat his benefice to hyre,
And leet his sheep encombred in the myre,
And ran to London, un-to sëynt Poules,
To seken him a chaunterie for soules,
Or with a bretherhed to been withholde;
But dwelte at hoom, and kepte wel his folde,

He drew folk to heaven by his good example, but if any were obstinate, he would rebuke them sharply. 'Snibben' is expressive, meaning 'snub' or rebuke. A 'spyced conscience' is an easy conscience.

To drawen folk to heven by fairnesse
By good ensample, was his bisinesse:
But it were any persone obstinat,
What-so he were, of heigh or lowe estat,
Him wolde he snibben sharply for the nones.
A bettre preest, I trowe that nowher noon is.
He wayted after no pompe and reverence.
Ne maked him a spyced conscience,
But Cristes lore, and his apostles twelve,
He taughte, and at first he folwed it himselve.

ix *The Ploughman*

The Parson had a brother who was a Ploughman. We would call him now a small farmer. He had loaded many a cart-load of dung and was a good worker. 'Fother' is a cart-load. 'Swink' is work. 'Swinker' is a worker.

With him ther was a Plowman, was his brother,
That hadde y-lad of dong ful many a fother,
A trewe swinker and a good was he,
Livinge in pees and parfit charitee.

He paid his tithes (the tenth part of his produce payable to the Church) and rode in a 'tabard' (a loose upper coat without sleeves).

His tythes payed he ful faire and wel,
Bothe of his propre swink and his catel.
In a tabard he rood upon a mere.

5 The Miller and his party

i *The Miller*

The Miller is such an amusing character that I must set out Chaucer's description of him. But it needs a good deal of translation. He was a stout 'carl' (countryman). He always won the prize (a ram) at any wrestling show. He would heave any door off its hinges (harre) or running at it break it with his head (heed). He had a broad red beard. He had a wart on the right tip (cop) of his nose with a tuft of hair on it as red as the bristles of a sow's ear. His nostrils (nose-thirles) were black and wide. His large mouth was like a big furnace. He was a wrangler and buffoon (goliardeys) telling stories of sin and prostitution. He was a good hand at stealing corn and took three times his due. And a good thumb for testing it, by God! (par dieu). For all this he was good at bagpiping and played the pilgrims out of town.

The Miller was a stout carl, for the nones,
Ful big he was of braun, and eek of bones;
That proved wel, for over-al ther he cam,
At wrastling he wolde have alwey the ram.
He was short-sholdred, brood, a thikke knarre,
Ther nas no dore that he nolde heve of harre,
Or breke it, at a renning, with his heed.
His berd as any sowe or fox was reed,
And ther-to brood, as though it were a spade.
Up-on the cop right of his nose he hade
A werte, and ther-on stood a tuft of heres,
Reed as the bristles of a sowes eres;
His nose-thirles blake were and wyde.
A swerd and bokeler bar he by his syde;
His mouth as greet was as a greet forneys.
He was a janglere and a goliardeys,
And that was most of sinne and harlotryes.
Wel coude he stelen corn, and tollen thryes;
And yet he hadde a thombe of gold, pardee.
A whyte cote and a blew hood wered he.
A baggepype wel coude he blowe and sowne,
And there-with-al he broghte us out of towne.

ii *The Manciple*

We never use the word 'Manciple' nowadays but it means the head steward or officer who buys victuals for a college or institution. The character who went on the pilgrimage was the 'Manciple' of the Inner (or Middle) Temple of the Inns of Court. The nearest equivalent today is the Under-Treasurer. He was a 'lewed' man, that is, an unlearned man as compared with the 30 Benchers who were his masters as they are today. They had much legal wisdom, and could help in any case in a shire. But in native wit this Manciple could outdo them all.

A gentil Maunciple was ther of a temple,
. . .

Now is nat that of God a ful fair grace,
That swich a lewed mannes wit shal pace
The wisdom of an heep of lerned men?
Of maistres hadde he mo than thryes ten,
That were of lawe expert and curious;
Of which ther were a doseyn in that hous
Worthy to been stiwardes of rente and lond
Of any lord that is in Engelond,
. . .
And able for to helpen al a shire
In any cas that mighte falle or happe;
And yit this maunciple sette hir aller cappe.

iii *The Reeve*

The Reeve was the estate manager of land in 'Northfolk'. I do not pause on him except to notice his long thin legs (like a stick) and his good keeping of corn in bins and granary.

Ful longe were his legges, and ful lene,
Y-lyk a staf, ther was no calf y-sene.
Wel coude he kepe a gerner and a binne;
Ther was noon auditour coude on him winne.

And he always came in last.

And ever he rood the hindreste of our route.

iv *The Somnour*

The Somnour pleases me. It does not mean that he was somnolent. It means 'summoner'. He was the court bailiff who summoned offenders to trial before an ecclesiastical court. Those courts had jurisdiction in cases of adultery and immorality, and could punish by excommunication. Chaucer gives this nice description of him in the *Prologue* to the Friar's Tale. He ran up and down summoning people for fornication. He was so unpopular that he got beaten up at the end of every town.

A Somnour is a renner up and doun
With mandements for fornicacioun,
And is y-bet at every tounes ende.

Turning back to the *Prologue*, the opening describes him as being as hot (hoot) and lecherous as a sparrow, and having a red carbuncled face. 'Sawcefleem' means carbuncles.

A Somnour was ther with us in that place;
That hadde a fyr-reed cherubinnes face,
For sawcefleem he was, with eyen narwe.
As hoot he was, and lecherous, as a sparwe;

He drank strong wine. When he was thoroughly drunk he spoke a few Latin words which he had learnt when reading some decree. He would cry out '*Questio quid iuris*' (what is the question of law?). But he was open to bribery. If he was given a quart of wine he would let a good fellow have a concubine for twelve months and dispense with any punishment.

> And whan that he wel dronken hadde the wyn,
> Than wolde he speke no word but Latyn.
> A fewe termes hadde he, two or three,
> That he had lerned out of som decree;
> . . .
> Ay 'Questio quid iuris' wolde he crye.
> He was a gentil harlot and a kinde;
> A bettre felawe sholde men noght finde.
> He wolde suffre, for a quart of wyn,
> A good felawe to have his concubyn
> A twelf-month, and excuse him atte fulle:

v *The Pardoner*

The Pardoner had come straight from Rome. He was the good companion of the Somnour. The Somnour summoned the offenders. The Pardoner pardoned them – for a fee. They sang a duet, 'Come hither, love, to me' with the Somnour in a loud supporting role (burdoun).

> With him ther rood a gentil Pardoner
> Of Rouncival, his freend and his compeer,
> That streight was comen fro the court of Rome.
> Ful loude he song, 'Com hider, love, to me'.
> This somnour bar to him a stif burdoun,
> Was never trompe of half so greet a soun.

The Pardoner had his wallet brimful of pardons all hot from Rome. He had a squeaky voice – like a goat's; he had a smooth chin – like a woman's – which made Chaucer doubtful of his sex.

> His walet lay biforn him in his lappe,
> Bret-ful of pardoun come from Rome al hoot.
> A voys he hadde as smal as hath a goot.
> No berd hadde he, ne never sholde have,
> As smothe it was as it were late y-shave;
> I trowe he were a gelding or a mare.

vi *The Relics*

He was the most effective Pardoner from Berwick down to Ware. He had a trunk full of religious relics which he sold to a credulous public. Chaucer's description of these relics is fascinating but needs translation. In his trunk (male) the Pardoner had a pillow-case (pilwe-beer) which he said was the veil of the Virgin Mary. He also had a fragment (gobet) of the sail which St Peter had when he walked upon the sea until Jesus Christ helped him. Also a metal (latoun) cross set with stones. And in a glass he had 'pigges bones'.

> But of his craft, fro Berwik into Ware,
> Ne was ther swich another pardoner.
> For in his male he hadde a pilwe-beer,
> Which that, he seyde, was our lady veyl:
> He seyde, he hadde a gobet of the seyl
> That sëynt Peter hadde, whan that he wente
> Up-on the see, til Jesu Crist him hente.
> He hadde a croys of latoun, ful of stones,
> An in a glas he hadde pigges bones.

vii *He sells the relics*

With these relics he made more money in one day than a poor parson would in two months: and so made monkeys (apes) of the people.

> But with thise relikes, whan that he fond
> A povre person dwelling up-on lond,
> Up-on a day he gat him more moneye
> Than that the person gat in monthes tweye.
> And thus, with feyned flaterye and japes,
> He made the person and the peple his apes.

viii *His singing*

He was a good speaker in church: but he was best at singing the offertory hymns. He made much silver by it. That is why he sang 'so merrily and loud'.

> But trewely to tellen, atte laste,
> He was in chirche a noble ecclesiaste.
> Wel coude he rede a lessoun or a storie,
> But alderbest he song an offertorie;
> For well he wiste, whan that song was songe,
> He moste preche, and wel affyle his tonge,
> To winne silver, as he ful wel coude;
> Therefore he song so meriely and loude.

ix *The number*

At the outset Chaucer said they were 29 pilgrims. So far I have counted 30 pilgrims. To them Chaucer adds himself. Thus making 31. Then afterwards the Host joins in, so Chaucer cannot have revised his script very carefully.

6 The Host

i *They have supper*

Chaucer ends the *Prologue* by telling of the supper they had that evening at the Tabard and of the welcome given to them by the Host. 'Vitaille' is of course 'victuals'. He says what a merry man he was. And the humorous speech he made to them after they had paid their bills.

Greet chere made our hoste us everichon,
And to the soper sette us anon;
And served us with vitaille at the best.
Strong was the wyn, and wel to drinke us leste.
A semely man our hoste was with-alle
For to han been a marshal in an halle;
A large man he was with eyen stepe,
A fairer burgeys is ther noon in Chepe:
Bold of his speche, and wys, and wel y-taught,
And of manhod him lakkede right naught.
Eek therto he was right a mery man,
And after soper pleyen he bigan,
And spak of mirthe amonges othere thinges,
Whan that we hadde maad our rekeninges;

He suggested that each of them should tell two stories on the way out to Canterbury and two on the way back: and they would all stand a dinner for the best story-teller. The Host would go with them and be the judge.

This is the poynt, to speken short and pleyn,
That ech of yow, to shorte with your weye,
In this viage, shal telle tales tweye,
To Caunterbury-ward, I mene it so,
And hom-ward he shal tellen othere two,
Of aventures that whylom han bifalle.
And which of yow that bereth him best of alle,
That is to seyn, that telleth in this cas
Tales of best sentence and most solas,
Shal have a soper at our aller cost
Here in this place, sitting by this post,
Whan that we come agayn fro Canterbury.
And for to make yow the more mery,
I wol my-selven gladly with yow ryde,
Right at myn owne cost, and be your gyde.

ii *They go to bed*

They all agreed to the Host's suggestion, drank up their wine and went to bed.

. . . and thus, by oon assent,
We been acorded to his jugement.
And there-up-on the wyn was fet anon;
We dronken, and to reste wente echon,
With-outen any lenger taryinge.

iii *Next morning*

The next morning they rode out and at the first stop, drew lots as to who should tell the first story. The truth (sothe) is that the lot fell on the Knight which pleased everyone.

Anon to drawen every wight bigan,
And shortly for to tellen, as it was,
Were it by aventure, or sort, or cas,
The sothe is this, the cut fil to the knight,
Of which ful blythe and glad was every wight;

iv *The tales themselves*

That ends the *Prologue*. The Knight started his tale with the others following. The tales are separate stories in themselves, having nothing to do with the pilgrimage at all. For instance the Man of Law's tale has nothing whatever to do with the law. It is a fanciful story about the daughter of a Roman Emperor. I think that Chaucer must have composed these stories earlier at various dates, and then used the pilgrimage as an excuse for bringing them all together. Even the pilgrimage itself seems to me an excuse for bringing together the fascinating descriptions of typical folk of Chaucer's time. I very much doubt if they went together on a real pilgrimage.

Epilogue

In some ways I have been feeling my age. My eyesight is failing. My hearing is poor. I walk with a stick. I lean on a friend's arm. But my speaking is, I hope, as good as ever. And my brain still works tolerably well. At any rate I go to the debates in the House of Lords and contribute what I can. I have spoken there from time to time. Usually on topics where a lawyer can help. Such as kerb-crawling, telephone-tapping, corporal punishment in schools, top people's salaries, insolvency, criminal evidence and the prosecution of offenders. I sit on the cross benches because I am, and always have been, independent of any political party. I have noted how greatly the House has advanced in public esteem. The televising of its proceedings has shown the high quality of the discussions there.

With several other Peers, I always like to be there in time to hear one of the Bishops say prayers at the sitting of the House. He says this beautiful prayer which has come down the centuries, asking for guidance in all our counsels:

> Almighty God, by whom alone Kings reign, and Princes decree justice; and from whom alone cometh all counsel, wisdom, and understanding; We thine unworthy servants, here gathered together in thy Name, do most humbly beseech thee to send down thy Heavenly Wisdom from above, to direct and guide us in all our consultations; and grant that, we having thy fear always before our eyes, and laying aside all private interests, prejudices, and partial affections, the result of all our counsels may be to the glory of thy blessed Name, the maintenance of true Religion and Justice, the safety, honour, and happiness of the Queen, the publick wealth, peace and tranquillity of the Realm, and the uniting and knitting together of the hearts of all persons and estates within the same, in true Christian love and Charity one towards another, through Jesus Christ our Lord and Saviour. Amen.

Back home in Whitchurch, I have found much interest in improving the environs of our old Town Hall. We have built three delightful dwellings for elderly folk, set in a quiet courtyard. Also a charming little office next to the house where I was born. On the wall of the house our friends from the State of Alabama have put up a plaque saying:

The Right Honourable
LORD DENNING
Master of the Rolls 1962–1982
born here 23 January 1899
and lived here with his
parents, brothers and sister
for 24 years
Placed here by Lord Denning's American friends

It was unveiled at a special ceremony on Sunday 21 July 1985 before a most distinguished company, and all our Whitchurch folk.

Another recent occasion was when the Basingstoke Male Voice Choir (of which I am President) gave a concert which ended with the *Pomp and Circumstance March*. They sang well the famous song, *Land of Hope and Glory*, of which they had learnt all the words. All in the audience knew the chorus and joined vigorously in it. The poem was written by Arthur Christopher Benson, a distinguished Master of Magdalene College, Cambridge. That was in the days of the great British Empire and the words reflect the pride and patriotism of that time. He wrote the poem to be sung as the Finale of Elgar's *Coronation Ode (1902)* to music derived from the *Pomp and Circumstance March, op. 39. No. 1 in D Major*. The song owes its appeal to the triumphal music of Sir Edward Elgar who was – to my mind – the greatest English composer ever. It is very English and makes a fitting end to this English Anthology.

Land of Hope and Glory, Mother of the Free,
How shall we extol thee, who are born of thee?
Wider still and wider shall thy bounds be set;
God, who made thee mighty, make thee mightier yet.

Many of you will have seen on television the enthusiasm with which the young people of today sing this song at the last night of the Promenade Concerts in the Royal Albert Hall, waving their Union Jacks. Well may they still do so. We are no longer mighty in arms, as nations go, but we are still mighty in the things that matter in a civilised society – in freedom, culture, spirit and courage.

I am often asked: What are we coming to? With all this increase in crime and violence – vandalism and hooliganism – amongst the youth of today? I make answer: That is done by a very small minority. The young people of today are as good as ever we were, and maybe better. We have done our part. They will do theirs. It is in the hope that they may read it and know something of the glories of our literature and our history that I have compiled this book.

Index

Twenty Answers

1 The Queen of Hearts (not the Duchess) in *Alice in Wonderland* by Lewis Carroll.

2 Winston Churchill in the House of Commons on 18 June 1940.

3 St Paul before Festus, the Roman Governor, at Caesarea.

4 Lord Nelson in the *Victory* in the early morning of 21 October 1805 before the Battle of Trafalgar. He added the words, 'to my King and country'.

5 Oliver Cromwell on 20 April 1653 in the House of Commons. He ordered the leader of the musketeers to take away the Mace, thus ending the Long Parliament.

6 Portia at the court of the Duke in Venice, addressing Shylock. She added the words, 'Take thou thy pound of flesh'.

7 John Bunyan wrote it in *The Pilgrim's Progress* and Mr Valiant-for-Truth sang it.

8 Cecil Rhodes on 30 December 1895 on hearing of Jameson's raid into the Transvaal.

9 Queen Elizabeth the First – according to the Scholar (Venator) as recorded by Izaak Walton in *The Compleat Angler*.

10 An officer of the Foot Guards shouting to Monmouth's troops at the Battle of Sedgemoor, who replied, 'King Monmouth'.

11 In Jane Austen's novel, 'Pride' was personified by Mr Darcy and 'Prejudice' by Miss Elizabeth Bennet.

12 Tess in Thomas Hardy's novel, *Tess of the d'Urbervilles*, after accepting an evening lift with Alec d'Urberville.

13 Mr Samuel Pickwick in *The Pickwick Papers*. He had gone by mistake into a lady's bedroom at the Great White Horse at Ipswich.

14 The unpatriotic man in Sir Walter Scott's poem, *The Lay of the Last Minstrel*. He did not love his native land.

15 Thomas Orton who was the claimant in the *Tichborne case*. He claimed to be Sir Roger Tichborne, Baronet, but was found to be a perjurer.

16 The Lord Chancellor in the Old Hall of Lincoln's Inn in the case of *Jarndyce v Jarndyce* in *Bleak House* by Charles Dickens.

17 Dr Grantly, the Archdeacon of Barchester, in his study behind a locked door, in Anthony Trollope's novel, *The Warden*.

18 Swallows go to the warm climate of Africa. Gilbert White mistakenly thought that they hid in holes in England.

19 The Good Wife of Bath as described by Geoffrey Chaucer in the *Prologue* to *The Canterbury Tales*.

20 The trial of Warren Hastings in Westminster Hall in 1788. Whenever a point of law was raised, the judges walked out to consider it and nothing happened in the court.